A Reader's Guide to Thomas Mann's *Doctor Faustus*

Studies in German Literature, Linguistics, and Culture

A Reader's Guide to Thomas Mann's *Doctor Faustus*

Tobias Boes

Rochester, New York

Copyright © 2025 Tobias Boes

The eBook edition of this book is available under the Open Access Licence CC BY-NC-ND. Open Access publication of this book was made possible through generous grants from Notre Dame's Franco Family Center for the Liberal Arts and the Public Good, as well as from the Thomas Mann House (TMH) in Pacific Palisades.

Some rights reserved. Without limiting the rights under copyright reserved above, any part of this book may be reproduced, stored in or introduced into a retrieval system, or transmitted, in any form or by any means (electronic, mechanical, photocopying, recording or otherwise)

First published 2025
by Camden House

Camden House is an imprint of Boydell & Brewer Inc.
668 Mt. Hope Avenue, Rochester, NY 14620, USA
and of Boydell & Brewer Limited
PO Box 9, Woodbridge, Suffolk IP12 3DF, UK
www.boydellandbrewer.com

Our Authorised Representative for product safety in the EU is Easy Access System Europe - Mustamäe tee 50, 10621 Tallinn, Estonia, *gpsr.requests@easproject.com*

ISBN-13: 978-1-64014-180-3 (hardback);
978-1-64014-223-7 (paperback)

Library of Congress Cataloging-in-Publication Data
Names: Boes, Tobias, author.
Title: A reader's guide to Thomas Mann's Doctor Faustus / Tobias Boes.
Description: Rochester, NY: Camden House, 2025. | Series: Studies in German literature, linguistics, and culture; 254 | Includes bibliographical references and index.
Identifiers: LCCN 2024058721 (print) | LCCN 2024058722 (ebook) | ISBN 9781640141803 (hardback) | ISBN 9781640142237 (paperback) | ISBN 9781805437147 (pdf) | ISBN 9781805437154 (epub)
Subjects: LCSH: Mann, Thomas, 1875–1955. Doktor Faustus. | LCGFT: Literary criticism.
Classification: LCC PT2625.A44 D6326 2025 (print) | LCC PT2625. A44 (ebook) | DDC 833/.912—dc23/eng/20241213
LC record available at https://lccn.loc.gov/2024058721
  LC ebook record available at https://lccn.loc.gov/2024058722

Contents

List of Illustrations	vii
Acknowledgments	ix
Notes on References to *Doctor Faustus*	xi

Part One: Getting Started

1:	Why Read *Doctor Faustus* in the Twenty-First Century?	3
2:	Which Edition of *Doctor Faustus* Should I Buy?	16
3:	What Should I Pay Attention to as I Read the Novel?	19

Part Two: Contexts

4:	Composition and Publication History	23
5:	A Brief History of the Faust Theme	30
6:	*Doctor Faustus* and Literary Modernism	37
7:	The Historical Setting of the Novel	50
8:	Anti-Semitism and the Problem of Other People's Suffering	68

Part Three: Interpretations

9:	Five Masters from Germany: Leverkühn as Artist and Intellectual	77
10:	Music Theory and Political Allegory: Leverkühn as Fascist	96
11:	Illness and Redemption: Leverkühn as Christ	114

Part Four: Materials for Consultation

12:	Chapter Summaries and Page-By-Page Commentaries	125
13:	Cast of Characters	231

14: Timeline of Events in the Novel	243
15: List of Adrian Leverkühn's Major Compositions	247
16: Suggestions for Further Reading and Research	249
Index	271

List of Illustrations

Illustrations follow page 257

1	Albrecht Dürer, *Portrait of Philip Melanchthon*
2	Albrecht Dürer, *Portrait of a Young Venetian Woman*
3	Albrecht Dürer, *The Master-Builder Jerome of Augsburg*
4	Albrecht Dürer, *Knight, Death, and Devil*
5	Albrecht Dürer, *The Apocalypse, The Torture of St. John the Evangelist*
6	Albrecht Dürer, *The Apocalypse, St. John Devouring the Book*
7	Albrecht Dürer, *The Apocalypse, The Hymn in Adoration of the Lamb*
8	Albrecht Dürer, *The Apocalypse, The Whore of Babylon*
9	Albrecht Dürer, *The Apocalypse, The Four Horsemen*
10	Illustration, Pythagorean Tuning System
11	Photograph, The Schweighart Farm in Polling
12	Photograph, The Parlor of the Schweighart Farm

Acknowledgments

THIS BOOK WAS born from my experiences teaching *Doctor Faustus* to undergraduate students at the University of Notre Dame. My thanks go first and foremost to the talented students who discussed the novel with me in my upper-division seminars on "The World of *Doctor Faustus*" and in my first-year University Seminar on "The Faust Myth in and through History." They especially sharpened my attention to the novel's humor and to its religious dimensions—two aspects that often receive insufficient attention in the critical literature.

Several of my colleagues at Notre Dame gave generous guest lectures or guest performances for these classes. Daniel Schlossberg performed Beethoven's Op. 111 for us, while Berthold Hoeckner spoke about the concept of absolute music. Samantha Heinle unpacked the complexities of twelve-tone composition, while John Betz shed light on some of the theological questions discussed in the Halle chapters. Julia Schneider showed us Notre Dame's copy of the *Nuremberg Chronicle* and other treasures from the Hesburgh Libraries Rare Books & Special Collections. Cheryl Snay and Bridget Hoyt similarly displayed prize specimens from the holdings of the Raclin Murphy Museum of Art, including Dürer's *Apocalypse* cycle and his engraving *Knight, Death, and Devil*.

Other colleagues shared their subject expertise with me as I prepared to write this book. I'm especially grateful to Johanna Frymoyer, who put up with me over the course of two semesters of college-level musical theory. Needless to say, all musical errors and imprecisions in this volume are entirely my fault. C.J. Jones answered questions about Pietism and the Ephrata brethren. Mark Roche, whose article on laughter in *Doctor Faustus* I have long admired, provided helpful comments on an early draft of the manuscript.

Notre Dame sophomore Kephas Olsson served as my research assistant and sounding-board while I was writing this book. He suggested the basic shape of chapter 3 and provided invaluable feedback on the page-by-page commentary in chapter 12, helping me decide which passages needed glossing for a first-time reader.

In May of 2023, the city of Bad Tölz invited me to give a keynote lecture at its second annual Thomas Mann Festival. My stay in Bavaria allowed me to visit many of the sites commemorated in *Doctor Faustus*, such as Rombühel Hill, the Klammer Pool, and the Schweigestill Farmhouse. My sincere thanks go out to Eckhard Zimmermann for arranging the invitation, serving as my tour guide, and tracking down several of the historical images in this book. I'd also like to thank Christof Botzenhart and Ulrike Gänswein for their hospitality in Bad Tölz and in Polling respectively.

Open Access publication of this book was made possible through generous grants from Notre Dame's Franco Family Center for the Liberal Arts and the Public Good, as well as from the Thomas Mann House (TMH) in Pacific Palisades. I'd like to especially thank Benno Herz at the TMH for championing the project.

Notes on References to *Doctor Faustus*

FOR REASONS THAT are explained in Chapter 2, "What Edition of Doctor Faustus Should I Buy?," all page references in this book refer to the John E. Woods translation published by Vintage, followed by a second page number for the German edition in the pagination of the *Große kommentierte Frankfurter Ausgabe* (GKFA), published by S. Fischer Verlag.

Chapter numbers from *Doctor Faustus* are indicated by Roman numerals throughout the text. While these are more cumbersome than Arabic numbers, Mann chose the Roman numbering deliberately, since it serves an estranging effect and mirrors the formatting of the sixteenth-century chapbook.

Part One: Getting Started

1: Why Read *Doctor Faustus* in the Twenty-First Century?

THOMAS MANN'S NOVEL *Doctor Faustus: The Life of the German Composer Adrian Leverkühn, as Told by a Friend* (1947) was written with the grandest of intentions. When Mann first set pen to paper, in the second half of May 1943, he was sixty-seven years old and living in exile from the Nazis in Pacific Palisades, a suburb of Los Angeles. Commonly celebrated in America as "the Greatest Living Man of Letters" and universally recognized as a leading spokesman of what many people called "the other Germany"—that is, a Germany uncorrupted by fascism—Mann was perhaps most famous for his 1924 novel *The Magic Mountain*, in which he had minutely dissected the intellectual and cultural factors that had led to the outbreak of the First World War.[1] With *Doctor Faustus*, he tried to offer a similar explanation for the successive waves of illiberalism and mass hysteria that had rocked Europe during the interwar period, and of which Nazism was only the most prominent example. As Mann put it in a letter to his American patron Agnes E. Meyer at the time: "[My topic] is the idea of intoxication as such, and of the anti-reason admixed to it; this includes the political, the fascist, and therefore also the sad fate of Germany."[2]

When the novel was published, most of its early readers understandably took a narrower view of its ambitions, treating it exclusively as an allegory of Nazism, which had come to such an inglorious end only two years earlier. Mann at times supported this tendency. After all, he had become very famous as a commentator on Nazi Germany; an American newspaper had even declared him to be "Hitler's Most Intimate Enemy."[3]

---

1   On Thomas Mann's popular fame in America during the 1930s and 1940s, see Tobias Boes, *Thomas Mann's War: Literature, Politics, and the World Republic of Letters* (Ithaca, NY: Cornell University Press, 2019).

2   Letter to Agnes E. Meyer, April 28, 1943. Thomas Mann, *Selbstkommentare: "Doktor Faustus" und "Die Entstehung des Doktor Faustus,"* ed. Hans Wysling and Marianne Fischer (Frankfurt am Main: S. Fischer, 1998), 9. In a later letter to his friend Emil Preetorius (who makes a memorable appearance in the novel as the pseudo-fascist intellectual Sixtus Kridwiss), Mann similarly announced his intention to "capture the epoch in which I lived," by which he meant not Nazism proper but rather "the period from 1884 to 1945." See Mann, *Selbstkommentare*, 139.

3   Paul V.C. Whitney, "Distinguished Exile Speaks Here Tonight," *Deseret News*, March 21, 1938, 1.

But as time went on, he increasingly lamented the fact that nobody seemed to recognize the more universal aspirations of his tale.[4] By and large, the more limited focus has dominated critical interpretations into the present.[5]

The aim of this introductory guide, which is based on my experiences discussing *Doctor Faustus* with undergraduate students at the University of Notre Dame, is to change this state of affairs. My contention is that Mann's novel, besides being compulsively readable and wickedly funny, is also a work of vital relevance to the present moment. It deserves rediscovery not just because it might help us understand the "German Catastrophe," but also because of the way it reflects on the political turmoil of the twenty-first century. Like other important novels of the late 1940s and early 1950s (I'm thinking here especially of Camus's *The Plague*, Orwell's *1984*, and Ellison's *The Invisible Man*, works with which at first sight *Doctor Faustus* seems to have nothing in common), Mann's late masterpiece is indelibly stamped by the tumultuous time in which it was written. The ethical authority bestowed by this mark illuminates our own age as well.

My argument in a nutshell is this: the central theme of *Doctor Faustus* is the regression of progressive liberal culture into irrationality and barbarism. The novel uses early-twentieth-century Germany as a case study, but its message is of universal relevance. Its two major figures, the narrator Serenus Zeitblom and the protagonist Adrian Leverkühn, are born in the final third of the long nineteenth century (Zeitblom in 1883, Leverkühn in 1885), they witness the demise of this era of unprecedented social progress and economic prosperity in 1914, and they live through sixteen more politically precarious and intellectually reckless years until Leverkühn goes mad in 1930 and Zeitblom withdraws from public life in 1934. Like any other historical period, the years that provide the subject matter for *Doctor Faustus* were unique and need to be treated as such. The crimes of the Nazis, which were made possible by developments set in motion during the time period narrated in the novel, are certainly

---

4   See, for example, the letter to Jonas Lesser of May 1, 1948, in which he stresses that in the novel "Germany is only a paradigm. The constant message of 'the end is near, the end is coming' refers not only to it." In Mann, *Selbstkommentare*, 195.

5   Hans Rudolf Vaget, for example, writes that "[With *Doctor Faustus*] Mann chose to tell a particular part of German history in terms of 'German' music" and stresses that "the highly imaginative and professional musical encoding of the prehistory of the "German catastrophe" may be regarded as the novel's most original [...] feature." See Hans Rudolf Vaget, "'German' Music and German Catastrophe: A Re-Reading of *Doktor Faustus*," in *A Companion to the Works of Thomas Mann*, ed. Herbert Lehnert and Eva Wessell (Rochester, NY: Camden House, 2004), 221–44.

beyond compare. And yet history, to invoke a popular cliché, "may not repeat itself, but rhymes." Many of my students, who were born during the "golden quarter century" that came to an abrupt end in 2014/2015, when the Russian invasion of Crimea, the Brexit referendum, and the rise of Donald Trump signaled the renewal of darker times, have found the general structure of *Doctor Faustus* distressingly familiar.[6] Whether they, too, will witness the descent of the world into a general state of paralysis of the insane is as yet uncertain.

Doctor Faustus, so I believe, speaks to our present moment because its political analysis is constructed loosely enough to survive transposition onto the twenty-first century. Many prior critics have found fault with the novel precisely because of this vagueness. And, indeed, the explanations that the novel offers for the genesis of Nazism fall short of a comprehensive explanation. Economic factors, like the hyperinflation of 1923 or the Great Depression, play no role in the book; neither do the various crises of Weimar political culture. Anti-Semitism, too, is not systematically treated, and in fact Mann's depiction of Jewish characters consistently relies on anti-Semitic stereotypes.[7] The Holocaust, finally, is never directly mentioned—there's a reference to the Buchenwald concentration camp at one point, but this site is primarily associated with the persecution of political prisoners, not of Jews. What we get instead is a dogged focus on intellectual and cultural questions along with—somewhat puzzlingly—an attempt to narrate the rise of totalitarian ideology through a story about modern music. I will examine this curious and ethically troubling omission at greater length in chapter 8, "Anti-Semitism and the Problem of Other People's Suffering."

These seeming inadequacies turn into strengths, however, if we approach *Doctor Faustus* not as an attempt to offer a definitive account

---

6   I borrow the concept of a "golden quarter century" stretching from 1989/1990 to 2014/2015 from my colleague Vittorio Hösle, *Globale Fliehkräfte: Eine geschichtsphilosophische Kartierung der Gegenwart* (Munich: Karl Alber, 2021).

7   See Ruth Angress-Klüger, "Jewish Characters in Thomas Mann's Fiction," in *Horizonte: Festschrift für Herbert Lehnert zum 65. Geburtstag*, ed. Hannelore Mundt, Egon Schwarz, and William J. Lillymann (Tübingen: Max Niemeyer Verlag, 1990), 161–72; Egon Schwarz, "The Jewish Characters in *Doctor Faustus*," in *Thomas Mann's "Doctor Faustus": A Novel on the Margin of Modernism*, ed. Herbert Lehnert and Peter C. Pfeiffer (Columbia, SC: Camden House, 1991), 119–40; and Todd Kontje, *Thomas Mann's World: Empire, Race, and the Jewish Question* (Ann Arbor: University of Michigan Press, 2011), 168–75. Mann himself admitted that "the Jewish problem and the Jewish fate as such play no role in the novel" when he was confronted by the critic Ludwig Lewisohn in April 1948, though even then he appears not to have realized why this might be a problem. Mann, *Selbstkommentare*, 189.

of the rise of Nazism, but instead as a broader meditation on the question of why enlightened liberal cultures can relapse into authoritarian barbarism. Certainly, *Doctor Faustus* is an undeniably German story, and not just because its action takes place in Germany during the decades immediately predating the Third Reich. The novel analyzes a particularly Germanic path towards irrationality (one over which the philosopher Friedrich Nietzsche presided as a guiding star, for example), and it does so by telling a story about music, in part because music, in the early twentieth century, was considered to be "the most German of the arts."[8] But great literature always works by illustrating the general through the particular, and *Doctor Faustus* is no exception in this regard. Germanic as they may be, Leverkühn, Zeitblom, and the secondary characters that surround them are archetypes of intellectual culture more generally. Their sad fate over the course of the novel has much to tell us in the twenty-first century as well.

From Twelve-Tone Music to the "Politics of Eternity"

Such a reorientation can also help us make sense of the side of *Doctor Faustus* that poses perhaps the greatest difficulty to contemporary readers, namely the novel's focus on the invention of twelve-tone (or "dodecaphonic") composition around the time of the First World War. Mann's decision to attribute to his fictional character Adrian Leverkühn intellectual advances that had actually been undertaken by the real-life composer Arnold Schoenberg caused quarrels and confusion from the moment the novel was published. Schoenberg himself was convinced that it was done out of an attempt to deny him his rightful place in history.[9] Later critics, interested in exploring the allegorical connections between Leverkühn and the Nazis, instead reminded readers of Schoenberg's infamous proclamation from the 1920s that with twelve-tone music he had "made a discovery that will ensure the supremacy of German music for the next hundred years."[10] The arrogance that saturates these lines is indeed uncomfortably close to the megalomania of the Nazis. What better model, then, we might ask, than Arnold Schoenberg to use for a narrative

---

8   Pamela M. Potter, *Most German of the Arts: Musicology and Society from the Weimar Republic to the End of Hitler's Reich* (New Haven, CT: Yale University Press, 1998).

9   The most comprehensive treatment of the Mann-Schoenberg controversy can be found in E. Randol Schoenberg, ed., *The "Doctor Faustus" Dossier: Arnold Schoenberg, Thomas Mann, and their Contemporaries, 1930–1951* (Berkeley: University of California Press, 2018).

10   Quoted in Hans Heinz Stuckenschmidt, *Schoenberg: His Life, World and Work*, trans. Humphrey Searle (New York: Schirmer Books, 1977), 277.

in which the German cultural hubris is allegorized through the life of a modern composer?

In truth, however, Mann seems to have been unaware of Schoenberg's pronouncement, and he did not become interested in twelve-tone music because he somehow thought the story of its invention might make a good allegorical vehicle for the rise of Nazism. He held no ill wish toward Schoenberg, and although his allusions to real-world contemporaries in *Doctor Faustus* were often ethically dubious, surely he would have recognized that using the work of an exiled Jewish composer for such a purpose would have been crass beyond compare.[11] Mann was instead captivated by the ways in which modern intellectual life (including the various forms of modern art) had created an entire generation of thinkers incapable of formulating an adequate defense against a rising tide of irrationality. Central to Mann's concern was the increasingly wide intellectual gap that separated modern artists from their audience. Art, so he felt, needed to incessantly revise its formal language in order to escape becoming trapped in clichés. But in pursuing originality, it also became less and less accessible to the common man. This conundrum mirrored the condition of society at large, which, in becoming ever more specialized and technologically advanced, also became ever more obtuse and even frightening to the everyday observer.

Mann was naturally most interested in how this question played out in the realm of the novel. His essays and diary entries of the late 1930s and early 1940s document his increasing fear that the literary language he had developed during the first quarter of the twentieth century was by now useless—a concern we see most clearly in his increasing interest in the concept of "parody." (In *Doctor Faustus*, Adrian Leverkühn repeatedly expresses a similar fascination with parody.) At the same time, however, Mann mistrusted the more radical language developed by his contemporary James Joyce in works such as *Ulysses* (1922) and especially *Finnegans Wake* (1939), fearing the way in which these works sacrificed realist causality for an internal order based in mythic association and language games.[12]

Mann's treatment of dodecaphony in *Doctor Faustus* transposes this problem into the realm of modern music. In other words, Mann was

---

11 It's worth noting, however, that at least when he began the novel, Mann labored under the mistaken (and rather surprising) assumption that twelve-tone music was not only not persecuted but actually supported in the Third Reich. See the diary entry for May 8, 1943, in Thomas Mann, *Tagebücher*, ed. Peter de Mendelssohn and Inge Jens, 10 vols. (Frankfurt am Main: S. Fischer, 1977–95), V: 572–73.

12 Mann testifies to his preoccupation with Joyce in Thomas Mann, *The Story of a Novel: The Genesis of "Doctor Faustus"* (New York: Alfred A. Knopf, 1961), 91.

interested in Schoenberg and in twelve-tone composition not because he saw in them convenient vehicles by which to allegorize the rise of Nazism, but rather because he viewed Schoenberg as the musical equivalent of Joyce—a daring artist who had developed a novel and promising response to contemporary reality that, one suspects, is nevertheless not entirely sound. In pursuing this approach, Mann was greatly influenced by his neighbor in Pacific Palisades, the philosopher and music critic Theodor W. Adorno, who presented a similarly ambiguous picture of Schoenberg in his *Philosophy of New Music* (1949), which Mann read in manuscript version.

Once we learn to approach *Doctor Faustus* not as an allegory about a particular kind of historical evil, but rather as a narrative about the helplessness of advanced intellectual culture in the face of unreason, the relevance of the novel for the twenty-first century becomes much easier to see. In exploring this relevance with contemporary students, I have found the historian Timothy Snyder's arguments about the relationship between what Snyder calls a "politics of inevitability" and a "politics of eternity" extremely helpful. In a series of books, essays, and blog posts written in response to the rise of authoritarian regimes in Russia, the European Union, and America, Snyder has tried to provide a general account that would link these regimes to the dictatorships of the twentieth century without thereby becoming enmired in historical particularism.[13] His ingenious approach is to seek the common denominator for democratic backsliding not in political or economic factors, but rather in a society's relationship to *time*. As Snyder reminds us, modernity differs from pre-modernity perhaps most centrally by its teleological conception of history—by the idea that history is not a never-ending succession of ever-similar themes, but rather bends towards specific goals. This temporal understanding has great liberatory potential and has been the motor behind all great struggles for civil rights, justice, and liberty of the past few hundred years. But it can also be corrupted into smug self-security, into "a sense that [...] the laws of progress are known, that there are no alternatives, and therefore nothing really to be done." "In the American capitalist version of this story," Snyder elaborates, "nature brought the market, which brought democracy, which brought happiness. In the

---

13 See centrally Timothy Snyder, *On Tyranny: Twenty Lessons from the Twentieth Century* (New York: Tim Duggan, 2017), and *The Road to Unfreedom: Russia, Europe, America* (New York: Tim Duggan, 2018). Snyder also discusses the politics of inevitability and eternity on his YouTube Channel in a presentation archived at https://www.youtube.com/watch?v=Eghl19elKk8 (accessed July 9, 2024).

European version, history brought the nation, which learned from war that peace was good, and hence chose integration and prosperity."[14]

The confident pronouncements offered by the prophets of inevitability rarely match up with developments in the real world, however. At certain points in time, popular sentiments about the shape of history may indeed align with the talking points offered by pundits and political philosophers—Western Europe in the early 1990s, when a widespread sense of optimism in the future of liberal democracy provided a receptive environment for Francis Fukuyama's "end of history" thesis, might be a good example of such a moment.[15] But the actual progression of history is messy, and sooner or later facts will interfere with theory. And as the prophets of inevitability add ever more epicycles to their political theories, seeking to reassure ordinary people that the triumph of the market, the communist utopia, or the everlasting peace amongst nations is just around the corner, disaffection amongst those forced to put up with rampant inequality, "actually existing socialism," or the great game of aspiring superpowers grows. Eventually, the politics of inevitability collapse into a politics of eternity. "Whereas inevitability promises a better future for everyone," Snyder writes, "eternity places one nation at the center of a cyclical story of victimhood. Time is no longer a line into the future, but a circle that endlessly returns the same threats from the past."[16]

Snyder's theory of a transition from inevitability to eternity is broad enough to fit not only Russia in the 1990s and 2000s or (one fears) the United States in the 2010s and 2020s, but also Germany in the 1920s and 1930s. This aspiration towards universality, along with the strident tone of Snyder's pronouncements, raises the interesting question whether his model is not itself an example of the "politics of inevitability." However, I describe it here not because I think it is unquestionably correct, but because I think it provides a highly accessible summary of what Thomas Mann is trying to convey in *Doctor Faustus* by means of a much more densely woven allegorical account of the history of Western music.

Earlier in this chapter, I argued that Mann chose music as the allegorical vehicle for his tale "in part" because music in the early twentieth century was considered to be a particularly Germanic art. We know this to be true because of a lecture that Mann gave at the Library of Congress in May 1945, in which he stated (clearly making a disguised allusion to the novel he was then writing): "It is a grave error on the part of legend and story not to connect Faust with music. [...] If Faust is to be the representative of the German soul, he would have to be musical, for the relation

---

14 Snyder, *The Road to Unfreedom*, 7.
15 Francis Fukuyama, *The End of History and the Last Man* (New York: Free Press, 1992).
16 Snyder, *The Road to Unfreedom*, 8.

of the German to the world is abstract and mystical, that is, musical."[17] But this is not a sufficient, nor even a particularly satisfactory, explanation for the overall structure of *Doctor Faustus*. For Mann's novel does not offer a specifically "Germanic" treatment of its musical subject matter. Yes, Leverkühn makes musical advances that in real life were the intellectual property of a German composer, Arnold Schoenberg. And yes, his syphilitic infection recalls the life of the (Austrian) composer Hugo Wolf, as well as that of Robert Schumann. But Leverkühn's biography is just as much influenced by the Russo-French-American composer Igor Stravinsky and by the French composer Hector Berlioz. And while Mann devotes an entire chapter to a discussion of Ludwig van Beethoven, one of the "three Bs" that the nineteenth-century conductor Hans von Bülow had famously located at the heart of German musical identity, Bach and especially Brahms (the other two "Bs") receive comparatively scant attention. The same can be said of Wagner, though Mann does smuggle in a clever reference to the *Meistersinger* overture.[18] What we get instead are lengthy treatments of non-German composers such as Orlando di Lasso, Claudio Monteverdi, or Giovanni Pierluigi da Palestrina.[19]

Doctor Faustus, in other words, is a novel first of all about music as such, and about German music only in the sense that Mann believed the German people to have always had an especially intense relationship with a more universal problematic. In his Library of Congress lecture, Mann states: "Music is calculated order and chaos-breeding irrationality at once, rich in conjuring, incantatory gestures, in magic of numbers, the most unrealistic and yet the most impassioned of arts."[20] These lines, which I will explore at greater length in chapter 10, "Music Theory and Political Allegory," suggest that he chose music as the allegorical center

---

17 Thomas Mann, "Germany and the Germans," in *Thomas Mann's Addresses Delivered at the Library of Congress, 1942–1949* (Washington, DC: Library of Congress, 1963), 51.

18 Perhaps the reference was too clever, for even Adorno failed to recognize it when Mann sent him the passage in manuscript version (see the commentary for 142/195). Most critics treat Mann's description of this incident in *The Story of a Novel* as a humorous anecdote demonstrating Adorno's obtuseness. To me, it instead suggests that the philosopher was set up because Mann had given him no prior indication of how and why he might wish to integrate Wagner into the novel.

19 Thomas Mann criticism long neglected this extra-German dimension of *Doctor Faustus*. Important corrective accounts are offered by Hans Rudolf Vaget, "'Blödsinnig schön!' Französische Musik im *Doktor Faustus*," in *Seelenzauber: Thomas Mann und die Musik* (Frankfurt am Main: S. Fischer, 2006), 122–42, as well as by Eckart Goebel, *Esmeralda: Deutsch-französische Verhältnisse in Thomas Manns "Doktor Faustus"* (Göttingen: Wallstein Verlag, 2015).

20 Mann, "Germany and the Germans," 51.

of his novel because in its attempt to create "calculated order" out of the "chaos-breeding irrationality" of mere sound it directly resembles the struggles of the modern intellectual, who similarly wrestles to bring order to an ever-more-chaotic world. If there is one image that cuts to the very heart of *Doctor Faustus*, then, it is the one that I have chosen as the cover for this book, and which Adrian Leverkühn tacks to the wall above his piano in chapter XII (102/138) of the novel. Dürer's *Melencolia I* depicts an angel caught in a moment of melancholic contemplation, surrounded by various tokens of intellectual labor and scientific inquiry: a book, a compass, a rhombohedron, a brazier, and a balance scale, among other things. Above the angel's head hangs a magic square (an array of numbers that always adds up to the same sum, no matter if read horizontally, vertically, or along the major diagonals). Over the course of the novel, Mann will develop this magic square into a symbol of dodecaphonic composition, thereby stressing the link between music and intellectual work more generally.

Doctor Faustus documents how Leverkühn, the archetypal modern composer, becomes disenchanted by the rat race of tonal composition, in which novelty can only be achieved by ever greater harmonic subtlety, by a play with rules that have long since become too complex for ordinary listeners to genuinely appreciate. Seeking to overcome this dictatorship of tonal innovation, he turns towards a radically different compositional style, one that is based on predetermination and on endless recurrence. Thomas Mann calls this the "strict style"—his name for Schoenberg's innovation. Timothy Snyder, describing a similar development in the realm of politics, also locates predestination and the endless recycling of familiar arguments at the heart of his "politics of eternity."

Serenus Zeitblom and the Question of Accountability

In the essays that follow, I will therefore try to provide the first-time reader with all the tools necessary to understand the historical context in which *Doctor Faustus* was written and in which it takes place, along with some thoughts about the more universal significance of Mann's project. None of this means that the only enjoyment to be derived from this novel is of an intellectual sort, as we watch Thomas Mann work out a modern literary equivalent for the kind of work that political philosophers do with abstract thought. *Doctor Faustus* is, to return to my original claims, a compulsively readable and also wickedly funny book. Part of the humor comes from the many minor characters and historical vignettes with which the novel abounds. Think, for example, of Herr von Gleichen-Rußwurm, a charlatan whose rather outlandish plan for insurance fraud is ruined by a fatally uncooperative rodent. But the main source of enjoyment in Mann's novel stems from what I consider to be the true hero of the work, the narrator Serenus Zeitblom. For *Doctor Faustus* belongs to a class of modernist novels—Ford Madox Ford's *The Good Soldier* and Nabokov's *Lolita* and *Pale Fire* are other examples—in which the person telling the story is far more complex and far more interesting than the ostensible protagonist. Adrian Leverkühn, the poet Stephen Spender once claimed, resembles a "statue of genius carved in ice."[21] Nobody, by contrast, would mistake Zeitblom for a genius or accuse him of having a frozen soul. He runs hot and cold, and his decided mediocrity is not only what makes him human, but also what makes him such a fascinating character.

This is not coincidental, for Mann's purpose when he started writing his novel in March of 1943 was not only to reflect on what had happened in the past, but also to look forward into the future. The question of what Nazism's defeat might mean for the German people was just as important to him as the question of how the Third Reich had become possible to begin with. Serenus Zeitblom allowed him to tackle this question. Zeitblom is the "good German"—a term that, with Thomas Mann, should only ever be used in quotation marks. He is, in other words, a person who never gave up on the values of democratic liberalism, but who also has to confront the fact that these very values have proven so easily corruptible.

This is another dimension of *Doctor Faustus* that is highly pertinent to readers in the twenty-first century. If, as I have argued throughout this introduction, we are indeed already in a period of democratic backsliding, then the question of how we account for what has happened and how we justify our faults to future generations is of the utmost significance. In grappling with this vexing moral dilemma, Serenus Zeitblom provides a specimen case for all of us. His considerable faults should serve as a warning. His flawed humanity, however, also pulls us into the text and reminds us that *Doctor Faustus*, despite its glacial aspects, is ultimately as warm and engaging a novel as any ever written—if only we know where to look.

This allegorical dimension is not the only reason why Mann's narrator should be an especially fascinating figure for readers in the twenty-first century. In conversations with my students, I've found them to be finely attuned to the emotional nuances of Zeitblom's obvious sense of jealous possessiveness when it comes to his lifelong friend Adrian Leverkühn. The basic contours of this emotional disposition have long been known to scholarship: Zeitblom's almost obsequious devotion to Leverkühn, his willingness to follow him around from town to town, his pride at being

---

21 Stephen Spender, "Thomas Mann's *Doctor Faustus*," *The Nation*, December 4, 1948, 634–35.

allowed to address the composer with informal pronouns, his jealous dislike of Rudi Schwerdtfeger. What most academic readers have been reluctant to acknowledge, however (unlike my students, born into a different generation and unburdened by any reverence to canonical interpretations), is that Zeitblom's feelings for Leverkühn quite clearly reflect not Platonic friendship, but rather male-male desire.

Consider only the most obvious indices. Zeitblom is intensely jealous not only of Schwerdtfeger (with whom Leverkühn actually does begin a homosexual affair), but also of the only other man to win the composer's friendship: Rüdiger Schildknapp, a man whose boyish good looks and natural charm earn him numerous amorous solicitations from female acquaintances, all of which leave him "lethargic, frugal, reserved" (180/247). As if to compensate for this evident jealousy, Zeitblom repeatedly assures us of his ostensible heterosexuality and manly prowess. In chapter XVI, having just mentioned that amongst the students of the Winfried fraternity "there was no talk of women or wenches, girlfriends or love affairs" (156/214), Zeitblom practically trips over himself to report that he "had tasted of the apple, and that for some seven or eight months back then I had an affair with a lass from the common folk, a cooper's daughter" (157/214). Later in life, Zeitblom actually does wed a woman with the rather comical name Helene Ölhafen (her surname means "oil harbor" in German). By his own admission, he picks her in no small part because of the classical resonance of her first name. It's a legitimate question how happy this marriage actually is. The opening of chapter XXI, in which we briefly peek in on the Zeitbloms' domestic life, reads like a parody of Book IV of *The Odyssey* with its infamous depiction of the cold relationship between Helen of Troy and her husband King Menelaos of Sparta. Certainly, Zeitblom is willing to leave his wife and children at the drop of a hat whenever his composer friend calls. He even rents a bachelor pad in Munich so that he can more easily move about in the same social circles as Leverkühn.[22] None of these Munich friends, meanwhile, find it odd that Zeitblom usually appears without his wife. In fact, Heinrich Institoris is perfectly comfortable entrusting his own spouse to Zeitblom's company for an entire evening while he goes out to play cards. And then there is the name of the only other close friend Zeitblom has besides Leverkühn, and to whom he confides his innermost thoughts, including his secret

---

22 The vague geographic references that Mann scatters throughout *Doctor Faustus* would place this bachelor pad in the vicinity of the Englischer Garten, which, as Robert Tobin has pointed out in an analysis of Mann's novella *Death in Venice*, was well-known as a gay cruising ground at the time. See Robert Tobin, "Why is Tadzio a Boy? Perspectives on Homoeroticism in *Death in Venice*" in Thomas Mann, *Death in Venice*, trans. and ed. Clayton Koelb (New York: Norton, 1994), 207–32.

opposition to the Nazi regime. It is a Catholic priest hilariously named "Monsignore Hinterpförtner" (Monsignor Warden of the Back Door). His name fits right in with that of other self-evidently homoerotic ones in the novel, such as "Schwerdtfeger" (sword polisher; *Feger* is also a slang term for a cheeky young man) or "Zapfenstösser" (cone thruster).

It is remarkable to me that Zeitblom's sexuality, and by extension its larger importance for the novel, seems to have never received sustained attention in the critical literature. My students, on the other hand, unencumbered by any background knowledge about the collective guilt hypothesis, the debates surrounding humanism in the 1940s, or any of the other topics through which Zeitblom's role is customarily read, tend to latch onto details such as these with evident interpretive zeal. This indicates to me that twenty-first-century readers have much to contribute to the study of *Doctor Faustus* yet, not despite but rather precisely because they approach the novel without any knowledge of what one is "supposed" to say about it.

A reading of *Doctor Faustus* as the document of a queer friendship may appear frivolous to some, given the weighty intellectual questions that are undeniably being negotiated in the text. In truth, however, we are dealing with two sides of the same coin. We know, for example, that Thomas Mann in the early 1920s developed a theory of democracy that was closely tied to the conception of homosocial eros propagated by Walt Whitman in his 1871 essay "Democratic Vistas," in which the American poet describes "intense and loving comradeship, the personal and passionate attachment of man to man" as it had been shown, for example, by the soldiers of the Union Army, as the "most substantial hope and safety of the future of these [United] States."[23] This Whitmanesque theory, in turn, represented a decisive turning away from the national-chauvinistic theories of homosociality formulated by Hans Blüher, which Mann had studied with great fascination a few years earlier. Blüher argued that the German state could only be saved by tight-knit coteries of men operating outside the view of the public and willing to embrace violent means where necessary; his theories would eventually feed into the wave of reactionary militancy known as the "white terror" between 1919 and 1921.[24]

---

23 Walt Whitman, "Democratic Vistas," in *Leaves of Grass and Other Writings* (New York: Norton, 2002), 770.

24 Mann's intellectual debt to Hans Blüher has been analyzed in German by Hans Wißkirchen, "Republikanischer Eros: Zu Walt Whitmans und Hans Blühers Rolle in der politischen Publizistik Thomas Manns," in *"Heimsuchung und süßes Gift": Erotik und Poetic bei Thomas Mann*, ed. Gerhard Härle (Frankfurt am Main: S. Fischer, 1992), 17–40. For briefer treatments in English, see Anthony Heilbut, *Thomas Mann: Eros and Literature* (Berkeley: University of California Press, 1995), as well as Lawrence S. Rainey, "Introduction to 'On the German Republic,'" *Modernism/modernity* 14, no. 1 (2007): 109–32.

Mann's reflections on the role of homosocial eros took place a quarter century before the composition of *Doctor Faustus*, but were clearly much on his mind when he wrote the novel: Hans Reisiger, the friend and translator who introduced Mann to Whitman, served as the model for Rüdiger Schildknapp, and Mann exchanged several letters with Hans Blüher, whose notion of a *Männerbund* (male community) also influenced the depiction of the Winfried fraternity in chapter XIV.[25]

To approach *Doctor Faustus* as a queer text—an approach that I have found uniquely helpful in capturing the interest of my undergraduate readers—might therefore also allow us to come to novel conclusions about Mann's evolving democratic sensibilities, and about his ultimate judgment of Serenus Zeitblom. Does the narrator's affection for his composer friend more closely resemble the conception of homosocial eros advocated by Blüher or by Whitman? Or does it represent an advance over both? Settling this question would require interpretive work that is beyond the scope of an introductory guide. The act of posing it, however, already shows that plenty remains to be said about *Doctor Faustus*, and that the novel is likely to continue to enjoy a rich afterlife in the twenty-first century.

---

25   Blüher is quoted in the student newsletter that Mann consulted when he wrote the Winfried episode. Mann underlined the relevant passage and placed an exclamation mark next to it.

2: Which Edition of *Doctor Faustus* Should I Buy?

THERE ARE CURRENTLY two English editions of *Doctor Faustus* available on the American market: the 1948 translation by H.T. Lowe-Porter published by Everyman's Library (ISBN 978-0-679-40996-0), and the 1999 translation by John E. Woods published by Vintage (ISBN 978-0-375-70116-0). The choice between the two is not difficult. Helen Tracy Lowe-Porter deserves enormous credit for having translated *Doctor Faustus* quickly and (considering the work's immense linguistic difficulties) more or less accurately. But she had to do so under ruthless deadline pressure and without recourse to decades of philological scholarship that would have helped identify Mann's literary borrowings and gloss the precise meaning of some of his more arcane vocabulary. The John E. Woods translation is therefore preferable and should be chosen by any contemporary reader.[1]

In German, a bewildering number of editions have appeared over the years with Thomas Mann's lifelong publishing house, S. Fischer. All recent ones follow one of two different reference texts: the *Gesammelte Werke* (GW) edition published between 1960 and 1974, or the *Große kommentierte Frankfurter Ausgabe* (GKFA) edition, publication of which has been ongoing since 2001. (The volume containing *Doctor Faustus* came out in 2007).

Among academics, it is a subject of some debate which of these two reference texts should be preferred. In a scene that could have been taken straight from a Mann novel, I once witnessed two professors get into a shouting match over this question at an otherwise eminently respectable literature conference in Zurich. And in defense of these two gentlemen, the differences between the two versions are indeed significant. For one thing, the GW edition reproduces the text of the 1947 "Stockholm edition," the newer GKFA version the 1948 "Vienna edition." (Both editions, however, also reproduce the Author's Note containing Mann's nod to Arnold Schoenberg, which wasn't included until the "Suhrkamp edition" published later in 1948.) In the months that passed between the

---

1   Readers interested in a more comprehensive analysis of the differences between the Lowe-Porter and Woods translations should consult David Horton, *Thomas Mann in English: A Study in Literary Translation* (London: Bloomsbury Academic, 2016).

publication of the Stockholm and Vienna editions, Mann not only fixed many typographical errors but also made significant cuts, especially in chapters VIII and IX, which reduced the overall length of the novel by around twenty pages. The GKFA edition is thus shorter than the GW edition.

In addition, Ruprecht Wimmer and Stephan Stachorski, the editors of the GKFA *Doktor Faustus,* made some contentious editorial interventions. For instance, they restored the date that Serenus Zeitblom gives as the starting point of his biographical project to "May 27, 1943," just as it had been in all early editions of *Doctor Faustus,* even though most scholars agree that this was due to an error in the manuscript. The GW had therefore silently corrected the date to "May 23, 1943"—the day on which Mann, too, began writing his novel. The editors also changed the non-sensical phrase *Fugengewicht der Akkorde* (fugal weight of the chords) in chapter VIII to read *Eigengewicht der Akkorde* (inherent weight of the chords), the phrasing used by Theodor W. Adorno in the handwritten letter from which Mann got these words.

Despite my own disagreement with these particular changes, all page references to the German edition in this *Reader's Guide* are to the GKFA edition. I recommend that a reader interested in perusing the text in the original language (or just in comparing key passages to the English translation) purchase the paperback edition that bears the subtitle "In der Fassung der Großen kommentierten Frankfurter Ausgabe" (ISBN 978-3-596-90403-7). I have two reasons for favoring the GKFA. First, it is now preferred by the majority of scholars.[2] Second, Wimmer and Stachorski did yeoman's work in preparing the commentary volume for the GKFA edition. It is more than a thousand pages long and informs almost every aspect of the much shorter commentary I created for the present book. To key my paginations to a different edition than theirs would have been a sign of profound disrespect.

My choice creates some additional problems, however. When John E. Woods carried out his English translation in the late 1990s, the GKFA was not yet available. His reference text was thus the GW. This creates the unusual situation of a translated version that includes passages cut from the now-standard edition in the original language. For reasons of concision, I have chosen not to highlight all the discrepancies in my

---

2   Academics about to embark on their first forays into Thomas Mann scholarship (as well as undergraduates condemned to write a research paper on *Doctor Faustus*) may want to make note that the scholarly convention is to refer to volumes from the GW edition by Roman numerals, to ones from the GKFA edition by Arabic numerals. Thus, a reference to the first page of *Doctor Faustus* would appear as "(VI: 9)" if the GW edition is being quoted and as "(10.1: 11)" if the GKFA edition is being quoted.

commentary. Readers might be interested in knowing, however, that if one of my comments is keyed to a German page number that is higher than nine hundred (and therefore to an appendix in the GKFA commentary volume), the passage in question was cut by Mann in 1948 as being non-essential to the novel.

3: What Should I Pay Attention to as I Read the Novel?

THE FOLLOWING FIVE sets of questions should help first-time readers get their bearings in *Doctor Faustus*:

i. Narration

Serenus Zeitblom, the narrator of *Doctor Faustus*, is an extremely memorable figure. What are his main personality traits and how do they affect the story that he tells? What is the precise nature of his relationship to Adrian Leverkühn? What does Zeitblom think about the Nazi regime under which he lives? How does he approach the topic of demonic forces, which are an integral part of any Faust story?

More information about Zeitblom's narrative style can be found in chapter 6, "*Doctor Faustus* and Literary Modernism."

ii. The Faust Tradition

The relationship of *Doctor Faustus* to the Faust tradition is not necessarily immediately obvious. What characteristics make Leverkühn a Faust figure and what events in the plot resemble those of other Faust stories? Critics have declared the Faust legend to be both peculiarly German in nature and a foundational "myth of modern individualism" (Ian Watt). What stance does Thomas Mann take on this question?

Readers unfamiliar with the myth can find a summary in chapter 5, "A Brief History of the Faust Theme." I also examine some of the more peculiar aspects of Mann's treatment in chapter 11, "Illness and Redemption."

iii. Politics

We learn on the very first page of the novel that Serenus Zeitblom begins composing his text in May of 1943, amidst allied bombing raids on Nazi Germany. How does *Doctor Faustus* comment on the genesis of the Third Reich, and what larger lessons does it offer about politics? What does the novel have to say about liberalism, republicanism, nationalism, fascism, and other political traditions?

Chapter 7, "The Historical Setting of the Novel," may be useful for readers unfamiliar with German history of the early twentieth century. I offer a more sustained investigation of politics in *Doctor Faustus* in chapter 10, "Music Theory and Political Allegory."

iv. Music and Culture

Doctor Faustus is perhaps most famous as a novel about twelve-tone music, but in truth its artistic reach is far wider and Mann spends at least as much time talking about early modern polyphony as he does discussing avant-garde compositions. What is the larger narrative that he is trying to construct, and how does it comment on artistic and intellectual life more generally? What do the extremely detailed discussions of fictional musical pieces add to the story?

I analyze Mann's discussion of music in greater detail in chapter 10, "Music Theory and Political Allegory," and offer an account of how Leverkühn relates to the German cultural tradition in chapter 9, "Five Masters from Germany."

v. Redemption

Faust narratives are, at their core, stories about damnation and the possibility of redemption. These were not abstract questions for Thomas Mann, who wrote his novel as a refugee from Nazi Germany and was heavily preoccupied with the future of his native country. How does *Doctor Faustus* employ symbolism and Bible quotations to incorporate a religious element into an otherwise largely secular story? What does the novel have to say about damnation and redemption? Is Zeitblom's final prayer, "May God have mercy on your poor soul, my friend, my fatherland," justified?

Zeitblom's hopes and the question of Leverkühn's redemption are the subject of chapter 11, "Illness and Redemption."

Part Two: Contexts

4: Composition and Publication History

Composition

THE ROOTS OF the *Doctor Faustus* project reach back to about 1904, when Thomas Mann recorded in his notebooks a plan for a novel about a "syphilitic artist who, driven by longing, approaches a pure, sweet, young and unsuspecting girl, becomes engaged to her and shoots himself as the marriage approaches."[1] Sometime after this, he added a further characterization of the "syphilitic artist as Dr. Faust and as someone who has sold his soul to the devil. The poison works as an intoxicant, a stimulant, an inspiration: he is allowed to create wonderful works of genius in a state of rapturous passion, the devil leading his hand. But finally *the devil gets him*: paralysis. The matter of the pure young girl that he seeks to wed will precede this."[2] When he wrote these lines, Mann, born in 1875, was not even thirty years old, but had already made a reputation for himself as an author whose novels and stories commonly revolved around the tensions between artistic and "ordinary" ways of living. These earlier notes to *Doctor Faustus* clearly continue this preoccupation, even if they break new ground through the ambitious plan of incorporating allusions to one of the best-known stories from German literary history.

The next few years were artistically hard ones for Mann, however, who started and abandoned multiple projects as he attempted to write a follow-up to his biggest successes to date, the novel *Buddenbrooks* (1901) and the novella *Tonio Kröger* (1903). The Faust project fell by the wayside. Mann eventually pulled himself out of this period of relative infertility with the undisputed masterpiece *Death in Venice* (1912). Over the next few decades, he became one of the best-known writers in the world; his novel *The Magic Mountain* (1924) made him a household name in the literary centers of Western Europe, and in 1929 his career was crowned when he was awarded the Nobel Prize in Literature. Over the same time period, he underwent a process of political conversion. He had begun his life as a conservative German nationalist and vehemently defended this position as late as 1918, when he published the book-length *Reflections of a Non-Political Man*. But his experience of the abortive German

---

1   Thomas Mann, *Notizbücher*, ed. Hans Wysling and Yvonne Schmidlin, 2 vols. (Frankfurt am Main: S. Fischer, 1991–1992), II, 107.
2   Mann, *Notizbücher*, II, 121–22.

revolution of 1918/1919, along with his disgust for the ever-more reactionary elements that were infiltrating the social life of his adopted hometown of Munich, led to a process of democratic conversion. In 1922 he publicly embraced the Weimar constitution. Over time, his politics even drifted towards the social democratic. Still, memories collected during his conservative period would serve him well when it came to writing *Doctor Faustus*, where the chapters devoted to the reactionary Schlaginhaufen salon (XXVIII), the German revolution (XXXIII), and the proto-fascist Kridwiss Circle (XXXIV) all draw on personal experience.

Mann's literary fame, along with his embrace of democracy and his ensuing verbal attacks on the Nazis, placed him high on the list of public enemies when Hitler came to power in 1933. The author and his family became exiles from Germany, first in Switzerland (and briefly in the south of France), then, starting in 1938, in the United States, where Mann lived and taught at Princeton before moving to the Los Angeles area in 1941, eventually settling in the suburb of Pacific Palisades. For the first decade of his exile period, Mann was largely preoccupied with the massive *Joseph* tetralogy, a series of novels retelling the well-known story from the Old Testament with all the tools at the disposal of a modernist writer. Begun as an apolitical project, the *Joseph* novels soon morphed into an allegorical commentary on contemporary events, with Joseph's brothers, who toss him into the well, personifying the fascist rabble, Joseph himself taking on features of Thomas Mann, and the administrative reforms that he initiates in Egypt standing in for Roosevelt's New Deal. During those same years, Mann lectured far and wide on political events, recorded propaganda broadcasts for the BBC, and dined at the White House. Eventually he became so famous that his name was even tossed around as that of a future president of a democratic postwar Germany.

Mann concluded his work on the *Joseph*-novels in January of 1943 and immediately followed up on them with another Biblical tale meant to undermine the Nazis, the story "The Tables of the Law." Already in late October of 1942, however, his thoughts had returned to the Faustus project of his youth. At Stalingrad, the Red Army was doggedly resisting the Wehrmacht; a few weeks later, the Western Allies landed in Northern Africa as part of Operation Torch. A German defeat, unthinkable during the first years of the war, began to seem not only possible but actually likely. It was an ideal time, then, to begin a process of reckoning, and what better way to do so than through a retelling of the story of Doctor Faustus, a man who sells his soul to the devil for immeasurable temporal gain but ends up by being dragged into hell? In this way, a project that forty years earlier had been conceived on a fairly personal level became filled with world-historical significance.

Mann wasn't a stranger to huge novels commenting on contemporary history. *The Magic Mountain* had already fulfilled this function for the First World War and had played a major part in the struggles over collective memory that roiled the Weimar public sphere.[3] Writing an analysis of the German soul in its lowest depths from a position of exile was a task that presented special challenges, however—challenges that would have major repercussions for the history of the novel form.

In early 1943, Mann was not yet cognizant of what lay ahead of him. He spent several months collecting materials and then began writing on May 23, 1943, the same day on which he has Serenus Zeitblom commence his biographical reflections (although due to an oversight on Mann's part, some editions of the novel give this date as May 27 instead). Detailed research was integral to Mann's compositional process, for he was an author who much preferred adapting preexisting materials over inventing subjects out of thin air. Indeed, in his 1906 essay "Bilse and I," his first major work of self-commentary, he had argued that "if one searches for great 'inventors' in literary history one never ends up with the best names."[4] The most important source for such preexisting materials was Thomas Mann's own past life, a fact that has proven fortuitous for later scholars, since it meant that when the author destroyed large parts of his diaries in May 1945 (possibly because they contained compromising revelations about his homosexuality) he preserved the records for the years 1918–21, which he needed for the Munich chapters of *Doctor Faustus*. The novel is filled with thinly fictionalized accounts of autobiographical experiences and also contains many a biting portrait of people who considered themselves family friends. Mann privately referred to these portraits as "literary murders" and had to extend a great deal of energy smoothing things over after *Doctor Faustus* was published.

But in order to write as complex a novel as *Doctor Faustus*, Mann also had to engage in significant research into secondary sources. Academics have invested an enormous amount of detective work over the past few decades tracking down the hundreds of books and articles that Mann likely consulted. Since the particulars are of limited relevance for a first-time encounter with *Doctor Faustus*, I have refrained from providing a comprehensive listing.[5] Nevertheless, a partial catalogue of only the most impor-

---

3 For an excellent introduction to *The Magic Mountain* and its cultural significance see Morten Høj Jensen, *The Master of Contradictions: Thomas Mann and the Making of "The Magic Mountain"* (New Haven, CT: Yale University Press, 2025).

4 Thomas Mann, "Bilse und Ich," in *Große kommentierte Frankfurter Ausgabe: Werke—Briefe—Tagebücher*, ed. Heinrich Detering, Eckhard Heftrich, Hermann Kurzke, et al. (Frankfurt am Main: S. Fischer Verlag, 2002–), 14.1: 99. In all further notes, this edition will be abbreviated as GKFA, with references given to volume, sub-volume, and page number.

5 Readers who speak German can find a detailed list of all the titles that have been identified in GKFA 10.2: 1169–75. In English, the best source—still

tant titles would include the volumes *The Story of Music* and *Beethoven* by the music critic Paul Bekker, Ernest Newman's *The Unconscious Beethoven*, Arnold Schoenberg's *Theory of Harmony*, an explanatory guide to musical instruments by Fritz Volbach, a fifteenth-century inquisitor's manual known as the *Malleus Maleficarum* or "Hammer of Witches," biographies of the sixteenth-century artists Albrecht Dürer and Tilmann Riemenschneider as well as of Ludwig van Beethoven and Friedrich Nietzsche, the memoirs of Hector Berlioz and Igor Stravinsky, the letters of Martin Luther and of Austrian composer Hugo Wolf, a bevy of scientific articles that proved crucial for chapters III and XXVII, medical literature on the progression of syphilis, and the newsletter of a conservative student fraternity, which helped inform chapter XIV.

Just as important as these written sources were conversations and epistolary exchanges that Mann conducted with friends and family. His youngest son Michael (then a violist with the San Francisco Symphony) sent him a letter that included a lengthy introduction to musical theory. The theologian Paul Tillich contributed detailed information about the curriculum for German divinity students in the early twentieth century, which Mann incorporated into chapters XI–XIII. By far the most formative, however, were Mann's conversations with the philosopher and musical theorist Theodor W. Adorno, who had settled just a few miles down the road from him in Brentwood. Adorno served as an informal musical advisor to Mann. He performed and explained many of the musical pieces that are mentioned in the novel, gave Mann copies of his writings (most importantly the 1937 essay "Late Style in Beethoven" as well as a manuscript version of *Philosophy of New Music*, which would eventually be published in 1949), proofread Mann's manuscripts and even drafted paragraph-length descriptions of fictional compositions that Mann then incorporated wholesale into his novel. Most of what Mann knew about the twelve-tone technique, for example, derived from Adorno. The fact that *Doctor Faustus* never acknowledges this debt (except in the sense that Mann lends Adorno's facial features and distinctive horn-rimmed glasses to the devil in chapter XXV, which is hardly a flattering tribute) led to some friction between the two men.

Mann's complex relationship with Adorno illustrates what precisely the author meant when he privileged "adaptation" over "inspiration." Mann did not simply use ideas that he found in his secondary sources to shape his own writing. Instead, he frequently copied entire passages from his readings into his novel, altering them only slightly and otherwise

---

relevant and eminently readable more than sixty years after it was originally published—is Gunilla Bergsten, *Thomas Mann's "Doctor Faustus": The Sources and Structure of the Novel*, trans. Krishna Winston (Chicago: University of Chicago Press, 1969).

presenting them as if they were his own work. At times, it is clear that he did not even understand the full ramifications of what he was copying. For example, he relied heavily on Adorno to flesh out Wendell Kretzschmar's lectures on Beethoven in chapter VIII, and amongst other things included verbatim quotations from a letter that Adorno had written to him explicating Beethoven's piano sonata Op. 111. Unfortunately, he had a hard time deciphering Adorno's handwriting and rendered the philosopher's phrase *Eigengewicht der Akkorde* (inherent weight of the chords) as the non-sensical *Fugengewicht der Akkorde* (fugal weight of the chords) (59/84).

Among literary and musical theorists, this kind of deliberate cut-and-pasting is known as "montage"; I will explore it more fully in chapter 6, "*Doctor Faustus* and Literary Modernism." For present purposes, it is worth stressing that Mann's montage work extended even to his personal life, making *Doctor Faustus* a novel that veers precariously and excitingly from the extremely objective (e.g., passages from textbooks inserted into the narrative) to the painfully intimate. In chapter XXXV, for example, Mann quotes verbatim from the suicide note of his younger sister Carla, who poisoned herself in 1910 and was dragged into service as the real-life model for the character of Clarissa Rodde thirty-five years after her death. The ethical implications of this trigger vigorous debate even to the present day.

Work on the novel progressed steadily over the next four years, even as the Third Reich fell in May of 1945. A caesura of a more personal sort occurred in the spring of 1946, when Mann had to interrupt work in order to travel to Chicago and undergo surgery on his lungs. His family kept the true gravity of the situation from him: Mann had been diagnosed with cancer. Even without full knowledge of what was happening to him, however, the seventy-year-old author undoubtedly realized that his condition was serious. As soon as had he recovered from the immediate effects of the surgery, he propped himself up in his hospital bed and continued working on *Doctor Faustus* with grim determination. On January 29, 1947, he brought his project to a successful completion. His desire to give a literary shape to an epoch had clearly not been sated, however, for just a few months later he sat down again to write *The Story of a Novel*, his 1949 account of the composition of *Doctor Faustus*, which simultaneously serves as a vivid portrait of the émigré community in Los Angeles.

Publication History

By the time Mann finished *Doctor Faustus*, the Third Reich had been defeated and the question of what a postwar Germany might look like was no longer an abstract matter. The international book market had changed as well. For much of Thomas Mann's exile period, his works were banned in Nazi Germany. His German publisher, Gottfried Bermann Fischer, had to relocate first to Austria, then to neutral Sweden, from whence Mann's books were shipped to the ever-dwindling number of European countries where they could legally be sold. Both financially and reputationally, the English translations that were published by Alfred A. Knopf in the United States and by Martin Secker in Great Britain became more and more important. Mann was keenly aware of this fact and went to great lengths to manage his international reputation. He sent chapters of *Doctor Faustus* to his long-time translator Helen Tracy Lowe-Porter almost as soon as he finished them, hoping to get a lucrative English-language edition between covers as quickly as possible.

This rushed production schedule put a great deal of stress on Lowe-Porter and was not exactly beneficial for the quality of her translation. But it did mean that the English-language version could be released in 1948, just a year after the first German edition by Bermann Fischer came out in Stockholm. Even before that, Alfred A. Knopf had published a limited-edition German version of *Doctor Faustus* in America in order to secure the copyright, for Mann had become a U.S. citizen in 1944 and the laws of his adopted country specified that American authors who published their works abroad first would thereby forfeit any copyright protection in the United States. This provision was meant to shield the domestic book trade, but was evidently counterintuitive in a case like Mann's.

The year 1948 also saw the publication of a second and much revised German version of *Doctor Faustus*, which came out in Vienna (the city to which the Bermann-Fischer Verlag had relocated in preparation for an eventual return to Germany), as well as of a licensed edition published by Suhrkamp Verlag in Berlin. These later editions not only fixed the usual typographical errors (exacerbated by the fact that most of the production personnel in Stockholm could not read German) but also contained a number of cuts, which Mann specified because he feared that the original version might overwhelm the reader.

When the 1947 Stockholm edition came out, Germany still lay in ruins and there were only very limited distribution networks that could have carried the novel to readers in Mann's native country. Copies thus almost exclusively shipped to the wider European market, especially to Switzerland. It was really only with the Suhrkamp edition that *Doctor Faustus* reached its intended target audience. The Suhrkamp edition was also the first to append an "Author's Note" meant to appease the composer Arnold Schoenberg, who took a dim view of the novel's montage technique and regarded the various descriptions of twelve-tone composition that Mann had attributed to Adrian Leverkühn as simple plagiarism.

This convoluted production history raises a number of interesting questions about *Doctor Faustus*. Thomas Mann was a native of Germany who thought and wrote in German but had been stripped of his citizenship and was now a citizen of the United States. His novel was published in America in German before it came out in English, but the English-language version was financially far more lucrative than all other versions put together. It also received more press coverage. In Germany, readers would at first have had a very hard time getting their hands on *Doctor Faustus*, and an even harder time obtaining domestic versions of Mann's earlier works, which had not been available for years. At least some people, however, would have been able to acquire English versions of these books, which entered the country in the knapsacks of American soldiers, or U.S.-produced German-language editions, which arrived in the pockets of repatriated POWs who had received Mann's novels as part of political reeducation measures.[6]

Not that there was an excessive amount of interest. For a number of years, Mann would routinely be derided in West Germany as a subservient vassal of the occupying Americans. A sense of collective guilt, along with the recognition that the émigrés from Hitler's Germany had been refugees, not traitors, developed only slowly. In East Germany, by contrast, Mann was lionized, though often more for political reasons than out of true literary appreciation.

Is *Doctor Faustus*, then, a German novel or an American one? And was the Thomas Mann of the 1940s a German or an American? For much of the twentieth century, the answer was clear: Thomas Mann was considered an unmistakably German author. As twenty-first-century readers, however, we are much more accustomed to the vagaries of transnational citizenship and of hybrid identities. Our answer may instead be that he was both, for there is no logical reason why an author might not be a part of two national traditions, or why the category of "national literature" should be given priority over that of "world literature." Indeed, the complicated production history of *Doctor Faustus* foreshadows the contemporary moment, in which translations of successful authors frequently appear nearly simultaneously with the originals, and often outstrip them in sales and influence. In this way, too, *Doctor Faustus* points towards the future.

---

6 I trace the convoluted publication and consumption history of Mann's books in the immediate postwar era in the fifth and sixth chapters of *Thomas Mann's War*.

5: A Brief History of the Faust Theme

WHEN THE YOUNG Thomas Mann decided in or about 1904 that he would like to write a novel about a "syphilitic artist as Dr. Faust," he was invoking an archetype that had played a major role in both German and world literature for over three centuries. Beyond that, the allure of the Faust legend had long ago spread to the theater, to the visual arts, and—crucially for Mann's project—to classical music.

Historical sources tell us that an astrologer and magician by the name of George (Latin: "Georgius," German: "Jörg") Helmstetter was born in the small town of Helmstadt near Heidelberg around 1466 ("Helmstetter" simply means "of the town of Helmstadt"). He enrolled at the University of Heidelberg in 1483, graduating as a *magister* of philosophy in 1487.[1] Shortly afterwards, he began a career as an astrologer and chiromancer (palmist), infuriating traditional practitioners of these crafts by his unorthodox ways but winning powerful patrons. Helmstetter seems to have experimented with a number of pseudonyms during this stage of his career, eventually settling on the nom-de-plum "Faustus," which means "fortunate" in Latin and "fist" in German. By the early 1500s, he may well have added necromancy to his repertoire and may have boastfully compared his ability to perform miracles to that of Christ; the truth is difficult to ascertain because the main charges against him were written by a professional rival, the abbot Johannes Trithemius. Trithemius's 1507 indictment was widely circulated and eventually led to charges of pederasty, sodomy, and devil worship being leveled against Faustus. These charges seem to have done no irreparable harm to his career, however, for Faustus soon found himself at the court of Emperor Charles V, for whom he drew up several horoscopes.

The historical Faustus died sometime around 1540, most likely in the small town of Staufen im Breisgau, located in the southwestern corner of contemporary Germany. Even before that, the lengthy process by which his life would be turned into one of the most enduring archetypes of literary history had been set into motion. In the early 1530s,

---

[1] Detailed information about the historical Dr. Faustus, as well as about the early legends that formed around him, can be found in Frank Baron, "Faustus of the Sixteenth Century: His Life, Legend, and Myth," in *The Faustian Century: German Literature and Culture in the Age of Luther and Faustus*, ed. J. M. van der Laan and Andrew Weeks (Rochester, NY: Camden House, 2013), 43–46.

the Protestant reformer Martin Luther mentioned Faustus twice during his so-called "table talks," on both occasions referring to the magician as an instrument of the devil's futile attempts to destroy him. These table talks were published in 1566 but widely circulated in fragmentary form before then. One of the people who was clearly familiar with them was a certain Johannes Manlius, a student of Luther's close associate Philip Melanchthon. In 1563, Manlius published his own account of Faustus, ostensibly based on anecdotes told to him by his former teacher. Manlius changed Faustus' first name to Johannes and his alma mater from Heidelberg to Cracow, then rumored to be a center of the black arts. He also claimed that Faustus had lived at Wittenberg, a location not attested in the historical records. This last change would prove to be particularly important, for it firmly associated Faustus with central Germany and, more specifically, with the home of the Protestant Reformation, despite his having led a rather peripatetic life mostly on the southern edges of the German-speaking world. In Manlius's retelling, Faustus began to morph from a mere charlatan into a heretic, somebody who had transgressed against the very foundations of the new faith that was being proclaimed in Wittenberg.

The first book-length retelling of the story of Faustus was published in 1587 in Frankfurt by a printer named Johann Spies; its author is unknown but may well have been Spies himself. This *Historia von D. Johann Fausten* (History of Dr. John Faust) is often referred to simply as the *Volksbuch* or "chapbook"—a "chapbook" in this sense being a collection of heterogenous and frequently anonymous prose fragments intended for a mass audience.[2] (For simplicity's sake, I have capitalized all further instances of "chapbook" when referring specifically to this 1587 edition, rather than to the genre as a whole). The Chapbook became the keystone work for all further literary adaptations throughout the centuries and served as Mann's primary inspiration—he reread it in March 1943, just as he was beginning to write *Doctor Faustus*, and he also studied a nineteenth-century retelling of the work in the summer of 1945. Besides shortening and Germanizing the name of the protagonist, the Chapbook introduced a number of consequential changes to the previously existing narratives, most importantly by adding the idea of a devil's pact. According to this new trope, Faust sells his soul in exchange for twenty-four years in which the forces of darkness must do his bidding.

---

2 For a good introduction to the Chapbook, see Gerald Strauss, "How to Read a *Volksbuch*: The Faust Book of 1587," in *Faust through Four Centuries: Retrospect and Analysis*, ed. Peter Boerner and Sidney Johnson (Tübingen: Max Niemeyer, 1989), 27–39, as well as Marguerie de Huszar Allen, "The Aesthetics of the 1587 Spies *Historia von D. Johann Fausten*" in *The Faustian Century*, ed. van der Laan and Weeks, 149–75.

Much of the narrative is then taken up with an account of various Satanic adventures; Mann would allude to many of these in *Doctor Faustus*, even if in sometimes heavily altered form. For instance, Faust travels throughout the known world and to the limits of the macrocosm, yet always returns to Wittenberg (chapters XXVII with the expedition to the depths of the sea and into deep space, as well as XXXVII with the rejected temptation by Fitelberg); he learns about the true nature of hell and is told that he may never marry (chapter XXV); he encounters Helen of Troy (who in Mann's novel comically figures as the wife of Serenus Zeitblom); and he ultimately repents, drawing up his final will and testament (chapters XLIII through XLVII). Mann also borrows the names of some of his characters from the Chapbook and frequently quotes from it verbatim in those passages in which Leverkühn speaks in an archaic German—another important example of the montage technique already mentioned in the previous chapter.

In adding these accounts of Satanic dealings, the anonymous author of the Chapbook was directly responding to changing historical circumstances in the late sixteenth century. The early 1500s, when the historical George Faustus performed his tricks throughout Europe, had been a time of comparatively liberal theological attitudes. By the second half of the century, people who openly flirted with black magic were liable to see themselves persecuted as witches. The Chapbook was heavily influenced by contemporary accounts of witch trials, and it also amplified Manlius's example of framing the Faust story as a morality tale about the dangers of theological heterodoxy. Mann recognized that these characteristics provided a fertile basis on which to construct an allegory of a society's downfall into collective madness. He consequently conducted his own research into witchcraft trials, studying the *Malleus Maleficarum* (Hammer of Witches) by the fifteenth-century inquisitor Henricus Institoris and quoting extensively from this work when he drafted Eberhard Schleppfuss's lectures in chapter XIII, Adrian Leverkühn's final address in chapter XLVII, and several other passages.

The Spies Chapbook became an instant bestseller and went through ten printings in its first year alone. An English translation appeared in 1588 as *The History of the Damnable Life and Deserved Death of Doctor John Faustus*. One of its readers was the great Elizabethan playwright Christopher Marlowe, who immediately set out to turn the story into a play, which premiered on the London stage as *The Tragical History of Doctor Faustus* in 1589. From England, dramatic adaptations of the Faust myth made their way back to the European continent by means of itinerant puppet theaters. For several centuries, the Faust story, which provided ample opportunities for primitive stage magic and also obeyed a clear division into good and evil characters (eminently suited for wooden marionettes that do not have variable facial expressions and thus cannot easily convey emotional nuance), formed a major part of the European puppet repertoire.[3] Mann read Marlowe's play in November 1943; as a younger man he had almost certainly also seen a performance of one of the puppet plays. This latter experience likely inspired him to have Adrian Leverkühn write a puppet opera based on the *Gesta Romanorum* in chapter XXI. Mann was also led by these theatrical sources to the Elizabethan convention of mirroring a tragical plot with a comical one. In Marlowe's play, Faust's assistant Wagner, who has only a very minor part in the Chapbook, becomes a prominent source of comic relief. In Mann's novel, Serenus Zeitblom performs a similar function.

Over the following two centuries, a number of different adaptations of the Faust myth were published both in Germany and elsewhere. But the next momentous event in the history of this literary archetype did not come until 1770 or 1771, when a young Johann Wolfgang von Goethe attended the performance of a Faust play in Strasbourg. The production clearly left an impression, for Goethe remembered it two years later when he attended the trial of a woman who had killed her infant son. Interlacing these two stories, Goethe created a highly original revision of the Faust myth in which both Faust and the devil barely resemble their counterparts from the Chapbook. The version of the play that we now know as *Faust I* was eventually published in 1808, the even more audacious sequel *Faust II* in 1832. Both texts became landmarks of the German literary tradition and have also exerted a profound effect on world letters.[4]

Critics have often claimed that Mann avoided any direct engagement with Goethe's plays when he wrote *Doctor Faustus*.[5] However, this is true only in a superficial sense. It is certainly correct that Mann did not incorporate any of the distinctive plot elements from Goethe's plays into his novel, and he also included only a small handful of quotations from these works, whereas he frequently cited verbatim from the Chapbook. But

---

3   For more on the theatrical and filmic afterlife of the Faust legend, see Sara Munson Deats, *The Faust Legend: From Marlow and Goethe to Contemporary Drama and Film* (Cambridge: Cambridge University Press, 2019).

4   The literature on Goethe's *Faust* is far too vast to summarize here. Jane K. Brown, *Faust: Theater of the World* (New York: Twayne Publishers, 1992) provides an excellent starting point, as do the various essays and background materials compiled in Johann Wolfgang von Goethe, *Faust*, trans. Walter Arndt, ed. Cyrus Hamlin (New York: Norton Critical Edition, 2001).

5   One articulation of this view can be found in Bergsten, *Thomas Mann's "Doctor Faustus,"* 48–49. Textual evidence for it can be found in Mann's own commentaries on his novel. For instance, he wrote on February 5, 1948 that, "[Ludwig Marcuse] wrote that I had written the most un-Goethean *Faustus* possible, which I think is right. My composer owes much more to the Faust of the Chapbook than he does to the one from Goethe." See Mann, *Selbstkommentare*, 162.

Doctor Faustus does owe a large debt to at least four of Goethe's major structural transformations of the story. First, Goethe's Faust is no longer content to use his Satanic powers to accumulate wealth, fancy foodstuffs, or sexual conquests, as his early modern forebears had been. He instead aims to transform the world and leave a lasting legacy, something that is also very much the goal of Adrian Leverkühn. Second, Goethe wrote his Faust story not in order to illuminate Lutheran orthodoxy, but rather to create an allegory of the transformative historical forces that he saw at work everywhere around him. Similarly large-scale ambitions also animate *Doctor Faustus*, although Mann is interested in plotting the ultimate outcome of processes that Goethe witnessed in their infancy. Third, Goethe put his dramatic focus not on the damnation of his protagonist, but rather on the harm and suffering that Faust's actions inflict on the people in his vicinity. This, too, is true of Mann's novel, which is at its most emotionally resonant when it focuses on those who are hurt by Leverkühn, whether it be Rüdiger Schildknapp, Rudi Schwerdtfeger, Marie Godeau, Serenus Zeitblom or, most affectingly, little Nepomuk Schneidewein. Finally, Goethe, in perhaps his most significant departure from the Chapbook, explicitly allows his Faust to be redeemed at the end of the play. Mann does not go quite this far, but he does introduce ambiguities that are at odds with the early modern sources. I will explore these ambiguities more fully in chapter 11, "Illness and Redemption."

Beyond these thematic borrowings, Mann clearly also learned stylistic lessons from Goethe. The Chapbook is a heterogeneous text, whose component parts have often struck readers as arbitrary and ill-arranged. In *Faust II*, Goethe showed how such an eclectic compositional structure could be used to explode the confines of traditional theater and create what the critic Franco Moretti memorably called a "modern epic."[6] Mann's *Doctor Faustus*, too, uses a highly digressive and frequently unpredictable narrative structure to break with the limitations of the nineteenth-century novel and create an allegory of the twentieth century in all its extremes.

Goethe's *Faust* plays had such an immediate and forceful impact on world letters that it would be futile to try and catalogue all the subsequent adaptations that appeared over the next 125 years. There were poems and plays by Alexander Pushkin, Heinrich Heine, Frank Wedekind, Fernando Pessoa, and Gertrude Stein; prose versions by Ivan Turgenev, Oscar Wilde, Mikhail Bulgakov, and Mann's own son Klaus; musical adaptations by Franz Schubert, Hector Berlioz, Albert Lortzing, Robert Schumann, Franz Liszt, Charles Gounod, and Ferruccio Busoni; films by Georges Méliès and F.W. Murnau; drawings and paintings by

---

6   Franco Moretti, *Modern Epic: The World-System from Goethe to García Márquez*, trans. Quintin Hoare (London: Verso, 1996), 11–98.

Eugène Delacroix and James Tissot; philosophical ruminations by Oswald Spengler and Georg Lukács. Of all these possible sources of inspiration, the only ones that seem to have had a marked influence on *Doctor Faustus* were the musical ones.[7] Thomas Mann was a great lover of nineteenth-century music, and he treasured both Berlioz's opera *The Damnation of Faust* (1846) and Gounod's opera *Faust* (1859); he listened to the latter repeatedly while writing his novel. These works would, of course, have confirmed him in his ambition to link the Faust theme to the development of Western music. Just as importantly, they served as a constant reminder that the Faust story had become an international literary archetype, resonating just as strongly on the other side of the Rhine as it did in Germany—another example of how *Doctor Faustus*, although it focuses on a specifically German tale, really aims for a much wider significance. Passing references to both operas can be found throughout *Doctor Faustus*, especially in chapters XXVII and XXVIII, the two that are overtly concerned with French music.

Mann's novel was greatly influenced not only by these two explicit Faust-operas, however, but also by a range of other works that play with the devil theme. Mann was a passionate admirer of Berlioz's *Symphonie Fantastique* (1830), for example, which is also mentioned in chapter XXVIII. And he loved Wagner's opera *The Flying Dutchman* (1843), whose protagonist mocks God and finds himself condemned to a life of endless journeying until a young girl redeems him—a fate not at all unlike that of Goethe's Faust. Leverkühn attends a performance of *The Flying Dutchman* in chapter IX, and the redemption motif may well have influenced the story of Nepomuk Schneidewein in chapters XLIV and XLV. By far the most important of these ancillary musical sources, however, was Carl Maria von Weber's 1821 opera *Der Freischütz*, about a young hunter who makes a pact with a devil figure named Samiel. Not only is "Samiel" the name by which Thomas Mann's devil wishes to be called in chapter XXV, *Der Freischütz* also concludes with a prayer by a pious hermit set in the key of C major, the only scale not to feature any black keys. Leverkühn plays excerpts of this prayer on the piano in chapter XVI when he is trying to protect himself from the succubae in the brothel in Leipzig. C major is associated with purity and simplicity throughout *Doctor Faustus*, for example in the description of Schwerdtfeger's violin concerto in chapter XXVIII.

---

7   For an overview of the Faust theme in music, see Lorna Fitzsimmons and Charles Mc Knight, *The Oxford Handbook of Faust in Music* (New York: Oxford University Press, 2019). Among the literary works, Mann demonstrably knew the Faust adaptations by Pushkin, Heine, Wedekind, and, of course, his son Klaus. As a lifelong admirer of Turgenev, he likely also knew the Russian novelist's short story adaptation, though I have found no definitive evidence of this.

Doctor Faustus thus continues a literary tradition that was almost four hundred years old when Thomas Mann sat down to write his novel. Even more important than these continuities, however, are the numerous ways in which the work breaks new ground in Western literary history. *Doctor Faustus* is a novel that belongs squarely to the twentieth century and to the modernist movement in arts and letters. It is to this context that we must turn next.

6: *Doctor Faustus* and Literary Modernism

Doctor Faustus HAS always been a "novel on the margin of modernism."[1] Born in 1875, Thomas Mann belongs squarely to the generation of writers to which literary critics refer as the "high modernists," that is, the cohort that decisively broke with realist representation and devoted itself to inventing a new formal language. But generally speaking, the high modernists did their most important work in the 1920s, and when Mann sat down to write *Doctor Faustus* in 1943, contemporaries such as Marcel Proust (born in 1871), Virginia Woolf (1882), and Franz Kafka (1883) were already dead. A double sense of lateness thus hangs over the work, a fact that Mann comments on at great length in *The Story of a Novel*. First, *Doctor Faustus*, like any other work of modernism, provides a capstone to what Zeitblom calls the "epoch of bourgeois humanism" (372/512). But second, *Doctor Faustus* is also marked by a definite sense of coming late *within* the modernist movement, at a time when the formal tools invented by Mann's generation were no longer quite adequate to keep up with the pressures of the times, exemplified by global war, the rise of totalitarian propaganda, and the Holocaust.

Mann had ample occasion to reflect on both of these dimensions in his encounters with James Joyce, whom he did not read directly (his English was not good enough) but instead studied by way of a critical introduction written by Harvard professor Harry Levin.[2] He immediately recognized the great Irish writer as a "brother"[3] and noted with some satisfaction that both he and Joyce employed traditional narrative styles only parodically.[4] But as time went on, he also began to show traces of disenchantment with what he now called Joyce's "eccentric avant-gardism," cribbing one of Levin's judgments with resigned approval: "He has enormously increased the difficulties of being a novelist."[5] By the early

---

1 Thus, the title of a volume edited by Herbert Lehnert and Peter C. Pfeiffer, *Thomas Mann's "Doctor Faustus": A Novel on the Margin of Modernism* (Columbia, SC: Camden House, 1991).
2 Harry Levin, *James Joyce: A Critical Introduction* (Norfolk, CT: New Directions, 1941).
3 Diary entry for February 20, 1942, in Mann, *Tagebücher*, V: 395.
4 Diary entry for September 19, 1943, in Mann, *Tagebücher*, V: 627.
5 Both quotations from Mann, *The Story of a Novel*, 91.

1950s, Mann even seemed to turn his back on the modernist legacy altogether, now noting: "I am one of the last people, maybe the last person period, who still knows what a 'work' is."[6]

By then, of course, a new generation of novelists who rose to prominence in the years immediately following the war (Orwell and Camus, Sartre and Ellison, to name but a few) had started to engage with their times in frequently stripped-down prose that rebelled against both the conventions of traditional realism and the formal exuberance of high modernism. Joyce's Stephen Dedalus had once proclaimed history "a nightmare from which I am trying to awake"; this new generation instead sought tools with which to engage it, given the horrors that they had witnessed.[7] *Doctor Faustus*, in its attempts to process the recent German past and draw more general lessons from it, in some sense anticipates these works. Its formal language, however, is still that of the modernist moment, even if it frequently bends this language to innovative ends. For any reader, an awareness of how the style and structure of *Doctor Faustus* differs from that of more traditional novels is a prerequisite to making sense of the work.

Unreliable Narration

With the first lines of Mann's text, we encounter its rather idiosyncratic narrator, Dr. Serenus Zeitblom, a retired philologist who spent the better part of his professional life teaching Latin, Greek, and history at the high school and the theological seminary in Freising, a small town near Munich. Zeitblom is what literary theorists call a "homodiegetic" narrator, that is, a narrator who also figures as a character in the events that are recounted. Homodiegetic narrators, precisely because they are involved in the story that they tell, by their very nature need to be treated with some suspicion, and Zeitblom quickly reveals himself to also be of the unreliable kind—that is, he is a narrator "the reliability of whose account is undermined by various features of that account."[8] This is true in several different ways.[9]

---

6 Diary entry for April 3, 1951, in Mann, *Tagebücher*, IX: 43.

7 James Joyce, *Ulysses*, ed. Hans Walter Gabler (New York: Vintage Books, 1986), 2.377.

8 "Unreliable Narrator," in Gerald Prince, *Dictionary of Narratology: Revised Edition* (Lincoln: University of Nebraska Press, 2003), 103. Not all unreliable narrators are necessarily homodiegetic. In fact, Thomas Mann wrote one of the most frequently discussed examples of unreliable *hetero*diegetic narration with *Death in Venice*. Similarly, not all homodiegetic narrators are unreliable—Watson's frequent inadequacies in the Sherlock Holmes stories, for example, do not undermine our trust in his intentions.

9 Zeitblom's unreliable narration has been analyzed in a number of studies. My summary in the next four paragraphs is greatly influenced by Barbara Beßlich,

First, Zeitblom presents himself as a member of the so-called "inner emigration" who has withdrawn from society under the Nazi regime and now lives in quiet but morally upright resistance to the ruling order. He even tells us how politics have driven a wedge between him and his two sons, who are both loyal servants of the Third Reich. Yet Zeitblom's thoughts and expressions reveal that Nazi ideology has had a greater effect on him than he would like us to believe. In the very first paragraph, for example, he refers to the German dominions as "our beleaguered Fortress Europe" (5/11), employing a term coined by Joseph Goebbels and combining it with the first-person plural in a telling fashion. In subsequent chapters, we'll also witness Zeitblom express barely contained pride at German military accomplishments and lapse into anti-Semitic stereotypes.

Second, although he claims to be writing a factual account of the life of his good friend Adrian Leverkühn, Zeitblom imposes an allegorical (and thus clearly stylized) structure upon his narrative. The very title of the book is an example of this, since it primes the reader to approach the life of Leverkühn as a modern-day version of the Faustus myth. Zeitblom gives ample support for such an allegorical reading, for he stresses details such as the clubfoot of Eberhard Schleppfuss, and he also frames the report that Leverkühn composes during his visit to Palestrina in a way that strongly suggests a visitation by the devil, even though it may well just be the document of a fever dream. If we read the novel carefully, we in fact discover that there is no *definitive* evidence of a pact with the devil, or of the presence of demonic elements; instead, we become increasingly entangled in a web of postulates and leading assertions. This is not to say that Zeitblom is lying, and certainly the novel becomes a whole lot less entertaining if we assume (as some critics have done) that he is inventing all the Satanic episodes.[10] But it is to say that Zeitblom is *unreliable*—that is, we cannot simply take at face value what he is telling us and need to struggle for our own understanding of what is happening.

Third, Zeitblom does not shy away from inventing detailed descriptions of scenes that he cannot possibly have witnessed. A good example occurs in chapter XLI, in the imagined conversation between Leverkühn and Schwerdtfeger in which the former convinces the latter to propose to Marie Godeau on his behalf. Sometimes (as here) Zeitblom is forthright about such inventions, other times he is not.

Fourth, and in an inversion of the third point, Zeitblom sometimes misses crucial details. Thus, he does not notice that Frau von Tolna bears an uncanny resemblance to Hetaera Esmeralda. This, too, is a form

---

Der Biograph des Komponisten: Unzuverlässiges Erzählen in Thomas Manns Roman "Doktor Faustus" (1947) (Heidelberg: Universitätsverlag Winter, 2023).

10 See. e.g., Karin L. Crawford, "Exorcising the Devil from Thomas Mann's *Doktor Faustus*," German Quarterly 76, no. 2 (2003): 168–82.

of unreliable narration, for it means that an attentive reader will, over the course of the novel, become ever more mistrustful of Zeitblom's limitations.

Unreliable narration is not by itself an indicator of literary modernism. For instance, both Laurence Stern's *The Life and Opinions of Tristram Shandy, Gentleman* (1759–67) and Mark Twain's *The Adventures of Huckleberry Finn* (1884) employ unreliable narrators. That said, the technique is certainly strongly associated with the modernist period. The unreliable narration of *Doctor Faustus* can be described as distinctively modernist for two reasons, one of them pointing backwards towards the nineteenth century, the other forward towards the postwar period. The backwards-pointing reason is that this technique allows an author to create works that superficially resemble the creations of the bourgeois nineteenth century, but actually expose these conventions to doubt and even mockery. Mann, who like Zeitblom firmly believed that he lived at the end of the bourgeois era, was drawn to such parody and also thematizes it within *Doctor Faustus*.[11] For instance, Leverkühn's violin concerto mocks some of the more sentimental musical practices of the nineteenth century.

Arguably the more important reason why Mann chose to include an unreliable narrator in *Doctor Faustus*, however, is that this technique allowed him to raise ethical questions that were already pressing when he began the novel in 1943, but whose importance would rise exponentially in the years that followed. Serenus Zeitblom is a narrator who, though not directly culpable for any of the crimes committed by the Nazis, has nevertheless soaked up their rhetoric and ideology to a greater extent than he is willing to acknowledge. He frames the story of Adrian's life as an allegory for German history, but he does so in a way that puts the ultimate responsibility for its most terrifying aspects on the shoulders of external demonic forces. And he embellishes where it seems useful while shying away from deeper investigations into inconvenient questions. In all these respects, he resembles the millions of Germans who, in the years after the downfall of the Nazis, lied about or prettified their personal experiences while insisting that the real fault for the events of the last twelve years lay with others. Mann resented such moral pusillanimity, which he encountered in his interactions both with the postwar "inner emigration" and with fellow exiles in America—including many Marxist thinkers, who were more than

---

11   Mann already expressed his firm belief that he lived at the end of the bourgeois era when he was still a young man and became plagued with self-doubts whether his debut novel would stand the test of time in the twentieth century. See his letter to his brother Heinrich ("*Buddenbrooks* was a novel of the bourgeoisie and means nothing to the twentieth century") reprinted in Hans Wysling, ed. *Letters of Heinrich and Thomas Mann, 1909–1949*, trans. Don Reneau (Berkeley: University of California Press, 1998), 118–19.

willing to lay blame for the crimes of the Nazis exclusively at the feet of "capital" while downplaying the culpability of working-class Germans.[12] With the figure of Serenus Zeitblom, he sought to hold up a mirror to his contemporaries and compatriots. As I have argued in the introduction to this volume, his decision to do so is one of the major reasons why *Doctor Faustus* still speaks to our own era, which may well call for a similar process of moral reckoning.

Medium Specificity

In our enumeration of the various ways in which Serenus Zeitblom can be called "unreliable," we have not yet touched upon what is perhaps his most distinctive characteristic as a narrator. Already in the first paragraph, in which he interrupts himself several times and then asks the reader's permission to start anew, we encounter him as a person who struggles to give an appropriate shape to his material. Initially, episodes such as this one seem to testify only to the curious blend of boastfulness, insecurity, and pedantry that characterizes Zeitblom. As we delve deeper into the novel, however, we realize that Mann's narrator wrestles (or pretends to wrestle) with forces that are beyond his control; forces that seek to impose a certain shape upon his narrative. There is the convoluted passage at the start of chapter XIV, for example, in which Zeitblom tries to disavow any responsibility for the fact that Eberhard Schleppfuss, the novel's first unmistakable devil figure, is introduced in the chapter that bears the ill-omened number "XIII." Then there's the fact that Leverkühn's ostensible conversation with the devil occurs in chapter XXV, the midpoint of a novel that consists (depending on how we interpret the three-part chapter XXXIV) of either forty-seven numbered chapters plus an epilogue or forty-nine chapters plus an epilogue. And of course, the special status of chapter XXXIV is in and of itself suspicious, since that chapter number corresponds to the sum to which all horizontals, verticals, and main diagonals of the magic square that adorns Leverkühn's study add up.

It is ultimately up to the reader to decide whether these numerical eccentricities indicate the presence of a demonic force that is helping to shape the narrative, or whether they are another attempt by Zeitblom to distract attention from evils that actually have purely human causes. Either way it is clear that the chapter divisions in *Doctor Faustus* function differently than they do in realist novels, where they primarily serve to break down the narrative into digestible chunks. In *Doctor Faustus*, by

---

12 See Herbert Lehnert, "Thomas Mann, Bertolt Brecht, and the 'Free Germany' Movement," in *Exile: The Writer's Experience*, ed. John M. Spalek and Robert F. Bell (Chapel Hill: University of North Carolina Press, 1982), 182–202.

contrast, chapter divisions actively participate in the process by which the novel creates meaning.

This is an inherently modernist property, for it illustrates what the art critic Clement Greenberg called modernism's obsession with "medium specificity," that is, with those features of an artwork that are unique to a given medium and are ordinarily dismissed as mere carriers of meaning, rather than of meaning proper.[13] Greenberg was thinking about the ways in which abstract expressionists like Jackson Pollock or Willem de Kooning focused attention on the materiality of paint, but for a writer like Thomas Mann, such meta-literary components as chapter divisions serve an analogous purpose. Arnold Schoenberg's twelve-tone system can be similarly seen as a form of modernist medium specificity, for it privileges abstract considerations about the mathematical relationship between tones over the affective and expressive dimensions of music.

Doctor Faustus has, in fact, often been interpreted as an elaborate attempt to capture the essence of twelve-tone music in the form of written prose. For instance, some readers of the novel have pointed out that the number "forty-eight" (corresponding to forty-seven numbered chapters plus the epilogue) is highly significant in dodecaphonic composition, where each tone row consists of twelve tones and can be presented in four different versions (original, inversion, retrograde, and retrograde-inversion).[14] It is even possible to map the four-fold division of dodecaphonic theory onto the novel. One way to do so would be to argue that the first twelve chapters of *Doctor Faustus* document Leverkühn's growth into the world in the manner of a traditional German novel of formation, which conventionally ends when the protagonist has found a place in society. The next twelve chapters, starting with the encounter with the devil figure Eberhard Schleppfuss, invert this process of outward growth and depict Leverkühn's withdrawal into an inward-facing world of musical composition, abnormal psychology, and sexual aberration (the latter facet culminating in him willfully contracting syphilis). The next twelve chapters, which begin with another Satanic encounter in XXV, form a retrograde to the first twelve chapters and see Leverkühn retrace the steps that took him from Buchel to Munich in reverse order, until he ends up in Pfeiffering, the uncanny equivalent of his childhood home. The final twelve chapters, beginning with the visit by Saul Fitelberg, another devil figure, combine elements of inversion and retrograde when Leverkühn

---

13 See Clement Greenberg, "Towards a Newer Laokoon," *Partisan Review* (July–August 1940): 296–310.

14 Probably the first critic to point this out was Aline Valangin in the pages of *Die Auslese* in April 1948. An English translation of this text can be found in Schoenberg, *The "Doctor Faustus" Dossier*, 125–30. See also Bergsten, *Thomas Mann's "Doctor Faustus,"* 168–79.

renounces his nascent fame and focuses once again on his inner life, including his tragic relationships with Schwerdtfeger, Godeau, and Echo.[15]

Other critics propose that the three-part chapter XXXIV be counted thrice, resulting in a novel with forty-nine chapters plus an unrelated epilogue. Forty-nine, in turn, is the square of the number seven, which plays an important role in many Satanic rituals. Conceptualizing *Doctor Faustus* in this fashion not only hints at the magic square of chapter XII, but also moves the novel into the vicinity of the twelve-tone matrices that Schoenberg drew up to illustrate his theories.

Proponents of such readings rarely acknowledge that there is strong circumstantial evidence that Mann never intended them. For instance, he informed his American translator Helen Tracy Lowe-Porter on February 29, 1947, that he was toying with the idea of making his novel more accessible by dividing it into multiple "books," restarting the chapter numbers with each one. He even composed new transitional sections for this purpose.[16] Less than a month later, he backtracked on his previous letter, now observing that: "the work has, after all, been written in consecutively numbered chapters and the text contains several allusions to that."[17] By November, however, still bothered by the possibility that his novel might prove overly taxing to his readers (a consideration that also caused him to slash extended passages for the second edition), he reversed himself once again, now giving Lowe-Porter permission to expand the total number of sequentially numbered chapters to fifty for the American publication, explaining that "this would be a superficial change that would not make much of a difference" (Lowe-Porter never acted on the suggestion).[18]

Clearly, then, Mann regarded his self-referential games with chapter numbering as an indispensable part of *Doctor Faustus*, but he was willing to accommodate minor changes as long as they didn't interfere with the overall import of those games. A division into fifty numbered chapters, for example, would have kept chapter XXV at the center of the work and would have done nothing to interfere with chapters XIII and XXXIV. But if he had really intended the novel's structure to allude to the twelve-tone

---

15 The most recent variation on such a reading that I am familiar with is the one by my colleague Berthold Hoeckner, who goes so far as to argue that Zeitblom must himself be an incarnation of the devil, since he is the only character to appear in chapter I and thus the only character who might complete the symmetry that places a devil figure in each of the starting chapters of a twelve-chapter sequence. See Berthold Hoeckner, *Programming the Absolute: Nineteenth-Century German Music and the Hermeneutics of the Moment* (Princeton, NJ: Princeton University Press, 2002), 224–65.
16 Mann, *Selbstkommentare*, 104.
17 Mann, *Selbstkommentare*, 107.
18 Mann, *Selbstkommentare*, 125.

technique, he surely would have said so to his American translator. The fact that he did not actually increases the modernist cachet of his work. For "medium specificity" is by definition not transferable from one artistic medium to another. Tone rows obey an inner logic that is based in the principles of acoustics and the history of Western music; Schoenberg could never have invented an "eleven-tone system." This logic is lost when transferred to the realm of literature, where twelve chapters are no more of an inherently significant organizing unit than eleven or thirteen chapters would be. As Zeitblom's excursus at the start of chapter XIV illustrates, the chapter numbers in *Doctor Faustus* are instead based on a form of medium specificity particular to the novel: they flow from the complex decisions that are involved in the process of giving a meaningful shape to narrated human experience.[19]

Polyphonic Composition

Critics who remain wedded to the idea that *Doctor Faustus* is structured like an elaborate dodecaphonic matrix might draw support for their reading from a passage in *The Story of a Novel*. There, Mann describes the impact left upon him by Theodor W. Adorno's *Philosophy of New Music*, which he studied in the late summer of 1943: "Moreover, this reading nourished the musical conception which had long been my ideal of form and for which this time there was a special esthetic necessity. I felt clearly that my book itself would have to become the thing it dealt with: namely, a musical composition."[20] Given that Adorno's manuscript deals extensively with Schoenberg, is it not natural to assume that the "ideal of form" described here would be that of dodecaphonic technique?

In fact, Mann had taken inspiration from music throughout his long and varied career and had always turned to more traditional models than those provided by twelve-tone composition. Throughout the years in which Mann wrote *Doctor Faustus*, he repeatedly commented on the strange incongruity between his own musical conservatism and the subject matter of his novel, perhaps most emphatically in a diary entry for September 28, 1944, in which he declared that "the triad-world of the *Ring* cycle is, in truth, my musical home." The formal influence of Wagner can indeed be strongly felt in *Doctor Faustus*. In an introductory

---

19 Nicholas Dames, in *The Chapter: A Segmented History from Antiquity to the Twenty-First Century* (Princeton, NJ: Princeton University Press, 2023), points out that "a turn to the indexical or citational functions of chapters will present itself usually as self-consciously antique. In the case of the novel, it [...] serves as a reminder of the novel's historical lateness" (32). This, too, of course, would have been entirely congruent with Thomas Mann's intentions.

20 Mann, *The Story of a Novel*, 64.

lecture on *The Magic Mountain* that he delivered just a few years before he began writing his late modernist masterpiece, Mann spoke at great length on the debt that he owed to Wagner's method of composing in *leitmotifs*—recurring melodic fragments that add depth and continuity to the characters and concepts in Wagner's music dramas.[21] In *Doctor Faustus*, the repeated references to Schwerdtfeger's blue and Marie Godeau's black eyes serve a similar purpose.

Surely Mann had something more drastic in mind than this, however, when he spoke of a "special esthetic necessity" to engage with musical form in the *Doctor Faustus* project. At a different point of his *Story of a Novel* Mann writes: "But, above all, the interposition of the narrator made it possible to tell the story on a dual plane of time, to polyphonically weave together the events which shake the writer as he writes with those he is recounting."[22] This was not the first time Mann had used this metaphor to describe his novels; in a diary entry written a quarter-century before *Doctor Faustus*, he had already called *The Magic Mountain* "a polyphony of themes, thoughts, and impressions."[23] Nevertheless, the term here acquires a novel and more technical connotation than it had before.

Mann's phrasing indicates that he conceived of the two temporal planes that structure *Doctor Faustus*, and which I refer to in my commentary as "Time of Narration" and "Narrated Time," as two interdependent narrative lines. ("Polyphony" is the technical name for a musical texture in which each voice presents a different melody. The various parts are harmonized by the laws of counterpoint, not by the chordal logic of "homophonic" compositions.) Sitting in Freising in 1944, Zeitblom recalls events that took place in Munich and Pfeiffering in the early 1920s: two separate narrative lines that nevertheless advance in tandem with one another. Yet when Zeitblom's hands shake during the process of composition, it is impossible to tell whether they do so out of fear and loathing for Leverkühn's actions during the 1920s or because of the Allied bombing raids that are targeting nearby Munich in the 1940s. Or to be more exact: they shake for both of these reasons, for the two seemingly independent lines are instead harmonically connected and Leverkühn's misdeeds, so Zeitblom hints, may be the root cause of the Allied destruction.

Doctor Faustus makes use of this polyphonic technique to a far greater degree than even Mann's quote from *The Story of a Novel* would suggest. For its not just that Zeitblom and Leverkühn exist on two different

---

21   Thomas Mann, "The Making of *The Magic Mountain*," trans. H.T. Lowe-Porter, *Atlantic Monthly* (January 1953): 41–45.

22   Mann, *The Story of a Novel*, 31. The crucial word "polyphonically" is omitted in Richard and Clara Winston's translation.

23   Diary entry for March 25, 1919, in Mann, *Tagebücher*, I: 178.

temporal planes that are nevertheless in constant reference to one another; Leverkühn himself exists on multiple temporal and referential frames as well. Gunilla Bergsten therefore compares his function in the novel to that of a musical chord, though I personally prefer to avoid this term, since Mann strongly associates chords with the realm of homophony, not polyphony.[24] I'll expand on this particular aspect of the novel in chapter 9, "Five Masters from Germany."

"History," in *Doctor Faustus*, is thus treated not only horizontally (or "melodically"), as a matter of temporal unfolding, but also vertically (or "harmonically") as a question of the simultaneity of non-simultaneous elements. This polyphonic approach greatly expands the capacity of the novel form. Nineteenth-century realism generally comments on history by illustrating how certain events lead to particular consequences. *Doctor Faustus*, on the other hand, supplements this basic cause-and-effect structure with a mind-bogglingly expansive modernist vision, concatenating multiple frames of reference in a way no sociological analysis or realist tale ever could.

Montage

Perhaps the most important way in which Mann created the polyphonic structure of *Doctor Faustus* was through his use of what he called his "montage-technique."[25] Simply put, many names, sentences, and even entire passages in *Doctor Faustus* are copied whole cloth from external sources. Thus, when Ehrenfried Kumpf launches into one of his diatribes in an early modern idiom, he sounds as convincing as he does because Mann is quoting verbatim from sources such as the collected letters of Martin Luther, or from Christoffel von Grimmelshausen's 1669 novel *Simplicius Simplicissimus*. And when Zeitblom describes the progress of Leverkühn's syphilitic infection, he does so in sentences copied from Paul Deussen's 1901 memoirs of his friendship with Friedrich Nietzsche, *Recollection of Nietzsche*. In this way, different temporal layers can be brought into juxtaposition with one another, as Mann's text briefly collapses the distance that ordinarily separates the sixteenth or the nineteenth from the twentieth century.

Mann employed montage technique throughout his career. Perhaps the earliest famous example of it occurs in *Buddenbrooks*, where he cribs several pages of a medical textbook in order to vividly yet clinically render Hanno Buddenbrook's slow death from typhoid fever. He also described this technique in a host of literary manifestos, from "Bilse and I" in 1906

---

24   Bergsten, *Thomas Mann's "Doctor Faustus,"* 136.
25   In *The Story of a Novel*, Mann in fact calls montage "something specifically musical" (33).

to the 1940 essay "The Art of the Novel." Nevertheless, it remained perhaps the most controversial aspect of his craft throughout his life. For cultural conservatives, Mann's habit of copying from other sources was plagiarism at worst and evidence of a lack of imagination at best. Poets were supposed to be inspired inventors, not merely copyists who shuffled around pre-existing materials. Mann's detractors among the literary avant-garde, on the other hand (his fellow novelist Alfred Döblin most famously among them) thought that his notion of montage did not go nearly far enough, that it was mere "quotation." The Soviet filmmaker Sergei Eisenstein had developed a theory of montage in the 1920s that located the aesthetic effect of this technique precisely in the incongruity between juxtaposed elements. A sudden shift in style or perspective, so Eisenstein thought, could usefully destroy any lingering realist illusion in a film and instead force viewers to confront that they were dealing with an artistic construct. Mann was never interested in such avant-garde confrontation, and always tried to suture his quotations into his own literary texture.

The way in which the montage technique is deployed in *Doctor Faustus* nevertheless represents an important advance over Mann's previous work. In a letter to Emil Preetorius, Mann spoke of a "strange" development in his use of the montage technique and noted that "something like this has never happened to me before."[26] A few months later, writing to Erich Kahler, he claimed that "the idea of montage is in fact one of the premises of the book."[27] Indeed, the use of montage in *Doctor Faustus* differs both quantitatively and qualitatively from that in previous works. There is hardly a major text by Thomas Mann in which montage isn't used at some point, but in *Doctor Faustus* it is one of the structuring principles of the work, to be found in almost every chapter, and indeed on almost every page. Such extensive acts of quotation also change the fundamental nature of the novel. We have already discussed the important connection between montage and polyphonic style, which allows Mann to juxtapose several different temporal layers in his text. Another important consequence of this near-constant game of textual hopscotch is that the flow of the action in *Doctor Faustus* is repeatedly interrupted as Mann pauses the plot to insert yet one more passage from one of Adorno's essays, from a Nietzsche biography, or from a treatise on syphilis.

The first-time reader is bound to feel these interruptions most acutely whenever the discussion shifts to musical matters and the action comes

---

26 Letter to Emil Preetorius, December 12, 1947, in Mann, *Selbstkommentare*, 139.
27 Letter to Erich Kahler, March 6, 1948, in *Letters of Thomas Mann, 1889–1955, Volume II: 1943–1955*, ed. and trans. Richard and Clara Winston (New York: Alfred A. Knopf, 1970), 549.

to a halt for an extended period of time (as it does in chapter VIII, for example). It's easy to react to such interruptions with annoyance, since they subvert the expectations that we place in a well-made plot. Mann's digressions are undoubtedly clever, but shouldn't he also have anticipated that most readers would eventually grow bored with them?[28]

One of Mann's fundamental aims in *Doctor Faustus*, however, was to make us aware of a crisis afflicting art in the early twentieth century, and the montage structure of his novel should be seen as itself an expression and illustration of this crisis. Mann believed that the quest for ever more "advanced" forms of aesthetic expression over the course of the long nineteenth century had led the arts into a dead end, as it created a gap between what audiences demanded and what artists delivered. Within literature, this quest included the advent of such techniques as free indirect discourse and the stream of consciousness, as well as such movements as naturalism, symbolism, and literary impressionism. One possible solution to this dilemma lay in a new approach to production that would seek to create art out of the recombination of existing materials. Within the fine arts, the collage technique pioneered by the cubists expresses this tendency; within music, Stravinsky's neo-classical play with established musical forms represents a similar response to the crisis. Thomas Mann's montage technique, which substitutes appropriation for invention, intellectual reflection for spontaneous inspiration, also falls into this pattern.

Doctor Faustus, then, is a "novel on the margin of modernism" because it exemplifies modernist techniques but also desperately hopes to escape from the general intellectual condition of which modernism is ultimately a symptom. One of the main theses of the novel, as I have tried to argue in the introductory section of this book, is that the general disenchantment with the liberal ideology of progress that grabbed hold of Western societies in the early twentieth century led to an even more devastating "politics of eternity," in which seemingly timeless concepts such as blood, soil, and masculine honor became the basis of a fascist body politic. Adrian Leverkühn, the quintessential modernist composer, exemplifies this same development on an artistic level when he turns away from the nineteenth-century musical tradition and pioneers his "strict style," designed to exclude inspiration and novelty from the compositional process as much as possible.

Serenus Zeitblom, Leverkühn's humanistic biographer, observes this development with horror and tries to critically account for it. But just like

---

28 He did, in fact. For instance, he assured his young American admirer Fred H. Rosenau in a letter dated February 18, 1948, that, "it may sometimes seem that the essayistic portions of the book explode the novel form, but nevertheless even in these parts everything relates to the greater whole." Mann, *Selbstkommentare*, 169.

wide swathes of the German intelligentsia, he lacks the courage to fully acknowledge the role that people like him played in the political catastrophe that led to the rise of the Nazis. Zeitblom ultimately is an unreliable narrator, which in the context of *Doctor Faustus* means not only that we cannot fully trust his propositional statements, but also that his narrative—marked by metaliterary games such as the chapter numbering, by a polyphonic style, and by montage and digression—recapitulates many of the developments that Zeitblom ostensibly condemns. An alternate way to describe *Doctor Faustus*, then, would be as a "novel overcome by modernism": the supreme example of a historical period and an artistic style that its very content indicts in the strongest possible terms.

7: The Historical Setting of the Novel

THE PLOT OF *Doctor Faustus* stretches from the late 1880s to 1945, with the majority of the action taking place during the years from 1905 to 1930. These were some of the most eventful decades of German history, and they are vividly if sometimes selectively rendered in a work that brims over with colorful vignettes and minor characters. While Mann's discussions of music theory and theology are of undeniable importance to *Doctor Faustus*, the first-time reader of the novel would do well not to become overly intimidated by its more difficult passages. Mann always understood himself to be working in the great epic tradition of Goethe, Tolstoy, and Fontane.[1] For him, the novelist was a creator of worlds. And the world that he depicts in *Doctor Faustus* is as rich and as deep as any dreamt up by one of his great forebears.

Kaisersaschern (1883–1905)

Serenus Zeitblom is born in 1883 and Adrian Leverkühn in 1885. Both spend their childhood years in a Germany that had only recently (in 1871) been united into a single nation under Prussian rule. In his debut novel *Buddenbrooks*, Mann had depicted the process of national unification from the perspective of one of its victims, a merchant family in the formerly independent city-state of Lübeck on the shores of the Baltic Sea. The Saale River Valley, however, where the two central characters of *Doctor Faustus* grow up, had been a part of the Kingdom of Prussia since the early eighteenth century. There is thus no reference to Germany's inner colonialism in the novel. In terms of geographic origin as in terms of class, its protagonists are born into the very heart of the German Empire.

In 1895, the ten-year-old Leverkühn moves to Kaisersaschern, the hometown of his childhood friend Zeitblom. Kaisersaschern is a fictional place, though a heavily overdetermined one. For its description in chapter VI, Mann excerpted passages from encyclopedia entries about Nuremberg, Eisleben, Quedlinburg, and Wolfenbüttel—all towns near the center of Germany that flourished in the fifteenth through seventeenth centuries and are intimately associated with prominent cultural figures from that period such as Albrecht Dürer, Martin Luther, or Johann Sebastian Bach.

---

1   Mann's essays on these three writers are included in *Essays of Three Decades*, trans. H.T. Lowe-Porter (New York: Alfred A. Knopf, 1948).

Other influences were Naumburg, where Friedrich Nietzsche spent his childhood years, and Mann's own hometown Lübeck, which also held a distinguished place in early modern German history. In fact, when he needed to describe Lübeck for his 1945 Library of Congress lecture on "Germany and the Germans," Mann simply copied out some of the sentences from his manuscript.

The purpose of this montage work was to support Zeitblom's assessment of Kaisersaschern as a town that "maintains its identity, which was the same three hundred, nine hundred years ago, against the river of time sweeping over it and constantly affecting many changes" (39/57). This is an early example of the spiritual rebellion against progress and the recourse to mythical thinking that will come to afflict Leverkühn over the course of the novel. Kaisersaschern's "timelessness," as Zeitblom also calls it, has more direct consequences as well, however. In one central passage, Zeitblom complains that "there hung in the air [...] a hysteria out of the dying Middle Ages, something of a latent psychological epidemic" (39/57–58). Over the next few pages, he connects this "psychological epidemic" first to the ordinary people of Kaisersaschern who "voted the Social Democratic ticket at the polls, [but] were capable at the same time of seeing something demonic in the poverty of a little old lady" (41/59–60), and then to a series of vividly characterized eccentrics, among them "a man of indeterminate age, who at any sudden shout would feel compelled to perform a kind of jerky dance with knees pulled high" (41/60). He is, in other words, drawing a direct line between the medieval character of Kaisersaschern and the experience of Nazism, which inspired ordinary people to denounce their neighbors and to behave like marionettes as they performed the Hitler salute or goose-stepped across parade grounds.

The idea of connecting Nazism to medieval German history and to small-town culture was certainly not unique to Thomas Mann. In the same year that *Doctor Faustus* was published, his fellow exile Siegfried Kracauer finished his "psychological history of the German film" *From Caligari to Hitler*, which rests on a similar premise.[2] And Mann's own brother Heinrich had excoriated German small-town life as an incubator of authoritarian tendencies in novels such as *The Loyal Subject* and *The Blue Angel*.[3] These authors certainly had a point. The base of the Nazis' power

---

2 Siegfried Kracauer, *From Caligari to Hitler: A Psychological History of the German Film* (Princeton, NJ: Princeton University Press, 1947). In most other regards, Kracauer and Mann's respective analyses are quite different, as Hans Rudolf Vaget has pointed out in "'German' Music and German Catastrophe," 223–24.

3 Heinrich Mann, *The Loyal Subject*, trans. Helmut Peitsch (London: Continuum, 1998); *The Blue Angel* (New York: Howard Fertig, 2011).

did rest in small towns, and the electoral district of Merseburg, where the fictional town of Kaisersaschern would have been located, posted some of the highest returns for Hitler of any district in Germany during the 1932 presidential elections. The Nazis did explicitly try to connect their "Third Reich" to the Holy Roman Empire of the early modern period, as anybody who has seen Leni Riefenstahl's propaganda film *Triumph of the Will* (1935) can confirm. And small-town life in Germany during the final third of the nineteenth century did on a number of occasions tip over into pogroms that can only be characterized as "medieval."[4]

Precisely because it is so central to the conception of the novel, the Kaisersaschern chapter has also been met with a lot of criticism over the decades. For as Ernst Fischer pointed out as early as 1949, it vividly illustrates one of the main premises of *Doctor Faustus*, namely that Leverkühn's pact with the devil and his willed regression towards early modern structures indict Germany as a whole.[5] This, so Mann's detractors have argued, ignores Germany's various social and emancipatory movements, from Thomas Münzer in the sixteenth century to the 1848 revolutionaries.

Hans Rudolf Vaget has replied in Mann's defense that the depiction of Kaisersaschern is internally more complex than such charges would admit.[6] He argues that Mann believed German culture to be fundamentally cosmopolitan in nature, and that he thought of precisely this quality when he described the Third Reich as "[good] turned into evil through devilish cunning."[7] To support his point, Vaget draws attention to the fact that Mann rather strangely made the fictional Kaisersaschern the gravesite of the Holy Roman Emperor Otto III (980–1002), who actually lies buried in the West German town of Aachen. So important was this figurative exhumation to Mann that he even drew attention to it in the town's name (Kaisersaschern means "emperor's ashes"). Otto III, however, thought of himself as the leader of a cosmopolitan empire and not as a German.

Leverkühn will follow in the footsteps of the Holy Roman Emperor. In chapter XX, Zeitblom tells us that "it was not for nothing that he was

---

4   For a vivid illustration of one such case, see Helmut Walser-Smith, *The Butcher's Tale: Murder and Anti-Semitism in a German Town* (New York: Norton, 2002).

5   Ernst Fischer, "*Doktor Faustus* und die deutsche Katastrophe: Eine Auseinandersetzung mit Thomas Mann," in *Kunst und Menschheit: Essays* (Vienna: Globus-Verlag, 1949), 37–97.

6   Hans Rudolf Vaget, "Kaisersaschern als geistige Lebensform: Zur Konzeption der deutschen Geschichte in Thomas Manns *Doktor Faustus*," in *Der deutsche Roman und seine historischen und politischen Bedingungen*, ed. Wolfgang Paulsen (Bern: Francke Verlag, 1977), 200–35.

7   Mann, "Germany and the Germans," 64.

the son of the town in which Otto III lay buried. His distaste for the Germanness that he embodied [...] appeared in two divergent forms: an eccentric reticence to deal with the world and an inner need for the wide world beyond" (175/240–41). Leverkühn's "inner need for the wide world" will manifest itself throughout the novel in various ways, such as in his love for French and Italian music, and in his self-identification with Felix Mendelssohn, the Jewish composer and conductor who led the Bach revival of the early nineteenth century. But as Zeitblom already notes, it is fatally aligned with an unwillingness to deal with the world in a practical, "external" fashion. We see this in chapter XXVIII, in which the devil appears to Leverkühn in the guise of the concert agent Saul Fitelberg, offering him a brilliant musical career in Paris. Leverkühn rejects this offer, much as Germany opted to disengage from the wider world in the 1930s, instead choosing the hysteria and psychological illness that also afflict Kaisersaschern.

Halle an der Saale (1903–1905)

In 1903, the eighteen-year-old Leverkühn graduates from high school in Kaisersaschern and moves to nearby Halle an der Saale to study theology. He is soon joined by Zeitblom who, two years his senior, has spent the past two years as a student at the universities of Jena and Gießen. Halle, unlike Kaisersaschern, is a real place and the largest city in what Zeitblom himself calls "Luther country" (10/18). Choosing it as the location for Leverkühn's student days thus allowed Mann to reinforce the close link between his protagonist and early modern German history that he already established in the Kaisersaschern chapters. The University of Halle had the added appeal of having been institutionally merged with the University of Wittenberg, the town that had traditionally served as Faust's home ever since the days of Johannes Manlius.

There were other reasons to choose Halle as a setting for the novel. The theological faculty there had an exceptionally strong and multifaceted history. An early bastion of the Lutheran reformation, the university in the late seventeenth century also became the home of August Hermann Francke. Francke was a leading figure of German Pietism, the protestant reform movement better known to many Americans as the "Moravian Church." And from 1804 to 1806, the Reform theologian Friedrich Schleiermacher, the greatest religious thinker of German Romanticism, served on the faculty there.

Zeitblom refers to all of these figures at great length and also muses about the general desirability of reform movements in the history of Christianity. Did Luther's Reformation, he asks, not have the unintended effect of breathing new life into a moribund Catholic Church, thereby giving rise to the Counter-Reformation and a new era of persecutions and witchcraft trials? These may seem to be somewhat unusual thoughts for a man who will eventually take up a teaching post at a Catholic seminary, but Zeitblom has since the first pages of the novel self-identified with sixteenth-century humanists such as Erasmus of Rotterdam and Crotus Rubianus, who kept their distance from the narrow-minded dogmatics in both the Catholic and protestant churches.[8] Zeitblom's musings, at any rate, are relevant not only to the life of Adrian Leverkühn (who will himself become an overzealous reformer in his chosen field), but also to politics. For Zeitblom and Leverkühn belong to the same generation that would produce real-life thinkers such as Arthur Moeller Van den Bruck, Carl Schmitt, and Oswald Spengler, all of whom became leaders of the so-called "Conservative Revolution" in political thought during the 1920s. This movement began with the goal of fanning the dying embers of German conservatism but largely ended up as a handmaiden of the Nazis. We'll engage more closely with it later in this chapter.

During their studies, Zeitblom and Leverkühn encounter a number of fictional theology professors, whose names and demeanors once again foreground a connection to the early modern era. Perhaps the most memorable of these is Ehrenfried Kumpf, a professor of systematic theology who is clearly modeled on Martin Luther and even invites our two protagonists to a dinner straight out of Luther's sixteenth-century *Table Talks*. Kumpf represents the crudest and most dogmatic tendencies of the Reformation period, and thus exactly those tendencies which Mann feared Germany had taken too much to heart. Tellingly, later in the novel, when Leverkühn starts talking in an old-fashioned German idiom, he sounds exactly like Kumpf (and both of them sound like Luther, whose writings Mann took as a model for these passages).

Kumpf is matched in interest to the reader only by a lowly lecturer named Eberhard Schleppfuss, who holds forth on the philosophy of religion and introduces to the novel a number of important themes related to early modern religiosity, cultic excess, and the suggestibility of ordinary people. Schleppfuss is also important because he is the first unmistakable devil figure in the novel (though earlier characters, such as the hunchbacked stableboy Thomas and the charmingly persuasive Wendell Kretzschmar, have at least a whiff of the demonic about them as well).

By no means was Halle only of interest to Mann because of its rich symbolic resonance, however. In drafting his description of university life, Mann also relied on his correspondence with a fellow exile to America,

---

8   For more on Zeitblom's self-identification with these figures, as well as on the role of Halle as a theological institution more generally, see Peter Eagles, "The 'Dunkelmänner' of *Doktor Faustus*: Humanists versus Theologians," *German Life and Letters* 75, no. 1 (2022): 88–115.

the liberal protestant theologian Paul Tillich.[9] Tillich had himself studied theology in Halle during the years in question, and sent Mann a first-hand account of his student days. Chapters XI–XIII of *Doctor Faustus* should, therefore, also be read as a commentary on German university life during the early years of the twentieth century, and characters such as Kumpf and Schleppfuss might be read as caricatures of certain professorial types of the day.[10] Kumpf enjoys the almost boundless devotion of a coterie of students who are drawn to him less by the originality of his thought or his mastery of his subject matter, and much more by the force of his personality and his eccentric behavior. Schleppfuss, on the other hand, deploys his rapier-like wit in the service of a post-Nietzschean critique that seeks to reduce ultimate values to mere products of human psychology.[11] Neither of the two, one senses, are doing very much to give their students what professors of theology might be expected to give them, namely a solid anchoring point that would prevent them from being blown away by the tempests of the early twentieth century.

While in Halle, Zeitblom and Leverkühn join the Christian student fraternity "Winfried," a thinly disguised version of the real-life fraternity "Wingolf," of which Tillich was a member. In his letter to Mann, Tillich opined that "that which I have become in a theological, philosophical and human sense, I owe only partly to professors. A much greater part was played by the fraternity, where theological and philosophical debates past midnight and personal conversations at dawn played a decisive part for my entire life."[12] Many members of Mann's and Tillich's generation would have found this a familiar sentiment, for fraternities played an important

---

9   By sheer coincidence, Tillich had supervised part of the dissertation of Mann's informal musical advisor, Theodor W. Adorno. This bit of trivia neatly illustrates just how small (and at times downright incestuous) the community of exiled German intellectuals in America really was. This fact surely had an important influence on the form of *Doctor Faustus*.

10   The character of Eberhard Kump was greatly influenced by Tillich's teacher Martin Kähler. For the academic community of that time and place as a breeding ground for reactionary sentiment, see Fritz K. Ringer, *The Decline of the German Mandarins: The German Academic Community, 1890–1933* (Cambridge, MA: Harvard University Press, 1969). The sociologist Stefan Breuer has drawn attention to the fact that an unusually high number of far-right intellectuals during the Weimar years had studied theology. See Stefan Breuer, *Anatomie der konservativen Revolution* (Darmstadt: Wissenschaftliche Buchgesellschaft, 1993), 27–28.

11   There is also a lot of Kierkegaard in the Schleppfuss chapter, though Mann dialed back on it after he learned from Tillich that Kierkegaard was not really known in Halle until after the First World War. When the devil reappears in chapter XXV, he will again be quoting Kierkegaard.

12   GKFA 10.2: 371–72.

part in German life of the day. The history of these organizations (which dates back to the days of the Napoleonic Wars) and their internal structure is significantly different from that of American student organizations, but there are still many similarities. Mann milks every bit of humor possible out of Zeitblom's and Leverkühn's respective struggles to fit in with the chummy conviviality of the Winfried brothers, and one wonders whether the other students are secretly more annoyed by Leverkühn's inability to stick to informal pronouns or by Zeitblom's insistence on accompanying their songs on his viola d'amore.

The reason why student fraternities were so important to German history is that they decisively shaped the outlook of the Zeitblom-Leverkühn generation, that is, the generation that went to war in 1914 and then dominated the intellectual and cultural life of the Weimar Republic.[13] Generational identity is, in fact, a major topic of the midnight debates that the Winfried brothers conduct on their regular hiking trips. In an exchange with Adrian, who as always is acting older than he actually is, one of the students proclaims that "to be young means to be primordial, to have remained close to the wellspring of life, means being able to rise up and shake off the fetters of an outmoded civilization." These qualities, furthermore, are supposedly archetypally German, for "the German is, if you will, the eternal student, the eternally striving student among the nations" (127/174). Just to be sure we don't fail to realize that this is intended as the description of an ideological formation, not just an individual point of view, Mann gives the character in question the name "Konrad *Deutsch*lin."

Other topics discussed by the Winfried brothers include the general tendency of modern societies to subordinate the common good to the demands of groups that each have a "specific sense of life" (125/171), the question whether economic rationality should or should not be applied to matters of public well-being (131–32/177–78), and the question whether societies should be structured around liberal or communitarian principles (133–34/180–81). There is also a general celebration of vitalism, of action over theory, of audacity over calculation. These discussions are framed in terms that are particular to their own time and place, but they nevertheless hold a universal relevance.

The ultra-nationalist position tends to win out in these debates, especially since later in the chapter Deutschlin receives reinforcement from another character named "Teutleben" (= German life). Mann has sometimes been accused of putting his thumb on the scale by using as his main source of inspiration a fraternity newsletter called *Die freideutsche Position* (The Free-German Position) from 1931, and thus from a time at which

---

13 For more on this cohort, see Robert Wohl, *The Generation of 1914* (Cambridge, MA: Harvard University Press, 1979).

most student movements were already infiltrated by Nazism. While this is fair criticism, it is also true that German student fraternities had been moving towards increasingly chauvinistic and anti-Semitic positions since the 1890s.[14] Here as elsewhere in the novel, Mann is presenting a complex and intriguing portrait of an era that he himself experienced.

Leipzig and First Stay in Munich (1905–1911)

In the fall of 1905, Leverkühn abandons his studies of theology and moves to an even larger city, Leipzig in nearby Saxony, to continue his music instructions with Wendell Kretzschmar. He continues to move in the footsteps of the literary Faustus: Goethe set a memorably scene of *Faust I* in Auerbach's Cellar, a real-world tavern in Leipzig. The key scene of Leverkühn's Leipzig days takes place in an even more illicit setting, namely the brothel where the budding composer first lays eyes on the prostitute Esmeralda. One year later, Esmeralda initiates Leverkühn into the devil's pact when she infects him with syphilis during a sexual encounter in Pressburg, modern-day Bratislava. Sometime after that, she also indirectly leads Leverkühn to the discovery of the "strict style," which the young man first conceptualizes when he inserts the musical motif B-E-A-E-E♭ (or H-E-A-E-Es, for "Hetaera Esmeralda," in the German transliteration) into one of his Brentano Songs and thereby hits upon the idea of writing in "musical words." And more than a decade after her original appearance, Esmeralda likely resurfaces as the mysterious Frau von Tolna, who removes obstacles from Leverkühn's musical career and brings him closer to Rudi Schwerdtfeger.

The Leipzig chapters, in other words, are symbolically even more overdetermined than the ones set in Halle an der Saale. Nevertheless, there is a historical reference point for them, even if it too is highly mediated by literature. For the salient details of the first encounter with Esmeralda (an accidental visit to a brothel, awkward communications between prostitute and customer, a chord struck on a piano, flight from the establishment) are taken from Paul Deussen's aforementioned *Recollections of Nietzsche*. Nietzsche spent his own student days in Leipzig and supposedly found himself in the same risqué situation as Leverkühn. Chapter XVI, in which this episode takes place, thus marks a high point of the composer's similarity with the German philosopher and is a central chapter for any reader that seeks to interpret *Doctor Faustus* as a "Nietzsche novel."

After four years of study about which we learn relatively little (Zeitblom is traveling through Greece for part of this period), Leverkühn

---

14 See in this context the chapter on "University Students and Professors on the March," in George L. Mosse, *The Crisis of German Ideology: Intellectual Origins of the Third Reich* (Madison: University of Wisconsin Press, 1964), 192–205.

relocates to Munich, thereby breaking free from the geographical confines of the Chapbook. For a brief while, he rents a room in the bohemian district of Schwabing. Mann modeled Leverkühn's landlords—the widowed Frau Senator Rodde and her daughters Inez and Clarissa—on his own mother Julia and his sisters Julia Elisabeth and Carla. This kind of superimposition of close relatives onto the story of a devil's pact is inherently awkward. But Mann's decision gets even more vexatious by virtue of the fact that both of his sisters committed suicide. Carla Mann poisoned herself in 1910 when she was blackmailed by a former lover, an episode that made it into *Doctor Faustus* in nearly unaltered form, down to the wording of the suicide note. Julia Elisabeth hanged herself in 1927, having been thrust into economic destitution by the 1923 hyperinflation. Mann gave her a different fate in his novel, making Inez Rodde a central figure in a murderous love triangle inspired by real-life events that he had first heard about during a visit to Julia Elisabeth's house.

The Rodde episodes are amongst the most ethically troublesome in all of *Doctor Faustus*. They raise serious questions about the limits of Mann's montage technique and of the liberties permissible to fiction when adapting real-world events. If Mann's actions are defensible, they are so only because he did not draw on his sisters' biographies for salacious reasons, but rather because he thought their fates expressed something of deeper significance about the Zeitblom-Leverkühn generation and its place in German history.

Inez and Clarissa's lives are tragically dominated by their attempts to mediate between the nineteenth-century bourgeois sphere into which they were born and a rapidly evolving modern world. Their mother was a "celebrated member of a patrician society and manager of a household full of servants and duties" (210/286). After the death of her husband, however, she falls upon hard times and is forced to sublet her Munich apartment. Inez resents this, she "made a point of looking back to the old paternal world of bourgeois dignity and rigor" (211/287). But her only way to return to this paternal world is through marriage to the art historian Dr. Helmut Institoris who, despite holding a solid academic post, is very much a creature of the tempestuous fin-de-siècle. Regarding their unlikely liaison, Zeitblom observes that "it was, to put it in the briefest terms, the dichotomy between aesthetics and ethics, which to a great extent governed the cultural dialectics of the era and was more or less personified in these two young people—the contradiction between a scholarly glorification of 'life' in its glittering thoughtlessness and a pessimistic veneration of suffering" (305/420). Readers familiar with Nietzsche will immediately recognize in Zeitblom's dualism of "thoughtlessness" and "suffering" a variation of the opposition between "blond beasts" and "ascetic priests" described in *The Genealogy of Morals*. Institoris, however, though he tellingly has carefully coiffed blond hair, is ultimately no "blond beast," but merely an example of the "scholarly glorification" thereof. He stands symbolically for a generation of German scholars who may not have directly participated in the rise of the Nazis, but who nevertheless provided intellectual cover for it by failing to subject the rising tide of unreason to adequate forms of critique. Later in the novel, we will consequently encounter Institoris as a hanger-on in the company of much more dangerous figures, the members of the Kridwiss Circle.

Clarissa Rodde, meanwhile, chooses a different path from Inez. Like Mann's sister Carla, she seeks an escape from the nineteenth-century bourgeois sphere in the bohemian world of the theater. When she belatedly realizes that her talents are insufficient to secure her a career, she is reduced to the standard fate of struggling actresses of the time: selling her body to a rich admirer. Events take their course, and Clarissa ultimately commits suicide when her final desperate attempt to marry back into the bourgeois sphere founders on the shoals of blackmail. The widening gulf between bohemian and bourgeois life worlds in the late nineteenth century led to many dissolute existences in the fin-de-siècle and was a subject of lifelong fascination for Thomas Mann. He was well aware that one of the most characteristic products of this dynamic was Adolf Hitler, who, after many years living as a struggling artist, succeeded in translating his bohemian inclinations into a new form of community when he took over the Nazi party.[15]

Palestrina, Pfeiffering, and Munich Society Prior to the November Revolution (1911–1918)

Following his initial brief stay in Munich, Leverkühn spends a year in Italy in the company of his close friend Rüdiger Schildknapp. They pass the summers of 1911 and 1912 in Palestrina, a small town in the Apennine Mountains roughly twenty miles east of Rome. Palestrina is the birthplace of the sixteenth-century Italian composer of the same name—a fact that is of obvious significance given that Leverkühn has taken an increasing interest in early modern polyphonic compositions and will discuss their significance during his conversation with the devil in chapter XXV. There is also a biographical element here, for Mann, too, had spent a summer in Palestrina as a young man, working on his debut novel *Buddenbrooks*. Not for the first time, Mann thus superimposes elements of his own life onto that of his fictional composer—another example of the anguished self-identification with the subject of his novel that I describe at greater length in chapter 9, "Five Masters from Germany."

---

15 Mann explores Hitler's fundamentally bohemian character in the 1938 essay "Brother Hitler," published in English translation as "A Brother" in *Esquire* 11 (1939): 31, 132–33.

Following his return to Germany, Leverkühn sets up residence in the fictional village of Pfeiffering, located about thirty miles southwest of Munich. From there, he regularly commutes to the Bavarian capital to take part in its social life. Pfeiffering is closely modeled on the real-world hamlet of Polling, where Mann's mother settled in the early twentieth century and where Mann himself spent many an enjoyable weekend afternoon. In bringing the place to life, Mann drew on these memories, as well as on others he had of his own vacation home in nearby Bad Tölz. The vividly described topographical features that render Pfeiffering so memorable, such as Rombühel Hill or the Klammer Pool, can still be found in that part of upper Bavaria and are now the focal point of a modest kind of literary tourism. The Schweigestill farmhouse with its "winged-victory room" and "abbot's chamber" is extant as well (Figures 11 and 12). Part of the building is now given over to a luxury car tuning and restoration service, which might serve as a useful reminder that the literary cloth from which *Doctor Faustus* is made is interwoven everywhere with the living fabric of German history.

Pfeiffering is a highly significant location within the literary logic of the novel, since it duplicates the setting of Leverkühn's childhood days in Buchel and thereby highlights the themes of mythical return and the "ever-present now" that are so central to *Doctor Faustus*. From a historical perspective, however, Munich clearly outweighs it in importance, and will acquire an ever-greater significance in the second half of the novel. Munich was a thriving metropolis at the beginning of the twentieth century, second in Germany only to Berlin in terms of political and economic power. Culturally speaking, its influence arguably exceeded that of the capital. Its university was one of the very best in the country, and many of Germany's painters, writers, and composers sought shelter from the repressive Prussian government in the comparatively liberal atmosphere of Bavaria.

The young Adolf Hitler was one such artist attracted to the Bavarian freedoms. He settled in Munich in 1913, trying to avoid the military draft in his native Austria and hoping to improve his middling fortunes as a postcard painter. Ten years later, he had risen to head of the National Socialist Party. Yet another ten years later, he was Chancellor of Germany. Thomas Mann does not comment on the rise of the Nazi movement at all in *Doctor Faustus*, and Leverkühn's character traits are the opposite of Hitler's in almost every conceivable way. Leverkühn is not Hitler, and yet it is not a coincidence that Mann's fictional composer ends up in the same place at the same time as the historical dictator. For Munich, despite or perhaps precisely because its cultural and intellectual star shone so bright, would turn into a pivotal place for the rise of unreason and violent extremism over the next twenty years.[16] Nowhere else in the world were the most advanced forms of enlightened liberal culture in such close proximity to regression and barbarism, and nowhere else did they capitulate to the challenges posed by this barbarism quite as readily. This is what Mann hopes to show us in *Doctor Faustus*.

We see this very clearly in chapters XXIII and XXVIII, in which Zeitblom describes the society salons in which Leverkühn spends a good amount of time in 1913 and 1914. The hosts of these salons—the Rodde family, the Schlaginhaufens, the publisher Radbruch, and the paper manufacturer Bullinger—are cultured people. Their guests include artists such as the painters Leo Zink and Baptist Spengler, the novelist Jeannette Scheurl, and the opera singers Harald Kjoejelund and Tanya Orlanda, as well as intellectuals such as the numismatist Dr. Kranich and the cultural philosopher Dr. Chaim Breisacher. But something is off right from the start. Mann's depiction of the various artists and intellectuals is mocking. There's the off-handed quip about "writers who wrote nothing at all" (215/294), for example, or the biting description of the painter Leo Zink, who is repeatedly compared to a randy faun. One senses that none of these people has much of an inner conviction or a devotion to an artistic ethos.

Nor are the intellectuals any better. Kranich is what the Germans call a *Fachidiot*, a blinkered specialist with no practical expertise outside his narrow academic field—a fact that he will repeatedly use as an excuse in situations where concrete action would be called for. Breisacher, however, is even worse. A charismatic and intellectually subtle lecturer, he holds forth on *völkisch* ideas, extolling such virtues as racial purity, primitivist immediacy, and thoughtless dynamism.[17] The centerpiece of chapter XXVIII is the conversation between Breisacher and the intendant of the Munich Court Theater, Baron von Riedesel, whose last name is a portmanteau of the German words for "reed" and "donkey." Riedesel is a traditional conservative, comfortable with the Bavarian monarchy and the state of society as it currently is—or rather, as it was in some hazily idealized not-too-distant past. At the Schlaginhaufen salon, he gets intellectually steamrolled by Breisacher, who argues that the goal of politics shouldn't be to cling to what exists, but rather to overthrow the existing social order and restore a more primordial and authentic state of affairs. If Riedesel is a conservative, then Breisacher is an unabashed reactionary, and the conversation between

---

16 The process by which this happened in traced in great detail in David Clay Large, *Where Ghosts Walked: Munich's Road to the Third Reich* (New York: W. W. Norton, 1997).

17 Breisacher is modeled on Oskar Goldberg, a Jewish philosopher of religion with whom Mann repeatedly crossed paths in the 1920s and 1930s and to whom he privately referred as a "mystic and fascist." See Helmut Koopmann, "Ein 'Mystiker und Faschist' als Ideenlieferant für Thomas Manns *Josephs*-Romane: Thomas Mann und Oskar Goldberg," *Thomas Mann Jahrbuch* 6 (1993): 71–92.

the two men showcases how one form of right-wing politics—associated, in Germany, with defenders of the monarchy and members of the German National People's Party—would, as the century wore on, increasingly lose ground to a more dangerous and reactionary kind.

Riedesel, of course, is not only a theater intendant and an amateur pianist, but also a nobleman. He belongs to the upper strata of society, not to the bohème. The same is true of the wealthier of the Munich society hosts, the Bullingers, the Radbruchs, and the Schlaginhaufens. The surname of the latter couple, which features especially prominently in these chapters, can be translated as "punch the rabble." This little joke highlights that the dangerous ideology which Breisacher imports into the salons, and which the artists and intellectuals are neither willing nor able to counter in any form, would ultimately find a receptive audience amongst those seated quite comfortably within the halls of power.

The internal hypocrisy of Munich salon society is revealed with the outbreak of the First World War, when Serenus Zeitblom, of all people, is the only one who sees military service. His friends find various excuses to resist conscription; they are perfectly comfortable playing with incendiary ideas as long as it is others who end up getting burned. In one especially funny scene, Zeitblom runs into Breisacher in the streets of Munich. The prophet of reaction has decked himself out in cockades, the early twentieth-century equivalent of flag pins, in an attempt to leave no doubts about his patriotism and forestall anti-Semitic aggression by the very mob he so fervently praised in his prewar sermons. The contrast would be grotesque if it weren't also so distressingly familiar from our contemporary television screens.

The First World War and the Failed German Revolution (1914–1919)

Real-world events play only a very minor role during the first half of *Doctor Faustus*. Mann is much more concerned with highlighting the perilous social context in which art was produced during the early twentieth century, and with investigating the inner life of the post-Nietzschean generation that would end up willingly trading liberalism for authoritarianism during the 1920s. This changes with the outbreak of the First World War in chapter XXX. The war was the defining event of the Zeitblom-Leverkühn generation. Thousands of young men volunteered for military service not only because they wanted to serve their country but also because they were intoxicated by the "Spirit of 1914"—the idea that the war experience would forge a new spiritual community out of the splinters of modern German society, eliminating distinctions of class, creed, and education in the process.

Zeitblom personally partakes in this mad atmosphere and in one of his lengthy digressions also gives us an important conceptual tool with which to describe it, namely that of the "breakthrough" (325/449). "Breakthrough," in *Doctor Faustus*, refers not only to the military aim of breaking through the enemy ranks, but also to the utopian social aspirations that accompanied the mobilization of 1914. In a third sense, it refers to Leverkühn's quest to "break through" to a new kind of music. Mann explicitly links this artistic sense to the socially utopian one: while the German youth march off to war, he has Leverkühn write *Gesta Romanora*, a "puppet opera" for wooden marionettes greatly influenced by the essay "On the Marionette Theater" by the Romantic poet Heinrich von Kleist. Kleist's essay treats the graceful movements of marionettes on their strings as a parable for the possibility of human redemption from a fallen earthly existence. It would not have been lost on Mann that this redemption is possible only because the marionettes have wooden heads—like ideal soldiers, they merely carry out the directions of others.[18] The very real human stakes in all this talk about "breakthroughs" are illustrated by one of the more haunting vignettes in *Doctor Faustus*: Zeitblom's depiction, at the start of chapter XXXI, of a "gaunt French woman standing on a hill" who curses the advancing German troops with raised fists, shouting the words "*Je suis la dernière!*" (I am the last one; 327/451) to no avail.

Another historical event that Mann describes in significant detail is the German revolution of 1918 and 1919, which came about as a result of the power vacuum that followed upon the abdication of the Kaiser and took an especially dramatic form in Munich.[19] On November 8, 1918, the journalist and Independent Socialist Party politician Kurt Eisner proclaimed the birth of a Bavarian Republic to be led by a council of workers, soldiers, and peasants. The Wittelsbach dynasty, which had ruled Bavaria for almost 750 years, was unceremoniously deposed, with King Ludwig III fleeing across the nearby border to Austria. Eisner's actions came in advance even of those of Philipp Scheidemann, the Social Democrat who one day later proclaimed a German republic from the balcony of the Reichstag in Berlin. Over the course of the next three months, the

---

18 Paul de Man, a critic uncommonly attuned to the similarities between the respective rhetorics of Romanticism and of Nazism, noted about Kleist's essay: "Aesthetic education by no means fails; it succeeds all too well, to the point of hiding the violence that makes it possible." See Paul de Man, "Aesthetic Formalization: Kleist's *Über das Marionettentheater*," in *The Rhetoric of Romanticism* (New York: Columbia University Press, 1984), 289. I'm grateful to Todd Kontje for bringing this quote to my attention.

19 For a comprehensive overview of the events of 1918 and 1919, see Robert Gerwarth, *November 1918: The German Revolution* (New York: Oxford University Press, 2020). Large, *Where Gosts Walked*, provides a compelling narrative of the events in Munich.

relationship between the nascent German government in Berlin and its more radically left-wing cousins in Munich became increasingly frayed, a fact that empowered the reactionary *Freikorps* militias who refused to accept the armistice or the formation of a democratic (to speak nothing of a socialist) state on German soil. Eisner was assassinated by a militant reactionary in broad daylight on February 21, 1919. To prevent a putsch by rightist elements, his comrades first declared a general strike and then proclaimed the formation of a council republic on the Soviet model on April 7. The Munich Soviet Republic lasted for less than a month; it was smashed by *Freikorps* forces assisted by regular army units that the central government in Berlin dispatched to restore order in Bavaria.

As a resident of Munich, Mann got a first-hand impression of the events of 1918 and 1919. For the rest of his life, he believed that the revolution held the key to many subsequent developments of German history. For purposes of *Doctor Faustus*, arguably the most important thing about the revolution was that it was led by artists and intellectuals. Kurt Eisner was a freelance journalist who had studied philosophy. Ernst Toller, the leader of the Munich Soviet Republic, was a playwright, as was his close associate Erich Mühsam. Ordinary citizens soon referred to the new regime as the "Schwabing Soviet" (after the bohemian district surrounding the university) and to its leaders as "coffeehouse anarchists."[20] The abject failure of their endeavors illustrates one of the central theses of *Doctor Faustus*, namely that modern artists and intellectuals, as a result of over-specialization and increasing withdrawal from the affairs of common men, have lost both the claim and the ability to meaningfully guide modern societies. In chapter XXXIII, Mann reveals the intellectuals' desperate attempt to return wholeness to a fragmented society as doomed farce. In a central passage, we peek in on a meeting of the Munich "Council for Intellectual Workers" at which "a belletrist spoke, not without charm, indeed with dimpled sybaritic fuzziness, on the topic of 'Revolution and Brotherly Love'" while "a little girl recited a poem, a man in field gray was prevented only with difficulty from reading a manuscript that had begun with the greeting, 'my dear citizens and citizenesses,' and doubtless would have lasted all night; an angry graduate student ruthlessly took to task every single speaker who had preceded him, but never once deigned to offer those assembled a single positive opinion of his own" (359/494–95). Art and thought are revealed to be either utterly trite (as in the case of the young girl or the man in field gray) or completely useless (as with the belletrist and the graduate student). Either way, intellectual work seems to no longer have any utility.

One artist who keeps himself above the fray, of course, is Adrian Leverkühn, who spends much of the fateful fall of 1918 in bed with

---

20 Large, *Where Ghosts Walked*, 105.

severe headaches caused by the outbreak of tertiary syphilis (see chapter 11, "Illness and Redemption"). By spring 1919, he is at work composing the *Apocalipsis cum figuris* (Apocalypse with Pictures) and also nowhere to be seen in Munich. To some extent, the *Apocalipsis* can be seen as an indirect commentary on revolutionary events. Leverkühn's oratorio is inspired by a cycle of Dürer woodcuts of the same title, which in the logic of the novel are in turn linked to the peasant's uprising of the 1520s. Like the Munich Soviet, the peasant revolt ended in bloodshed. Leverkühn's fascination with antiquated musical forms, his belief that an escape from the progressive liberal culture of the nineteenth century will only be possible through a return to pre-modern elements, also parallels the Munich Soviet's attempt to replace mass democracy with a system of occupation-based councils.[21] But the Soviet is ultimately a dead-end street, its utopian aspirations unfulfilled and unredeemed. The *Apocalipsis*, on the other hand, is a transitional work. It serves as a capstone to the "middle period" of Leverkühn's creative striving, but it also marks the onset of his final phase, the one that will eventually lead him to paralytic collapse, and Germany to the catastrophe of Nazism.

The Kridwiss Circle and the Conservative Revolution (1920–1930)

Mann shows us an admittedly one-sided version of what the intellectual life of this final period looked like in chapter XXXIV, in which a description of the *Apocalipsis* is interwoven with Zeitblom's detailed account of the proto-fascist "Kridwiss Circle" of intellectuals in which he moves during these years.[22] The Kridwiss Circle bears some resemblance to the pre-war salons and indeed includes some of the same members. But everything here is much worse, much more grotesque. If the artists who mingled with industrialists at the Schlaginhaufens were mostly puerile and self-absorbed dreamers, the habitués of the Kridwiss Circle are relentless cynics. They not only have lost the interest and energy to defend progress and liberal society, but now actually celebrate its demise. There's the paleozoologist Dr. Egon Unruhe, who preaches a "sublimated Darwinism" in which "all the things that an advanced humanity had long since ceased to believe

---

21 Similar attempts would proliferate throughout the 1920s on both the far left and the far right of the political spectrum in Germany. See the chapter on "The Corporate State and the Conservative Revolution in Weimar Germany," in George L. Mosse, *Germans and Jews: The Right, the Left, and the Search for a "Third Force" in Pre-Nazi Germany* (Madison: University of Wisconsin Press, 1970), 80–98.

22 In an April 1, 1950, letter to Otto Reeb, Mann used the term "pre-fascist" to refer to the Kridwiss Circle. See Mann, *Selbstkommentare*, 301.

became true and real again" (382/527). Or Professor Georg Vogler, transparently modeled on the philologist Josef Nadler (1884–1963), who was the author of an infamous literary history that linked the stylistic particularities of German poets to the Germanic tribes from which they had ostensibly descended and the landscape in which they had grown up. Not surprisingly, this work became quite popular during the Nazi period. Mann reserves most of his satirical venom for the poet Daniel zur Höhe, however, whom he modeled on an old enemy, the poet Ludwig Derleth (1870–1948).[23] Zur Höhe is the author of a "lyrico-rhetorical outburst of voluptuous terrorism" in which he adopts the persona "of an entity named *Christus Imperator Maximus*, an Energy who enlisted and commanded troops prepared to die in the cause of subjugating the globe [...] and could not get enough of unquestioned, unbounded obedience to his fist-pounding demands" (383/528).

Describing the Kridwiss Circle, Zeitblom notes "that there was a lively sense that the war had disrupted and destroyed what had seemed to be life's fixed values" (384/529), but also acknowledges that "the war had only completed, clarified, and forged as a common drastic experience something that had long been developing and establishing itself as the basis of a new sense of life" (384/530). Thinking back to Mann's earlier description of Kaisersaschern, we might realize that this "long development" can be seen as the surface manifestation of an even older tendency. The Kridwiss Circle represents merely the most extreme version of a human propensity towards unreason that has always cast a shadow over the accomplishments of modernity.

Unsurprisingly, then, the members of the Circle not only despise liberal democracy but also mock the bourgeois progressive tradition that led to things like "culture, enlightenment, humanity, and dreams like the improvement of nations through scientific civilization" (384/530). They believe that dictatorship is the only logical response to the chaos of modernity and congratulate themselves on possessing not only the intellectual acuity to have recognized this clearly, but also the moral resolve to hasten its arrival: "Everything ended in dictatorship, in violence, in any case; for with the demolition of traditional forms of government and society by the French Revolution, an age had dawned that [...] was moving toward despotic tyranny over atomized, disconnected masses leveled to a common denominator and as powerless as the individual" (385/531).

The Kridwiss Circle offers a satirical summary of the aforementioned current in 1920s intellectual life known as the "Conservative Revolution."[24]

---

23 Mann had already parodied Derleth forty years earlier, in the short story "At the Prophet's" (1904).

24 See Roger Woods, *The Conservative Revolution in the Weimar Republic* (New York: St. Martin's Press, 1996).

The best-known conservative revolutionaries in the English-speaking world are the novelist Ernst Jünger, the jurist Carl Schmitt, and the philosopher Oswald Spengler, though there were many others. The name given to their movement is a much-discussed paradox, but it accurately identifies the distinctive feature of these reactionary intellectuals, namely their determination to oppose modernity not only by hanging on to traditional values in danger of being erased, but rather by smashing the status quo and building anew. They believed that only a strong dictatorial figure who could count on the same adulation and unquestioned obedience that kings and popes had (supposedly) enjoyed in the Middle Ages could redeem society from its contemporary fallen condition. This combination of backward glance and wish for radical erasure of existing forms is what unites them with Leverkühn's artistic project during his final years.

Doctor Faustus ends with a grand finale in which nearly all of the figures who have populated the Schlaginhaufen salon and the living room of Sixtus Kridwiss make a pilgrimage to Pfeiffering to listen to a performance of excerpts from Leverkühn's symphonic cantata, *The Lamentation of Doctor Faustus*. Over the course of the previous ten years, Mann's fictional composer has perfected a "strict style" that successfully implements in musical terms much of what the Conservative Revolution strove for. It consists of a radical simplification of musical material, which it subjects to iron-clad control. At the same time, it rolls back a century and a half of homophonic musical innovation, restoring a polyphonic dimension to modern music that Beethoven thought he had successfully overcome. Tellingly, however, the man who presents this innovation to the assembled German artists and intellectuals is not a *Christus Imperator Maximus* like the one envisioned by Daniel zur Höhe, but rather a gaunt syphilitic whose frail body very much resembles that of the mortal Christ.

With the exception of Zeitblom and a few other faithful hangers-on, the invited guests all flee the scene before Leverkühn even has the opportunity to strike the first chords on the piano. They are unwilling to honestly confront this ghastly realization of their openly voiced wishes, unwilling also to take any responsibility for it. This final scene renders *Doctor Faustus* a provocative indictment not only of the intellectual abnegation that led to the Third Reich, but also of the refusal to take responsibility that Mann saw everywhere around him when he finished his novel in 1947. When Mann told an American audience that the dark events in Germany were not alien to him, but that he had been "through it all," he was not merely thinking about long-gone history, the kind of events for which he had to consult thirty-year-old diaries. The long effects of those days were still with him, and they are with us now as well, if we only know where to look.

8: Anti-Semitism and the Problem of Other People's Suffering

MORE THAN THIRTY years ago, Egon Schwarz, a German-American literature professor who had fled the Third Reich as a young man, predicted that, "in a future time whose Thomas Mann readers have not lived through Fascism themselves one fact will stand out more prominently than in ours: that in this German world of *Doctor Faustus* [...] the Jewish figures resemble neither Einstein nor Freud [...], but play instead the roles of a phony music impresario and a hair-splitting forerunner of Fascism."[1] And indeed, contemporary readers of *Doctor Faustus* are invariably and rightly scandalized by Mann's highly unflattering depiction of his Jewish characters. It is also hard to account for the fact that the Holocaust is never directly mentioned in the novel, which otherwise offers such a scrupulous reckoning with Germany's slide into Nazism.

Although he could not have known the exact nature of what went on in the death camps when he started writing *Doctor Faustus*, Mann was aware of the scale of the destruction unleashed upon the Jews of Europe even then. On June 18, 1943, he addressed over ten thousand people at a rally in San Francisco with the words: "the number of those who have perished partly by direct massacre, partly by planned starvation ran into millions even by the end of last year, and under constant intensivation [*sic*] of the awful action, it has substantially increased since then."[2] By the time that he finished *Doctor Faustus* in 1947, the world knew the truth about Auschwitz. Mann himself had in fact, been one of the first people to draw unsparing attention to it in his 1945 essay "The Camps."[3] Why, then, the curious silence in his novel?

To answer this question, it is useful to first sketch a general outline of Mann's relationship to Judaism. To the average American observer at the time that *Doctor Faustus* was published, Mann would have appeared as a steadfast supporter of Jewish life and culture. In addition to his speeches and writings about the Nazi extermination campaign, he had

---

1 Schwarz, "Jewish Characters in *Doctor Faustus*," 138.
2 Thomas Mann, "The Fall of the European Jews," in *Gesammelte Werke*, ed. Peter de Mendelssohn, 20 vols. (Frankfurt am Main: S. Fischer, 1974), XIII: 495.
3 Most easily accessible to English-speaking readers as Thomas Mann, "Address to the German People," *The Nation*, May 12, 1945, 535.

also accumulated a record of appearing on behalf of Zionist causes.⁴ Furthermore, his widely reviewed fiction of those years (the *Joseph* tetralogy and the Moses-story "The Tables of the Law) featured sympathetic depictions of well-known figures from the Old Testament. A particularly knowledgeable interlocutor might have also been able to point out that Mann was married to a Jew (Katia Pringsheim), counted many Jews among his friends and neighbors (including Theodor W. Adorno, his close collaborator on *Doctor Faustus*), and had remained loyal to Jewish publishers in both Europe (Gottfried Bermann Fischer) and America (Alfred A. Knopf) at a time when other writers deserted them so as not to endanger access to the German book market.

The truth was far more ambivalent, however. Mann's earliest fictions, at the time little known in the United States, abound with characters—such as Frau Hagenström in the novel *Buddenbrooks* or the writer Detlev Spinell in the novella *Tristan* (1903)—who, although rarely explicitly identified as Jewish, are nevertheless described with anti-Semitic dogwhistles. Perhaps the worst example of this is Mann's 1906 story "Blood of the Walsungs" which revolves around a pair of incestuous twins, one of whom delivers the narrative's climactic line in a mixture of Yiddish and German. The offensiveness of this story is increased exponentially by the fact that the easily recognizable models for its protagonists were Mann's own wife and her twin brother Klaus Pringsheim. Mann withdrew the manuscript from publication after a confrontation with his in-laws, and in a response to a newspaper inquiry the following year he declared himself to be a "convinced and unhesitating 'philo-Semite.'"⁵ Still, "Blood of the Walsungs" was eventually published in 1921, although Mann replaced the Yiddish phrase with a more innocuous German one. That same year, he wrote another essay on "The Jewish Question" with which he hoped to burnish his philo-Semitic credentials, but which he had to withdraw when his wife took issue with the stereotyped language Mann had deployed in the portraits of three of his Jewish childhood friends.

Mann's letters and diaries provide a similarly ambivalent picture. In a diary entry written on April 28, 1919, in the midst of the abortive Munich revolution that *Doctor Faustus* so vividly reconstructs, Mann notes with clear disapproval that ordinary people were referring to the

---

4   Mann's public utterances and appearances on behalf of Zionist organizations are examined in a recent blog post by Kai Sina, "Precarious Advocacy: Thomas Mann and Zionism," https://medium.com/vatmh/precarious-advocacy-thomas-mann-and-zionism-bec11d7cd454 (accessed November 12, 2024). I have not been able to consult Sina's forthcoming book on the same topic.

5   Thomas Mann, "Die Lösung der Judefrage" [The Solution of the Jewish Question], GKFA 14.1: 174. Historical hindsight makes the title of this inquiry unfortunate, but it was a perfectly innocent phrase in the context of its time and was, at any rate, chosen by the Jewish journalist Julius Moses.

leaders of the uprising as "bloody Jews" (*Saujuden*).[6] And in a letter to Hermann Broch written after the end of the Second World War, in November 1945, he declares that "international law must henceforth brand anti-Semitism as a criminal tendency lest we be overwhelmed by barbarism."[7] Yet in immediate proximity to such utterances we find him referring to the journalist Wilhelm Herzog, one of the intellectual leaders of the Munich revolution, as a "Jewish rascal" (*Judenbengel*)[8] and grappling with the question whether the Jews should really be described as a "people" (*Volk*) or not rather as a "race" (*Rasse*), for "there is something different about them after all, and not just something Mediterranean."[9]

Trying to make sense of all this, a number of critics have voiced the hypothesis that Mann was comfortable with Judaism only for so long as he could treat it as an abstract and remote phenomenon—as he did, for example, in his fiction of the 1930s and 1940s or in his political speeches. By contrast, whenever Jews began to exert a palpable influence on his life, whether through politics in the 1918/1919 revolution, or as literary critics in the Weimar Republic, he reacted with reflexive anti-Semitism.[10] I do not wish to minimize in any way the highly problematic nature of Mann's attitude towards Judaism. Nevertheless, I believe that we need to take a fundamentally different approach when we deal with *Doctor Faustus*.

Let us briefly recap the problematic elements in that novel. First, there is the fact that although the plot of *Doctor Faustus* stretches into the weeks following the end of the Second World War, when news of the true extent of Nazi crimes finally make their way to Serenus Zeitblom, the Holocaust is never directly addressed. It is true that Zeitblom mentions Buchenwald and refers to Germans being marched past piles of corpses by American soldiers, but he does not identify those corpses as Jewish. Buchenwald was, in fact, primarily an internment camp for political prisoners. In Mann's depiction then, the Nazis transgress against reason, against the rule of law, and against the fundamental essence of humanity, but not against the Jewish people per se. Nor does Mann make the persistent anti-Semitism in German society, or the troubling rise of this phenomenon over the course of the 1920s, in any way a subject of his novel. The closest that we get is a passing reference in chapter XX, where

---

6   Diary entry for April 28, 1919, in Mann, *Tagebücher*, I: 215.
7   Letter to Hermann Broch dated November 18, 1945, in Thomas Mann, *Die Briefe Thomas Manns: Regesten und Register*, ed. Hans Bürgin and Hans-Otto Meyer, 5 vols. (Frankfurt am Main: S. Fischer, 1976–87), III: 45/536.
8   Diary entry for November 8, 1918, in Mann, *Tagebücher*, I: 63.
9   Diary entry for October 27, 1945, in Mann, *Tagebücher*, VI: 269.
10 See, for example, Michael Brenner, "Beyond Naphta: Thomas Mann's Jews and German-Jewish Writing," in *A Companion to Thomas Mann's "Magic Mountain,"* ed. Stephen D. Dowden (Columbia, SC: Camden House, 1999), 141–57.

we learn that Rüdiger Schildknapp "ate his midday meal here and there at houses all over Leipzig, even at the tables of rich Jews, although he had been heard to make anti-Semitic remarks" (181/248). Commenting on this, Zeitblom disdainfully notes that "people who feel they are held back and not given their due, and who at the same time present a distinguished appearance, often seek redress in racist self-assertions" (181/248). We know that this was more or less also Mann's take on the virulent anti-Semitism of his time, for in a 1937 address to a Zionist gathering in Switzerland he argued that anti-Semites take as their guiding maxim the formula: "I may be nothing, but at least I'm not a Jew!"[11] As an intellectual analysis of modern prejudice, this is hardly groundbreaking stuff.

Secondly, *Doctor Faustus* contains at least three highly problematic portraits of Jews. The first such figure is the "polyhistor" Chaim Breisacher, whom we first encounter in chapter XXVIII. Breisacher, whose "advanced, indeed reckless, intellect" and "fascinating ugliness" (294/405). Mann goes out of his way to mention, is the "hair-splitting forerunner of Fascism" mentioned by Schwarz. This means, in turn, that a Jew serves as the most visible exponent of a pseudo-Nazi ideology in the novel. This fact bothered readers even during Mann's lifetime; the author brushed aside such objections with the unconvincing reply that there were, after all, plenty of unsympathetic gentile characters in *Doctor Faustus* as well.[12]

The second problematic Jewish character in *Doctor Faustus* is Kunigunde Rosenstiel, one of the two female admirers of Leverkühn whom we first meet in chapter XXXI. Rosenstiel, whom Mann partly modeled on his part-time archivist Ida Herz and partly on the literary critic Käte Hamburger (both Jews), is the part-owner of a "firm that produced sausage casings" (330/455), a position that not only makes her seem slightly ridiculous but can possibly also be read as an anti-Semitic joke about Jewish dietary strictures. Like many of Mann's other characters, she possesses a rather singular tic, namely the "elegiac habit of beginning every sentence with a plaintive 'ah!'" (331/456). In a novel in which the protagonists grasps his way towards a possible redemption by way of a musical piece that is explicitly marked as a "lamentation" (see in this context chapter 12, "Illness and Redemption"), this seeming throwaway reference to an "elegiac habit" is significant. In the essay from which I quoted at the start of this chapter, Egon Schwarz follows up on his prediction regarding the future reception of *Doctor Faustus* with the observation that in this novel, Jewish figures "are even excluded from mourning their own hopeless fate and that of the culture which they have served,

---

11   Thomas Mann, "Zum Problem des Antisemitismus" [On the Problem of Anti-Semitism], in *Gesammelte Werke*, XIII: 481.
12   See Klüger, "Jewish Characters in Thomas Mann's Fiction," 164.

painful feelings which Leverkühn and Zeitblom are so movingly allowed to suffer."[13] The example of Kunigunde Rosenstiel shows that the truth may be even worse. Not only is there no room for Jews in Leverkühn's *Lamentation of Doctor Faustus* or in Zeitblom's fervent prayer in the epilogue, Jewish mourning is, in fact, treated as a source of cheap humor.[14]

The final character to have often given readers pause is Saul Fitelberg, the Jewish impresario who offers Leverkühn a brilliant career in Paris in chapter XXXVII, and whom Mann modeled partly on an acquaintance, the film agent Saul C. Colin, and partly on a character from an eighteenth-century play by Gotthold Ephraim Lessing, the French mercenary Riccault de la Marlinière. Like Marlinière, Fitelberg is an over-confident name-dropper who speaks in a curious mixture of French and German. This emphasizes his foreignness and has also invited comparisons to stereotypical portraits of Jews, who are often depicted as speaking a "defective" German characterized by the admixture of "foreign" (usually Yiddish or Hebrew) elements. Fitelberg's worldliness and his uninhibited desire to make money off of Leverkühn's art round out the problematic nature of his appearance. With Fitelberg, too, Mann encountered pushback already during his own lifetime, especially after he made a habit of reading from chapter XXXVII, which offered him all sorts of opportunities for theatrical interludes, whenever he had friends over for dinner. His son Klaus pointed out to him that the chapter might be regarded as anti-Semitic, causing Mann to note in his diaries that "I cannot share those concerns."[15]

Problematic as he may be, Saul Fitelberg differs from the other Jewish characters in *Doctor Faustus* in one important respect: because his torrential stream of words is quoted as direct discourse, we experience him on his own terms, not on those dictated by Serenus Zeitblom. And these terms include several remarkable statements that come at the very end of the chapter, in his parting words to his two awestruck interlocutors. There, Fitelberg claims that Jews "are international—but we are pro-German, like no one else in the world, if only because we cannot help seeing the similarity of the roles Germanness and Jewishness play in the world. *Une analogie frappante!* They are both equally hated, despised, feared, envied, are both equally resented and resentful. One speaks of the age of nationalism. But in reality, there are only two nationalisms, the German and the Jewish" (428/591). Fitelberg's neat separation of "Germanness" and "Jewishness" (a conceptual division we also find in Mann's non-fictional

---

13 Schwarz, "Jewish Characters in *Doctor Faustus*," 138.
14 For a fuller analysis of Kunigunde Rosenstiel, see Yahya Elsaghe, "'La Rosenstiel' and Her Ilk: Jewish Names in Thomas Mann," *Publications of the English Goethe Society* 80, no. 1 (2009): 53–63.
15 Diary entry for August 18, 1946, in Mann, *Tagebücher*, VII: 31.

writings) is undoubtedly problematic, for it presupposes not only that these are monolithic identity formations, but also rules out any possibility that one could be both a German *and* a Jew. Nevertheless, the thesis that Germans and Jews are "equally hated, despised, feared" by the world is unusual enough to warrant more detailed study.

Even stranger sentences are yet to come, however. "The Germans," Fitelberg concludes, "with their nationalism, their arrogance, their fondness for their own incomparability, their hatred of being second or even placed on a par, their refusal to be introduced to the world and to join its society—the Germans will bring about their own misfortune, a truly Jewish misfortune, *je vous le jure*" (428/592). We may well nod along with this until we get to the final two phrases. Has Fitelberg really just drawn a parallel between the German descent into Nazism and the "Jewish misfortune," which culminated, after all, in the Holocaust?

In a recent study, the critic Todd Kontje has offered the most compelling interpretation of these strange lines to date. Mann included Jewish characters in the novel, so he argues, because he wanted to illustrate the fundamental choice the German people were facing, a choice that Jews had already been familiar with for many centuries. The options were either to double down on a chauvinistic view of the world that differentiates between a "Chosen people" and everyone else, or to seek a cosmopolitan engagement with other nations. Chaim Breisacher, whose German nationalism and anti-rationalism goes hand in hand with an equally arrogant love of "the old and genuine Hebrew presence of Yahweh," as opposed to the later "Biblical personages revered by every Christian child" (297/409), represents the former option. Saul Fitelberg, who urges Leverkühn towards a cosmopolitanism that is already foreshadowed by the composer's origins in Kaisersaschern (see chapter 7, "The Historical Setting of the Novel), represents the latter. Kontje even proposes that Mann's decision to pick the Fitelberg chapter for his public readings possesses "a strong element of self-parody [...] that arises from Man's long-term unease with himself in the role of [a] public intellectual and advocate of democracy and the Enlightenment."[16]

If we adopt such a reading, it would go a long way not towards excusing Mann's harmful stereotyping of Jewish characters, but at least towards blunting the full impact of his actions. Ultimately, we might then say, Mann was including caricatures of Jews in his novel because he wanted to thereby illustrate what he regarded as a fundamentally German dilemma. But such an interpretive move in turn raises other important questions about the treatment of anti-Semitism and the Holocaust in *Doctor Faustus*, questions that I think are best approached by means of an

---

16   Todd Kontje, *Thomas Mann's World: Empire, Race, and the Jewish Question* (Ann Arbor: University of Michigan Press, 2011), 171.

exchange that took place between Mann and his Jewish colleague Jakob Wassermann, one of the most popular authors of the Weimar period. Wassermann had complained about the many obstacles Jewish writers faced if they wanted to be successful in Germany. This irritated Mann, who sent his friend a letter in which he claimed that "many of your complaints refer to circumstances in Germany as such, and could just as well have been made by any non-Jewish writer." Wassermann responded by pointing out the differences between personal and social injustice, asking Mann: "How would you have felt if somebody had called for a vote of no-confidence in you simply because you were from Lübeck and a North German?"[17]

Mann, as this exchange suggests, possessed no notion of what we nowadays call "structural" racism or anti-Semitism. Injustices for him were personal, and because he had created characters like Breisacher, Rosenstiel, or Fitelberg with an allegorical purpose and not out of malice, he was impervious to any charges that their mere existence was harmful. Furthermore, because he was not particularly receptive to Jewish suffering as a structurally specific form of experience, he was entirely comfortable folding it into larger categories such as the "German" or the "European." This, I think, also helps explain why the Holocaust is curiously absent from the novel, although Mann was undoubtedly aware of its true scope. For him, the Holocaust wasn't a singular catastrophe, but simply a part of the larger complex of destruction unleashed by the Nazis. Since he saw such a close parallelism between Jewish and German identity, he likely would also not have understood Schwarz's complaint that Jewish suffering remains unredeemed at the end of the novel. That he thereby drew a perverse equivalence between the corpses at Buchenwald and the people who were made to march by them seems to have not occurred to him.

This deficiency of *Doctor Faustus* is, I think, closely related to (though certainly of a different order of magnitude than) another problem that I already mentioned in the previous chapter, and which contemporary readers frequently find both fascinating and revolting. I'm referring to Mann's unflinching willingness to adapt intimate details not only from his own life but also from those of people close to him into his fiction. Carla Mann's suicide note and Frido Mann's speech patterns come to mind in this context. These are individual cases, of course, not examples of structural suffering, but Mann nevertheless had no problems using them in order to strengthen the allegorical texture of his novel, just as he had no compunctions about resorting to stereotyping. His audacity resulted in some of the most memorable secondary characters in twentieth-century fiction. But the price was enormous.

17   I owe this quotation to Klüger, "Jewish Characters in Thomas Mann's Fiction," 164.

Part Three: Interpretations

9: Five Masters from Germany: Leverkühn as Artist and Intellectual

In chapter 6, "*Doctor Faustus* and Literary Modernism," I examined Mann's use of a "polyphonic" style in the composition of his novel. In *Doctor Faustus*, so I argued, different temporal layers exist simultaneously yet independently of one another, though they are woven together by the major characters of the narrative. The most obvious example of this is Serenus Zeitblom, who exists simultaneously on a temporal plane that stretches from 1883 to 1934 (the narrated time) and on one that stretches from 1943 to 1945 (the time of narration). Events from the earlier temporal plane, such as Leverkühn's dealings with the devil, are superimposed upon those from the later one, such as the bombing of cities by the Allied powers, resulting in physical reflexes with ambivalent causes.

An even more complex example of polyphonic style is presented to us by the character of Adrian Leverkühn, who exists on at least six different temporal planes simultaneously. For again and again throughout the story, we find references to important figures from German cultural and intellectual history to whom he bears an uncanny resemblance, whether in external appearance or through biographical particulars. A polyphonic composition in which the various musical voices present variations and repetitions of a single common melody is known as a "fugue," and as a result we might describe *Doctor Faustus* as having a "fugal" texture. Taken together, these fugal elements combine to present an allegorical argument that takes in three centuries of German cultural history.

Consider the example of chapter XVI, a large chunk of which is taken up with the transcription of a letter that Leverkühn sends to Zeitblom shortly after his arrival in Leipzig in the fall of 1905. The letter is written in an archaic idiom reminiscent of the sixteenth century, a stylistic choice that Zeitblom somewhat paradoxically calls both "a parody [...] a self-stylization" and "a manifestation of [Leverkühn's] inner disposition" (148/204). His inability to decide on one of these options is telling. Throughout the 1930s and 1940s, Mann consistently expressed dissatisfaction with the theory that Nazism had been entirely foreign to the German character, that it had overwhelmed and corrupted a fundamentally good nation whose ultimate innocence could still be found in certain sheltered parts.[1] Instead, he argued in his 1945 Library of Congress lecture on "Germany and the Germans" that "there are *not* two Germanys, a good one and a bad, but only one, whose best turned into evil through devilish cunning."[2] Going even further, he claimed that "not a word of all that I have just told you about Germany or tried to indicate to you came out of alien, cool, objective knowledge, it is all within me, I have been through it all."[3] *Doctor Faustus* makes the same point in fictional form. Leverkühn is *not* just the fundamentally good, basically innocent childhood friend as which Zeitblom would like to remember and protect him. He instead carries within him a strong legacy of the irrational and the demonic, elements which the novel highlights by repeatedly associating him with the early modern period, the era of black magic and witchcraft trials. Mann himself therefore went so far as to call *Doctor Faustus* a novel that "always has one foot in the sixteenth century."[4]

That is not all that we can extract from Leverkühn's letter to Zeitblom, however. Studying it carefully, we soon stumble upon the budding composer's first encounter with the prostitute Esmeralda, over the course of which Leverkühn steps up to a piano and strikes up a sequence of chords. Readers well versed in German intellectual history may feel a certain sense of familiarity when confronted with this passage, and indeed it is another example of Mann's borrowings from Paul Deussen's memoirs, which we already encountered as an important source for *Doctor Faustus* in the previous chapters. This act of copying adds a second temporal layer to the texture of the novel, however. Within the context of a letter in which Leverkühn seems to oscillate between the sixteenth and the twentieth centuries, he now also appears to repeat actions that were actually performed by Friedrich Nietzsche, a real-world figure from the nineteenth century!

This proliferation of layers tends to baffle first-time readers of *Doctor Faustus*. We are used to allegorical narratives in which a surface element

---

1   Mann would have had good reason to contemplate this thesis, for he encountered it repeatedly while in American exile—during the late 1930s in his dealings with Count Hubertus zu Löwenstein and his *American Guild for German Cultural Freedom*, which held steadfast to the notion that the "true" Germany had fled beyond the borders of the Reich; during the early 1940s in his interactions with Marxist intellectuals like Bertolt Brecht, who saw Nazism as an outgrowth of international capitalism, not as something endemic to the German nation; and finally in the mid-1940s within official Allied policy, which tried to foment a popular uprising in the Third Reich by reassuring ordinary Germans that they were not the real enemy.

2   Mann, "Germany and the Germans," 64.

3   Mann, "Germany and the Germans," 65.

4   Letter to Hans Ulrich Staeps, October 8, 1947, in Mann, *Selbstkommentare*, 121.

(known to literary theorists as the *vehicle*) represents exactly *one* deeper element (the *tenor*). In George Orwell's *Animal Farm*, for example, the pig Napoleon represents Stalin, Snowball represents Trotsky, etc. This is by no means the only way in which allegory can work, however. Early Christian theorists (with whose ideas Mann was eminently familiar from the twenty-six years he had spent researching and writing his *Joseph* novels) in fact developed a four-fold model of allegory, in which a single vehicle represents as many as four different tenors. *Doctor Faustus* can be seen as having a similar structure.[5] Besides a "literal" level, in which tenor and vehicle are identical, medieval thinkers postulated three further layers: the "typological," the "tropological" (or "moral"), and the "anagogical." The particular kind of allegory that I wish to examine here closely corresponds to what Christian theorists called the "typological" reading. I will describe a moral approach in the next chapter, "Music Theory and Political Allegory" and an anagogical one in chapter 11, "Illness and Redemption."

Typological allegory works by way of a mechanism called *figura*. In *figura*, according to the philologist Erich Auerbach, "something real and historical [...] represents and proclaims in advance something that is also real and historical."[6] For Christian theorists, it was the events of the Old Testament that proclaimed in advance the story of Christ. *Figura*—and thus typological allegory—can usefully explain what is happening in the letter Leverkühn writes to Zeitblom from Leipzig. In its pages, he *becomes* Nietzsche, or we might say just as readily: Nietzsche becomes him.

The argument that I want to develop in the rest of this chapter is that typological allegory can be productively used to analyze the fugal structure of *Doctor Faustus* as a whole. Leverkühn's internal division, the fact that he exists on multiple temporal planes at once, comes about by virtue of the fact that he combines within himself multiple historical personalities who are nevertheless simply variations of the same theme. I will first describe the various historical layers and then offer some concluding thoughts as to their ultimate significance.

Albrecht Dürer

Perhaps the earliest occasion on which a first-time reader of *Doctor Faustus* will become aware of the fact that the novel interweaves

---

5   For a particularly strong reading of *Doctor Faustus* as a twentieth-century variation on the four-fold schema, see the chapter on "Allegory and History: On Rereading *Doktor Faustus*" in Fredric Jameson, *The Modernist Papers* (London: Verso, 2007), 113–33.

6   Erich Auerbach, "*Figura*," in *Time, History, and Literature: Selected Essays of Erich Auerbach*, ed. James I. Porter, trans. Jane O. Newman (Princeton, NJ: Princeton University Press, 2014), 79.

different temporal layers occurs in chapter VI, in the description of Adrian Leverkühn's hometown of Kaisersaschern. In that chapter, Zeitblom tells us rather directly that the town "seems to bear *nunc stans*, the famous scholastic formula for timelessness, on its brow. [It] maintains its identity, which was the same three hundred, nine hundred years ago, against the river of time sweeping over it and constantly affecting many changes" (39/57). And indeed, Thomas Mann used early modern Nuremberg as an inspiration when he created the fictional Kaisersaschern.[7]

Perhaps the most famous resident of Nuremberg during the sixteenth century was the painter and printer Albrecht Dürer (1471–1528). Dürer's presence can be felt everywhere in *Doctor Faustus*. While writing the novel, Mann kept a copy of Wilhelm Waetzoldt's 1935 biography of the artist close at hand, and the names of many secondary characters (as well as that of the narrator, who gets his peculiar cognomen from Dürer's contemporary Bartholomäus Zeitblom) are taken straight from its pages. That's not all, however, for as Fritz Kaufmann pointed out as early as 1949, the peculiarly detailed descriptions of Leverkühn's family members in chapters III, IV, and VII were inspired by various Dürer portraits (see Figures 1–3).[8]

Mann had, in fact, been interested in the Renaissance artist for much of his life, and in a 1928 essay had lifted him into the company of "Goethe, Schopenhauer, Nietzsche, Wagner" as one of five German thinkers and artists in whom one might find "the whole fateful complex and constellation, a whole world, the German world, with all its vaulting self-dramatization, its enthralling intellectualistic climax and dissolution at the end."[9] This juxtaposition of otherwise diverse figures (an artist, a poet, two philosophers, and a composer, whose lives spanned three and a half centuries) already foreshadows the fugal ambition of the later *Doctor Faustus*.

Like the fictional Leverkühn, Dürer was an audacious innovator who gained crucial inspiration on a trip to Italy undertaken when he was in his mid-twenties. And also like Leverkühn, his external appearance bore a certain resemblance to canonical depictions of Jesus Christ, a fact that Dürer consciously emphasized in paintings such as his "Self-Portrait at Twenty-Eight." There are further similarities, such as a biographical connection to syphilis, a disease that first surfaced in Europe during Dürer's lifetime. The artist created the first known depiction of a syphilitic in

---

7   Other models included Mann's own hometown of Lübeck, nineteenth-century Naumburg, the hometown of Friedrich Nietzsche, as well as medieval Aachen, the town where the real-world grave of Emperor Otto III (which Mann relocates to Kaisersaschern) can be found.

8   Fritz Kaufmann, "Dr. Fausti Weheklag," *Archiv für Philosophie* 3 (1949): 5–28.

9   Thomas Mann, "Dürer," in *Past Masters and Other Papers*, trans. H.T. Lowe-Porter (New York: Knopf, 1933), 150.

Western art in 1496, and there is some speculation that he may have himself suffered from the disease.[10] Dürer, finally, died when he was fifty-six years old—at almost the exact same age as Leverkühn when he succumbs to his illness in 1940 at the age of fifty-five.

Typological allegory hinges less on empirical particulars, however, than on the overall interpretive shape that can be given to this data. Joshua and Jesus, for example, are linked through the trope of *figura* because both are redeemer figures who lead a population (the Jews and the Christian believers, respectively) out of bondage. Through Waetzoldt's biography (and later also through Walter Benjamin's study *Origin of the German Mourning Play*, which Adorno gave to him as a present in June 1946) Mann was familiar with the art historical studies of Erwin Panofsky, who saw in Dürer an early forerunner of the Faustian archetype—a conclusion that would not have been lost on the author, who in his 1928 essay had similarly emphasized the "Faustian *melencolia*" characteristic of Dürer's worldview.[11] Panofsky based his association on the fact that Dürer was well-known not only as a true "Renaissance Man" who pursued knowledge at all costs, but also as a melancholic who (much like the Faustus of the Chapbook) was repeatedly driven into pits of suicidal despair by the ultimate uselessness of all human striving. While the literary Faust made a pact with the devil to relieve his suffering, however, Dürer instead turned to the consolation offered by geometry and mathematics, which led him to important advances in pictorial perspective as well as to the audacious art-theoretical treatises of his final years.

Dürer and Leverkühn are linked with one another not only because both can be seen as Faust figures who tumble into extreme states of melancholic despair, but also because both seek refuge from these states in mathematically rigorous ordering systems. The link is made explicit in the novel by Leverkühn's admiration for Dürer's engraving *Melencolia I*, a detail of which the future composer pins to the walls of his student apartment in chapter XII (102/138).[12] *Melencolia I* depicts a brooding angel (the posture of which Leverkühn will imitate in the final chapters of the novel) who is surrounded by numerous references to geometry and the mathematical arts: a perfect sphere, a rhombohedron, a

---

10   Colin Eisler, "Who is Dürer's 'Syphilitic Man'?," *Perspectives in Biology and Medicine* 52, no. 1 (2009): 48–60.

11   Mann, "Dürer," 151.

12   By far the most comprehensive treatment of the multi-faceted connections between Leverkühn, Dürer, Faust, and the topos of melancholia is offered by Dieter Borchmeyer's chapter entitled "'Musik-Dämonie'—Saturn und Melancholie," in his *Thomas Mann: Werk und Zeit* (Berlin: Insel Verlag, 2022), 1175–1262. For an English introduction, see Michael Palencia-Roth, "Albrecht Dürer's *Melencolia I* and Thomas Mann's *Doctor Faustus*," *German Studies Review* 3, no. 3 (1980): 361–75.

compass and, most importantly, a magic square. Leverkühn is especially drawn to this magic square, which Zeitblom in chapter XXII connects explicitly with the composer's attempts at a "strict style" that would subject the horizontal (melodic) and vertical (harmonic) dimensions of music to the same laws.

Another Dürer engraving that plays a prominent role in *Doctor Faustus* is *Knight, Death, and Devil* (Fig. 4), which Leverkühn's fraternity brother Deutschlin singles out as an allegory of the German national character in chapter XIV (128/175).[13] *Knight, Death, and Devil*, too, is mentioned in the Dürer essay of 1928, where Mann not only links it to Friedrich Nietzsche and to Lutheranism, but also calls it an "essential element of the German and Dürer character-world, intimately bound up with [...] passion, odor of the tomb, sympathy with suffering, Faustian *melencolia*—and all of it composed into an idyll of peaceful domesticity."[14] Mann thus saw Dürer as the embodiment of a particularly Germanic attitude towards the world, outwardly composed and idyllic, but inwardly characterized by suffering, melancholia—even death and decay. It's not hard to see how he then transferred these attributes onto Adrian Leverkühn in *Doctor Faustus*.

The typological correspondences between Leverkühn and Dürer reach an obvious climax in the three-part chapter XXXIV, which describes the composition of Leverkühn's masterpiece *Apocalipsis cum figuris*, based on a cycle of Dürer woodcuts (figures 5–9) amidst the violence and confusion of the failed German revolution of 1918/1919. Here, the peasant revolts of the early sixteenth century (which actually took place a quarter century after the completion of the *Apocalypse* cycle) are equated with the communist uprisings that followed the First World War, while both Dürer and Leverkühn are presented to us as artists who transform social catastrophe into timeless art without, however, committing themselves to any sort of political engagement.

Martin Luther

A second historical person whose typological link to Leverkühn is related to that of Albrecht Dürer is the protestant reformer Martin Luther (1483–1546). Luther doesn't come into prominent focus in the novel until chapter XII, where Leverkühn's theology professor Ehrenfried Kumpf is clearly conceived as an overt parody of the great reformer— thrown ink well and dinner orations included. In subsequent chapters,

---

13 For a more detailed analysis of the role of this engraving, see Martin A. Ruehl, "A Master from Germany: Thomas Mann, Albrecht Dürer, and the Making of a National Icon," *Oxford German Studies* 38, no. 1 (2009): 61–106.

14 Mann, "Dürer," 151.

names and phrases from Luther's letters and writings also proliferate throughout the novel. But his presence is indirectly felt even earlier, for Leverkühn's childhood and youth is closely connected to a number of small towns in modern-day Thuringia and Saxony-Anhalt that played an important role in the protestant reformation.

As was the case with Dürer, Mann's essays provide important insight into the nature of the typological link between Luther and Leverkühn. The most important document in this regard is his 1945 Library of Congress lecture on "Germany and the Germans"—the same text in which he also justified his decision to employ the story of modern music as an allegorical device for political commentary. Martin Luther, whom Mann calls both a "gigantic incarnation of the German spirit" and "exceptionally musical" plays a major role in the lecture.[15] Mann, who was raised as a Lutheran (though some critics believe he had drifted towards Unitarianism by the time he wrote *Doctor Faustus*),[16] takes care to acknowledge his monumental achievements, conceding that he "not only reconstituted the Church; he actually saved Christianity," and also that "it was his momentous translation of the Bible that really first created the German language."[17] But he also stresses that Luther was a man who knew nothing of "political liberty, the liberty of the citizen" and argues that it was precisely the Reformer's intense focus on spiritual liberation at the expense of political emancipation that renders him a quintessential German figure.[18] Luther's myopic focus, so Mann argues throughout the essay, became characteristic of German culture as a whole during the nineteenth century, allowing a country that climbed to ever-new artistic and philosophical highs to simultaneously depart from the path of political liberalism trodden by other Western European nations. "National Socialism," Mann concludes, was the inevitable outcome of this process, for "in its exaggeration of this incongruity between the external and internal desire for liberty" it went so far "as to think of world enslavement by a people themselves enslaved."[19]

The physical and biographical parallels between Leverkühn and Luther are weaker than those between Leverkühn and Dürer. Luther was an immense man of immense appetites, known for his bawdy and choleric temper. Leverkühn, by contrast, lives an ascetic existence and he is refined and cosmopolitan in outlook. There are some connections, however, such

---

15 Mann, "Germany and the Germans," 52.
16 Heinrich Detering, *Thomas Manns amerikanische Religion: Theologie, Politik und Literatur im kalifornischen Exil* (Frankfurt am Main: S. Fischer Verlag, 2012).
17 Mann, "Germany and the Germans," 53.
18 Mann, "Germany and the Germans," 54.
19 Mann, "Germany and the Germans," 56.

as the fact that both men have an encounter with the devil during a period of self-enforced exile that will also prove formative for their intellectual output: Luther while hiding in the Wartburg in Thuringia, where he translates the Bible into German, and Leverkühn while sequestered in Palestrina, where he writes his first major work, the opera *Love's Labour's Lost*.

Symbolically and spiritually, the correspondences are much stronger. Both Luther and Leverkühn are zealous reformer figures, eager to revitalize and reconstitute what they regard as a moribund intellectual system— Christianity in Luther's case, classical music in Leverkühn's. Both achieve this task through an act of translation: Luther by transposing the Bible from Church Latin into vernacular German, Leverkühn by replacing the laws of tonality with those of dodecaphony. And both "save" what they value the most only at an immense price, namely the sacrifice of individual liberty that comes with the self-willed imprisonment in a carceral belief system that discourages any engagement with politics or with the social world more generally.

Ludwig van Beethoven

Many first-time readers will probably miss the majority of the references to Dürer and Luther that are scattered throughout the novel. The presence of Ludwig van Beethoven (1770–1827) is impossible to overlook, however, for Leverkühn's childhood mentor Wendell Kretzschmar devotes the first two of his four public lectures in chapter VIII to the great composer. Nor is it particularly hard to see that Leverkühn and Beethoven are typologically linked to one another. Zeitblom draws repeated comparisons to Beethoven's works when discussing Leverkühn's oeuvre, the total output of which can also be divided into three main periods following the schema that Kretzschmar, in large parts channeling Mann's musical advisor Theodor W. Adorno, outlines for Beethoven. There is an early period characterized by more or less faithful adherence to inherited conventions (for Leverkühn, this period encompasses his musical efforts prior to his syphilitic infection, with the 1906 symphonic fantasy *Phosphorescence of the Sea* as the most important work), a middle period characterized by ever-increasing innovation (from the syphilitic infection to the outbreak of tertiary syphilis and the composition of Leverkühn's chef-d'oeuvre, the 1919 oratorio *Apocalipsis cum figuris*), and then a complex late period characterized by a self-conscious and even parodic return to musical conventions, during which Leverkühn produces his 1924 violin concerto as well as his final work, the terrifying *Lamentation of Dr. Faustus*. The *Lamentation*, furthermore, is directly connected to the outstanding work of Beethoven's own late period, the Ninth Symphony, becoming its negative inverse when Leverkühn grimly declares his intention to Zeitblom that "I shall take it back [...] The Ninth Symphony" (501/692). The

Lamentation is also described as a "symphonic cantata," making it the formal inverse of the Ninth, which is a choral symphony.[20]

Mann also strives to make us see biographical correspondences between Beethoven and Leverkühn. Kretzschmar, in his lecture on "Beethoven and the Fugue," describes the final years of the composer in terms that recall the final days of Christ, and especially the events in the Garden of Gethsemane. Beethoven is described as isolated and irritable, followed by an entourage of disciples who dote upon him but do not really understand his predicament. Indeed Anton Schindler, Beethoven's earliest biographer whose writings Mann consulted extensively, frequently comes across as just such a disciple. Leverkühn, in the final chapters of *Doctor Faustus*, undergoes a similar Passion in the bucolic isolation of Pfeiffering, surrounded, in Chapter XLVII, by a group of uncomprehending hangers-on, of whom one, Zeitblom, even fulfills an Apostolic function. In the same lecture, meanwhile, Kretzschmar emphasizes Beethoven's late-life deafness, describing how the composer would tunelessly hiss and hum to himself in a manner that made him seem stark raving mad. Several of Beethoven's biographers, most notably Ernest Newman, whose *The Unconscious Beethoven* Mann studied carefully, attributed this deafness to syphilis. Beethoven, finally, was fifty-six years old when he died, closely approximating both Leverkühn and Dürer.

The biographical parallels also extend to the social plane. Beethoven lived during a pivotal period of Western social and political history. He was born into the Old Regime and was nineteen years old when the French people stormed the Bastille, thirty-four when Napoleon crowned himself emperor, forty-five when the Congress of Vienna brought an end to the revolutionary era with its graveyard peace. Some of the most important works of Beethoven's "middle period" (generally dated from 1802 to 1812) are marked by the revolutionary fervor of these tumultuous times.[21] There's the *Eroica* symphony of 1803–1804, for example, originally called the *Bonaparte* symphony. Or the 1805 opera *Fidelio*, which dramatizes the struggle for individual liberties and is repeatedly alluded to in *Doctor Faustus*. (Mann once remarked about *Fidelio*: "What amount of apathy was needed [by audiences] to listen to *Fidelio* in Himmler's Germany without covering their faces and rushing out of the hall!"[22]) Beethoven's later works, however, depart in a different direction. He

20 Leverkühn's oration in that chapter also contains similarities to Beethoven's so-called "Heiligenstädter Testament," an 1802 letter in which the composer bemoans his progressing deafness. See Edward Engelberg, "Thomas Mann's Faust and Beethoven," *Monatshefte* 47, no. 2 (1955): 112–16.

21 William Kinderman, *Beethoven: A Political Artist in Revolutionary Times* (Chicago: University of Chicago Press, 2024).

22 Letter to Walter von Molo, September 7, 1945. In Mann, *Letters of Thomas Mann, 1889–1955, Volume II: 1943–1955*, 482.

never wrote another opera following *Fidelio*, thereby turning his back on the musical form in which instrumental composition and human voices are most readily conjoined with dramatized political action. And while the greatest work of his final period, the choral Ninth Symphony, celebrates joy and human brotherhood, it does so in general and apolitical terms, a fact that has made it vulnerable to various reappropriations over the centuries, including by the Nazis.[23] The "Ode to Joy" that concludes the piece is an encomium to spiritual freedom rather than a call to action in the streets. In this sense Beethoven might be accused of repeating the fatal development Mann diagnosed in Martin Luther.[24]

Leverkühn lives through a similarly eventful period of European history. Like Beethoven, he is born into an "old regime" (the Wilhelmine Empire), and he witnesses the birth of a new world (the Weimar Republic, the first democracy on German soil) from the pangs of war and revolution. The ultimate outcome of these events is much more ambivalent and tragic than was the case with Beethoven, however. The French Revolution, for all the terror that it spawned, undeniably set the world on a new course, and all efforts to put the genie back into the bottle at the Congress of Vienna were doomed to failure from the start. By contrast, the abortive German revolution of 1918/1919 was a farcical affair, the only lasting effects of which were to strengthen the forces of reaction.

Leverkühn's trajectory as a composer reflects this important difference. While Beethoven, even after turning away from the direct depictions of political action, continued to seek an outlet for the spirit of his age by vastly expanding the expressive range of the symphony, giving this secular form the grandeur and urgency once only commanded by religious compositions, Leverkühn instead turns to the antiquated and constrained forms of the oratorio and the cantata. These are the genres in which he writes his masterpiece *Apocalipsis cum figuris* and his final work, *The Lamentation of Doctor Faustus*. Like the Ninth Symphony, the *Lamentation* might be called a spiritual work, though as its inverted double it turns inwards, towards self-doubt and the question of personal salvation, rather than outwards, towards the confident celebration of brotherhood and communal redemption.

---

23 Esteban Buch, *Beethoven's Ninth: A Political History*, trans. Richard Miller (Chicago: University of Chicago Press, 2004).

24 In *The Story of a Novel*, Mann confesses that he could "summon up no affection" for the "Ode to Joy," calling the piece "disjointed." Mann, *Story of a Novel*, 224.

Georg Conrad Beissel

Wendell Kretzschmar follows up on his two Beethoven lectures with one devoted to the topic of "Music and the Eye." His fourth lecture, on "The Elemental in Music," however, returns to a biographical subject, the German American religious leader Georg Conrad Beissel (1691–1768).

Unlike Dürer, Luther, and Beethoven, Beissel is a largely forgotten figure, so that Kretzschmar is forced to include the salient biographical details in his lecture. We learn that Beissel was born in the Holy Roman Empire and emigrated to North America as a young man, where he founded an anabaptist community named Ephrata in what is now Lancaster County, Pennsylvania. During his years as a leader of this community, Beissel became increasingly interested in music, eventually beginning to write hymns in a musical system of his own invention. As Kretzschmar summarizes it: "He decreed that there should be 'masters' and 'servants' in every scale. Since he had decided to treat the triad as the melodic center of every given key, he called the notes that belonged to that chord 'masters' and all other notes on the scale 'servants.' Every accented syllable in a text, then, would always have to be represented by a master and the unaccented ones by a servant" (73/100).

Thomas Mann discovered Beissel entirely by accident, through a magazine article that he stumbled upon shortly after beginning *Doctor Faustus*.[25] Unlike the other historical figures discussed in this chapter, Beissel was not originally central to the author's understanding of German history or the German national character. It's therefore perhaps not surprising that there are no overt biographical or physical links between Leverkühn and the American religious leader—no external similarities, no evidence of syphilitic infection on Beissel's part, nor even a comparable lifespan, since Beissel lived to ripe old age. There can be no question, however, that Mann recognized he was onto something significant when he first read about Beissel, and a couple of years later he showed himself deeply moved when he was given the opportunity to examine some of the preacher's manuscripts in the Library of Congress.[26]

Beissel, in fact, became a key figure for *Doctor Faustus* and a self-conscious point of identification for Leverkühn. We can already see this at the conclusion of chapter VIII, where Mann's protagonist defends the anabaptist against a skeptical Zeitblom: "At least he had a sense of order, and even foolish order is always better than none at all" (75/104), Leverkühn argues there, and "every law has a chilling effect, and music has so much warmth of its own [...] that it can use all sorts of lawful means for chilling

---

25 See Hans Theodore David, "Hymns and Music of the Pennsylvania Seventh-Day Baptists," *American-German Review* 9 (1943): 4–6, 36.
26 Mann, *The Story of a Novel*, 121.

things down" (76/104). Leverkühn's "strict" style will become just such a law, satisfying the intellect more than it does the senses and stripping music of the emotional appeal that Mann's character derides as a symptom of the homophonic age.

Beissel's significance for the novel reaches deeper than this, however. In his lecture on "Beethoven and the Fugue," Kretzschmar argues that Beethoven "had been the grand master of a profane epoch of music, in which that art had emancipated itself from the cultic to the cultural" (64/918). The Ninth Symphony, in which the concept of spiritual liberation is translated from the religious into the secular sphere, is the great example of this. Beethoven's fundamental distance from all things cultic is further indicated by the fact that according to Kretzschmar, he mastered counterpoint, the musical language of early modern religious music, in only one composition, the *Missa solemnis*. Beissel, however, created his eccentric musical system for explicitly "cultic" rather than "cultural" purposes. In this sense, he is an antipode to Beethoven, and Leverkühn, too, will pursue his "strict style" in the attempt to restore a cultic dimension to a modern life that he feels to be under the unhealthy sway of the "cultural."

Friedrich Nietzsche

The final and perhaps most obvious typological model for Adrian Leverkühn is Friedrich Nietzsche (1844–1900).[27] Subtle allusions to the philosopher are scattered throughout the early chapters of *Doctor Faustus*; both the recurring migraines of Jonathan Leverkühn (a condition from which Nietzsche also suffered) and the uncanny laughter of little Adrian (connected to many discussions of laughter in Nietzsche's works) are examples of such a connection.[28] As we have already seen, however, the correspondences emerge into full bloom with the Leipzig letter in chapter XVI, an episode that is closely patterned on a passage in Paul Deussen's *Recollections of Nietzsche*. Mann knew this work well and reread it in January of 1944, a few months before he started working on the

---

27 The secondary literature exploring Mann's fascination with Nietzsche is especially vast. A classic study, useful also for most other aspects of Mann's life and work, is T.J. Reed, *Thomas Mann: The Uses of Tradition* (Oxford: Clarendon, 1973). For a more recent introduction that focuses on *Doctor Faustus*, see Nicholas Martin, "'Ewig verbundene Geister': Thomas Mann's Reengagement with Nietzsche, 1943–1947," *Oxford German Studies* 34, no. 2 (2005): 197–203.

28 On Adrian's laughter, see Mark Roche, "Laughter and Truth in *Doctor Faustus*: Nietzschean Structures in Mann's Novel of Self-Cancellations," *Deutsche Vierteljahrsschrift für Literaturwissenschaft und Geistesgeschichte* 60, no. 2 (1986): 309–32.

chapter. More importantly, many German readers were familiar with the story too, and so the parallels between Leverkühn and Nietzsche became a focus of critical attention as soon as the novel was published. Mann did much to encourage such a focus, repeatedly referring to *Doctor Faustus* as a "Nietzsche novel" in the months after it was published.[29]

The biographical parallels between Nietzsche and Leverkühn are easy to see. Both are born in small villages in Saxony-Anhalt near the border with Thuringia (Nietzsche in Röcken, Leverkühn in the fictional Buchel), and both move to a nearby town during their school years (Nietzsche to Naumburg, Leverkühn to Kaisersaschern, which Mann modeled in part on Naumburg). Both initially study theology and join a fraternity (Nietzsche in Bonn, Leverkühn closer to home in Halle) before moving to Leipzig to pursue their true passion (classical philology for Nietzsche, musical composition for Leverkühn). After this, their life paths diverge, but both Nietzsche and Leverkühn will be irrevocably marked by the syphilitic infection that they contract during their student days in Leipzig, and to which both will succumb on the exact same day and month (August 25) at the age of fifty-five.

Much like Beethoven, Nietzsche was during the final years of his life also surrounded by admiring yet sometimes uncomprehending disciples. Early biographers like Paul Deussen or Paul Julius Möbius thus perform a very similar role to that performed by Anton Schindler for Beethoven, providing hagiographic and often gossipy descriptions of a famous figure that Mann could mine for material, but also serving as personal models for the character of Zeitblom. Women, finally, play an important role both in the life of the philosopher and in that of Mann's fictional character, though the influence of Nietzsche's sister Elizabeth Förster-Nietzsche would ultimately prove to be downright nefarious when compared to that of Else Schweigestill, Kunigunde Rosenstiel, or Meta Nackedey.

To get a grasp of the figurative significance of Friedrich Nietzsche in the novel, we need to turn no farther than to the lecture "Nietzsche's Philosophy in the Light of Contemporary Events," which Mann gave at the Library of Congress on April 29, 1947, just three months after he finished *Doctor Faustus* (and less than two years after speaking on Martin Luther and "Germany and the Germans" in the same venue). Midway through that lecture, Mann declares that, "basically remote from politics and innocently spiritual, [Nietzsche] functioned as an infinitely sensitive instrument of expression and registration; with his philosopheme of power he presaged the dawning imperialism and as a quivering floatstick indicated the fascist era of the West in which we are living and shall

---

29 For instance, in letters to Emil Preetorius on December 12, 1947, and to Kuno Fiedler on February 5, 1948, in Mann, *Selbstkommentare*, 138, 62.

continue to live for a long time to come."[30] More than being a mere "floatstick" (Mann is referring to a device for measuring fuel levels in the gas tanks of cars or airplanes), however, Nietzsche actually bore a certain responsibility for the events of the early twentieth century:

> If the words "By the fruit of their deeds ye shall know them!" are true, then Nietzsche is in a bad way. With Spengler, his clever ape, the *Übermensch* of Nietzsche's dream has become the modern "realist man of grand style," the rapacious and profit-greedy man who makes his way over dead bodies, the financial magnate, the war industrialist, the German industrial general manager financing fascism.[31]

The "Spengler" in question here is, of course, the cultural philosopher and latter-day Nietzsche disciple Oswald Spengler, whom Mann despised and who served as one of the models for the reactionaries caricatured in the Kridwiss Circle. Mann makes the connection to authoritarian politics even more explicit when he notes that the Nietzschean injunction to "live dangerously" (*lebe kühn*, from which Mann derived the name "Leverkühn") "was translated into the Italian and became a part of fascist slang."[32] The implication thus is that the protagonist of *Doctor Faustus*, like the historical Nietzsche, should be interpreted as both an early indicator and an active precursor of the coming age of fascism.

There is some amount of awkwardness involved here, for the correspondences between Leverkühn and Nietzsche are so much stronger than those between Leverkühn and other historical figures that there is simply no room left for the actual Nietzsche in the novel. Dürer, Luther, Beethoven, and Beissel are all extensively discussed in *Doctor Faustus*; Nietzsche is never mentioned. This is made even stranger by the fact that Mann documents the impact of Nietzsche's thought on the German intelligentsia of the early twentieth century in some detail in chapter XXXIV, which discusses the Kridwiss Circle. Clearly, then, Nietzsche (or somebody very much like Nietzsche) must exist as a historical figure within

---

30 Thomas Mann, "Nietzsche's Philosophy in the Light of Contemporary Events," in *Thomas Mann's Addresses Delivered at the Library of Congress, 1942–1949* (Washington, DC: Library of Congress, 1963), 94.

31 Mann, "Nietzsche's Philosophy in the Light of Contemporary Events," 94.

32 Mann, "Nietzsche's Philosophy in the Light of Contemporary Events," 94. "Live audaciously" would be a more literal translation than the one Mann uses.

the fictional world of *Doctor Faustus*, even though it never occurs to the superbly educated Zeitblom to mention him.[33]

Not all of "Nietzsche's Philosophy in the Light of Contemporary Events" focuses on the philosopher as a forerunner of fascism, however. In the lecture's opening argument, Mann refers to Nietzsche as "a personality of phenomenal cultural plenitude and complexity, summing up all that is essentially European"; a little later he also speaks of him as "a European proser and essayist of highest quality."[34] We here reencounter the duality that we already discussed in the opening chapter, where we observed that Leverkühn is on the one hand a deeply Germanic figure, but on the other hand a stand-in for the desperate condition of modern art in the early twentieth-century more generally. Indeed, Mann situates Nietzsche amidst a larger cultural progress in which "the dignified discipline and restraint of German humanistic tradition [...] slowly degenerates into an awesomely mundane and hectically humorous super-feuilletonism" and specifically points towards the philosopher's "Second Untimely Meditation: On the Uses and Disadvantages of History for Life" as his most important work, the one in which the "fundamental thought of his life [...] is pre-formed most perfectly."[35] In this text, Nietzsche proposes that an exaggerated respect for history ultimately leads to intellectual paralysis. Timothy Snyder proposes a very similar idea in his description of the "politics of inevitability," where he argues that contemporary pundits and intellectuals are frequently too caught up in their grand narratives to pay attention to the messy vicissitudes of history. Against the paralysis of modernity, Leverkühn proposes his "strict style" as a grand gesture, thereby fulfilling the prophecy of his Nietzschean name. But the strict style subordinates music (and by extension social life) to the dictatorship of an inalterable and endlessly repeated tone row. In the same way, the fascist regimes that took explicit inspiration from Nietzsche's proposals ended up enforcing a "politics of eternity" with no room left for utopian thinking.

The Meaning of Typological Allegory

Mann's use of typological allegory in *Doctor Faustus* is, as the foregoing reflections will have made clear, extremely complex and represents a significant obstacle for the first-time reader. The problem is not just that it is

---

33 The critic T.J. Reed has commented in this context that "complexity here begins to be confusion, of the kind which is born of mixing literary methods." See Reed, *Thomas Mann: The Uses of Tradition*, 370.
34 Mann, "Nietzsche's Philosophy in the Light of Contemporary Events," 69, 76.
35 Mann, "Nietzsche's Philosophy in the Light of Contemporary Events," 78, 81.

easy to miss many of the clues (such as details of physical appearance, or death at the age of fifty-five) that establish the links between Leverkühn and Dürer, Beethoven, Nietzsche, etc. The difficulty is, rather, that the manner in which these historical figures impact the text is heterogenous. Leverkühn essentially "absorbs" Nietzsche and comports himself as a kind of anti-Beethoven, but shares only surface similarities with Martin Luther. He seems inspired by Beissel but takes little notice of Dürer, whose influence is felt instead through Leverkühn's associates and through the localities through which he moves.

Mann's basic ambition is clear, however: he is trying to establish these figures as forerunners of a great intellectual crisis in the twentieth century, aspects of which they already embodied in their own lives and works. This is not to say that Mann wants us to condemn these figures; he certainly was a glowing admirer of Dürer, Luther, Beethoven, and Nietzsche, if perhaps not of Beissel. But he does want us to approach them as ambivalent figures, whose greatest accomplishments, to repeat the phrase from "Germany and the Germans," also "opened the way for devilish cunning." "There is no document of civilization," Walter Benjamin once famously said, "which is not also at the same time a document of barbarism."[36] This slogan accurately describes Thomas Mann's treatment of cultural history in *Doctor Faustus*.

The historical antecedents that I have describe in this chapter are all German, and there can be no question that Mann, when he drew up his genealogy, had his mind bent towards a particularly Germanic malaise. Like many conservative thinkers of the 1930s, Mann believed that Nazism had deep roots in its native culture, and he set out to expose these roots not only in *Doctor Faustus*, but also in his essays and lectures of the period. But had he meant for his novel to be read only as an indictment of a German "special path" towards Nazism, he would surely have drawn up a different genealogy—one that might have included intellectuals such as Paul de Lagarde, Julius Langbehn, or Ernst Bertram.[37] Mann certainly knew these figures (Bertram was a family friend) but they play only minor roles in *Doctor Faustus*. Zeitblom's final words, for example ("May God have mercy on your poor soul, my friend, my fatherland" [534/738]) are adapted from a Langbehn quote.

---

36 Walter Benjamin, "Theses on the Philosophy of History," in *Illuminations: Essays and Reflections*, trans. Harry Zohn (New York: Schocken Books, 1968), 256.

37 On the intellectual roots of Nazism in a particularly German strain of nineteenth-century culture, see Fritz Stern, *The Politics of Cultural Despair: A Study in the Rise of the Germanic Ideology* (Berkeley: University of California Press, 1961); Mosse, *The Crisis of German Ideology*; and—on Bertram—the translator's introduction to Ernst Bertram, *Nietzsche: Attempt at a Mythology*, trans. Robert E. Norton (Urbana: University of Illinois Press, 2009), xi–xxxvi.

Instead, Mann chose primarily figures of world-historical significance, and added to them a person of rather lesser importance, who was, however, active in the United States and not in Germany. Together, these choices illustrate that Mann's ultimate interest was in developments that characterized modernity proper and that (as Beissel's example shows) might even play out on the American continent. The fact that he refers to Nietzsche in his 1947 lecture not as a forerunner of Hitler, but more generally as a "quivering floatstick [for] the fascist era of the West" confirms this.

What, then, are these developments? Leverkühn's typological forerunners are important to Mann first because they are all—to once again invoke the Dürer essay—men with a tendency towards "vaulting self-dramatization" and "thrilling intellectual climax[es]." They are not just innovators, but self-conscious revolutionaries who aimed to fundamentally transform their respective disciplines. There is a dangerous loneliness that attends such grand ambition, as Mann tries to show us in the figure of Dürer's melancholic angel, his description of Beethoven's struggles with the *Missa solemnis*, and most importantly in his vivid depiction of Nietzsche's final descent into syphilitic paralysis, which Leverkühn reenacts. This loneliness, ultimately, is that of every modern artist or intellectual who strives to offer synthesizing descriptions of a world whose inherent complexity overwhelms the everyday observer.

Intellectual anomie is thus one danger of which *Doctor Faustus* warns. Its harm is so acute because it afflicts not only the modern thinker, but spreads also to society. Beethoven's Ninth Symphony is perhaps the central demonstration of this in the text. The Ninth Symphony is the consummate expression of its era, the distillation of everything that was good about the Age of Revolutions into a grand choral "Ode to Joy" and freedom. It's an undeniable masterpiece of Western civilization, but it also poses an intellectual problem, for the state of joy and harmony that it proposes as a remedy for human suffering is both unattainable and unsustainable in a world in which history does not stop. Having been written once, the Ninth Symphony cannot be composed again. It can only be performed—that is, reenacted. Every future performance of it comes with the unwritten historicist disclaimer that the joy that it celebrates is the joy of a past moment, one which we can only hope to approximate in the present. Future artists hoping to have a similar impact have to keep pushing the boundaries of their craft, creating ever more vertiginous compositions that will eventually start to alienate the very audience that they are meant to unite. As I discussed in chapter 6, "*Doctor Faustus* and Literary Modernism," Mann detected a very similar danger in the modern novel; his late masterpiece is written in the pained awareness that the very complexity of its insights will contribute to the problematic condition that it diagnoses.

Another important lesson to be drawn from the stories of Leverkühn's typological forerunners concerns the question of social engagement. The task of poets and thinkers is to offer a synthetic account of the world, a comprehensive picture that might help liberate us from the alienation and confusion that characterizes the modern world. But there are different forms that such a liberation might take. Martin Luther, a mighty thinker whose theses and sermons cut through the intellectual decay of the sixteenth-century Catholic church and offered a novel, energetic vision of what human salvation might look like, rejected the chance to give a socio-political significance to his theology during the Peasant Wars of the 1520s. In his lecture on "Germany and the Germans," Mann claims that Luther "hated the peasant revolution which, evangelically inspired as it was, if successful, would have given a happier turn to German history, a turn towards [political] liberty. Luther, however, saw in it nothing but a distortion of his work of spiritual liberation and therefore he fumed and raged against it."[38] As I have argued, we can detect in *Doctor Faustus* a similar criticism of Beethoven, whose Ninth Symphony likewise chooses spiritual liberation over the political liberty that is to be found in *Fidelio*. Mann, meanwhile, saw in Nietzsche's "self-conquest of Christian morality" a similar outgrowth of an original Lutheran error—the decision to rank spiritual truth and self-affirmation over the needs of the human community.[39]

A final lesson to be drawn from these case studies is that artists and intellectuals can sometimes be at their most dangerous when they recognize all the pitfalls that I have just described and try to free themselves from these fundamental limitations. This is the path that Leverkühn will ultimately take in the novel, and it is also the path that helps describe why Mann added the obscure Georg Conrad Beissel to his pantheon of otherwise instantly recognizable typological models. For Beissel was a historical figure whose genius lay in the unusual lengths to which he went to try and reverse the chasm that separates the intellectual and the artist from the general public under conditions of modernity. The music theory that he created self-consciously strives to rid Western music of everything "too complicated and artificial to be truly serviceable" and to create a new kind of music "more suited to the simplicity of [common people's] souls" (73/100). The technique that he comes up with is so radically simplified that it altogether erases the modern distinction between the specialized artist and the masses; at Ephrata, everybody is a composer.

Beissel's work might thus be called radically democratic, in the original Aristotelian sense of the term of a community in which power resides with all the people. But as Mann well understood (and sought to

---

38 Mann, "Germany and the Germans," 54.
39 Mann, "Germany and the Germans," 53.

communicate to American audiences in lectures such as "The Coming Victory of Democracy") a modern state that lacks representation, and in which all power is instead directly invested in the populace is not a utopia, but rather a totalitarian nightmare. The sinister division between "masters" and "servants" in Beissel's theory already hints at this. Wendell Kretzschmar's description of the Ephrata community in chapter VIII of *Doctor Faustus* is perhaps the earliest point in the novel at which we can discern a direct connection between music theory and political allegory. A long-overdue consideration of the musical elements that structure Mann's novel will help tease out this connection.

10: Music Theory and Political Allegory: Leverkühn as Fascist

No other aspect of *Doctor Faustus* is likely to vex the contemporary reader as much as Thomas Mann's decision to turn his protagonist into a composer of avant-garde music. The lengthy digressions on music history and theory that this entailed would have been taxing for most people even during Mann's lifetime, when classical music played a far more prominent role in American cultural life than it does today. For contemporary readers, who may have only the murkiest ideas about who Palestrina was, or about how a major scale relates to its relative minor, the obstacles are great indeed.

It may therefore come as a relief to know that Mann himself was not a musical expert and had to rely on outside guidance for even fairly trivial questions of music theory and history. He consulted a large number of sources for this purpose: introductory volumes by Paul Bekker and Ernest Newman as well as an instrument guide by Fritz Volbach, the *Theory of Harmony* by Arnold Schoenberg, the letters and memoirs of a number of different composers, perhaps most importantly those of Igor Stravinsky. He also conversed with friends and family. His youngest son, Michael, was a violist with the San Francisco Symphony, his brother-in-law Klaus Pringsheim conducted the Tokyo Chamber Symphony, and the world-renowned conductor Bruno Walter was his neighbor. Most importantly, he was able convince the philosopher, sociologist, and music theorist Theodor W. Adorno to serve as an informal consultant on the novel.

Even if his knowledge of musical theory was limited, however, Mann, like most educated Germans of his generation, was a great and omnivorous lover of classical music itself.[1] He also firmly believed that the musical arts were central to the intellectual life of the West.[2] *Doctor Faustus*, then, is a novel about music in roughly the same sense that *The Magic*

---

1 In October 1948, Mann submitted a list of his twelve "Favorite Recordings" to the *Saturday Review of Literature*; included were eleven musical records chronologically ranging from Mozart to Alban Berg, plus Roosevelt's "A Prayer for the Nation on D-Day." See GKFA 19.1: 407.

2 The secondary literature on Thomas Mann's lifelong obsession with classical music is vast, and includes, in German, Hans Rudolf Vaget's *Seelenzauber* and, in English, John A. Hargraves, *Music in the Works of Broch, Mann, and Kafka* (Rochester, NY: Camden House, 2002).

Mountain is a novel about tuberculosis: it focuses on this topic not as an end in itself, but rather to pose far larger questions about the modern condition, and especially about politics. As he put it in a May 1948 letter to his admirer Jonas Lesser: "No matter how much the book is also a novel about music, [music] is nevertheless only a paradigm."[3]

"Ambiguity as a System": Music as Order and Chaos

In the introductory chapter, I already drew attention to Thomas Mann's 1945 Library of Congress lecture, "Germany and the Germans," in which he called music "calculated order and chaos-breeding irrationality [...] rich in conjuring, incantatory gestures, in magic of numbers, the most unrealistic and yet the most impassioned of arts."[4] *Doctor Faustus* illustrates this definition in a number of different ways. "Incantatory gestures," for example, are to be found in several places in the novel, such as in chapter VIII, where the otherwise musically illiterate citizens of Kaisersaschern, upon leaving Wendell Kretzschmar's lecture on Op. 111, "dazedly hummed to [them]selves the evening's chief impression, the motif that constitutes the theme of the second movement" (60/86). Leverkühn's description of his "strict style" in chapter XXII illustrates the numerological character of music. And the notion that music is "calculated order" is most powerfully articulated in chapter XII, where Leverkühn's theology professor Kolonat Nonnenmacher lectures on Pythagorean music theory, including the Pythagorean notion of the cosmos as a collection of perfectly attuned "spheres sounding in a system of intervals beyond our hearing" (102/139).

Mann not only calls music "calculated order," but also "chaos-breeding irrationality," however. And indeed, *Doctor Faustus* is a novel about a devil's pact, and thus in part about the question of how chaos and evil creep into the systems dreamed up by musical theorists and utopian philosophers. Mann first hints at this in chapter VII, in which an as yet musically untutored Leverkühn discovers the importance of the perfect fifth for Western tonality, the relationship between the tonic and the dominant, and the importance of this relationship for harmonic modulation. Reflecting on his discoveries, Leverkühn calls music "ambiguity as a system" (51/74), a phrasing that neatly encapsulates the central duality that also underlies Mann's own definition of "calculated order and chaos-breeding irrationality." Leerkühn here refers to the principle of enharmonic equivalence. The pitches of a Western chromatic scale can be mathematically derived by taking a string and repeatedly shortening it

---

3   Mann, *Selbstkommentare*, 195.
4   Mann, "Germany and the Germans," 51.

by a ratio of 2:3. Doing so will create a series of rising tones that are each separated by a perfect fifth from the previous one. This process, however, will never yield at a frequency that exactly matches one that one might have created had one shortened the string by a ratio of 1:2, thus creating a series of octaves.[5] The "circle of fifths" does not naturally close, and if one stacks (for example) a series of fifths onto a starting tone of C, one will arrive, successively, at G–D–A–E–B–F♯–C♯–G♯–D♯–A♯–F, but never return to a C several octaves higher, only to a pitch fairly close to it. The gap that remains between the ideal and the actual is known as a "Pythagorean comma," and creates all kinds of problems for Western music (Fig. 10). Among other things, the asymmetry that it introduces means that if one were to perform the same operation in the other direction (lengthening strings to create a series of descending tones), one would arrive at pitches that are close to, but not entirely equal to, the ones from the original sequence. F♯, in such a system, is not the same frequency as G♭. The resulting divergence makes it extremely hard to modulate between different keys, i.e., between scales built on different base tones.

One solution to this problem is to spread out the Pythagorean comma between all twelve fifths, so that none is entirely perfect anymore. If one does this, symmetry is created, the circle of fifths is closed, and F♯ becomes the same as G♭. This is what Leverkühn calls "ambiguity as a system." Music theorists know it as "equal temperament," and it has been the basis of Western music since the time of Johann Sebastian Bach. Equal temperament is a powerful example of "calculated order" that nevertheless begets "chaos-breeding irrationality," for while it makes possible the harmonic masterpieces of the classical musical tradition, it also means that every equally tuned note is actually "irrational," in the sense that it no longer conforms to any idealized ratio between tones.[6]

It would not have been lost upon Thomas Mann that graphic representations of Pythagorean tuning and of the closed circle of fifths bear a striking resemblance to the pentagram, which was used to control dark forces in early modern magic rituals. He would have also been familiar with the passage in Goethe's *Faust I* (lines 1505–24) in which Mephistopheles, who finds himself entrapped by just such a pentagram, summons a pack of rats to gnaw through some of the lines traced out on the floor, in the process creating a figure that would have looked very

---

5   Mathematically speaking, the equation $(1/2)^m = (2/3)^n$ has no natural solution, for the denominator on the left will always be an even number, the one on the right always an odd one.

6   For a detailed (and amusingly polemical) introduction to these matters, see Ross W. Duffin, *How Equal Temperament Ruined Harmony (and Why You Should Care)* (New York: W. W. Norton, 2007).

much like a "broken" circle of fifths showing the Pythagorean comma. It's quite probable that he also knew that a perfect fifth that has been disfigured by the addition of the Pythagorean comma was known to early modern music theorists as a *Wolfsquinte*—the wolf, like the rat, being commonly associated with the devil. No wonder, then, that he was led to conclude that harmonic theory might be a perfectly fitting preoccupation for a modern-day Faustus figure.[7]

After their initial appearance in chapter VII, such considerations about intervals and the internal relationship between tones largely drop out of *Doctor Faustus*, to return only briefly in chapter XXXVIII, in the description of Leverkühn's violin concerto. There, Mann's avant-garde composer will indulge the rather simple-minded violinist Rudi Schwerdtfeger with a game of stacked fifths. Such music theoretical puzzles were ultimately not Mann's forte. He did, however, carefully study Paul Bekker's *The Story of Music*, which linked the development of equal temperament to the larger history of the West in a manner that would become hugely important for *Doctor Faustus*. Bekker argues that early modern music, precisely because it does not yet conform to equal temperament, "was based upon the original perception of tone as *sung*."[8] Even when written for musical instruments, in other words, such music is fundamentally "vocal" in nature, in the sense that it confines itself to a relatively limited range of pitches (at least in comparison to nineteenth-century symphonic music) and also that it privileges melody over harmony, horizontal development over vertical complexity. For when tones sound mostly successively, the presence of dissonances is much easier to disguise from the human ear than when they sound simultaneously.

In the eighteenth century, however, the nascent discipline of acoustics set in motion a conceptual shift by which "the resonant forms of air, too, were seen to be subject to the play of physical forces, whence sprang the conception of harmony with all its accompanying characteristics."[9] Leverkühn makes personal acquaintance with this "play of physical forces" in chapter III, where his father introduces him to the sound figures first discovered by the pioneer of acoustics, Ernst Chladni. During the time of Bach and of Händel, theorists and practitioners of music alike became interested in the complex effects that resulted from the superimposition of multiple frequencies. They also began to take a more mathematical attitude towards sound in general. The fruits of this were an expansion

---

7   In Carl Weber's Faust opera *Der Freischütz* (1821), which Mann alludes to on several occasions in *Doctor Faustus*, the Satanic figure Samiel similarly resides in a *Wolfsschlucht* (Wolf's Glen). In chapter XXV, the devil, discussing music theory with Leverkühn, identifies himself as "Samiel."
8   Bekker, *The Story of Music*, 86.
9   Bekker, *The Story of Music*, 91.

in expressive range, as well as a shift in emphasis from the horizontal (or melodic) dimensions of music to the vertical (or harmonic) ones. At around the same time, the fortepiano became a staple in every bourgeois household, a victory march only made possible by the adoption of equal temperament. As a result of all this, composers beginning with Haydn and his contemporaries "developed a preference for instrumental tone, because the composer's imagination [was inspired] by the concord of harmonically ordered tones."[10]

Within the logic of *Doctor Faustus*, then, both equal temperament and harmonically ordered tones are associated with a kind of protective magic, a way of keeping the devil at bay. The fundamentally irrational structure of the natural world, as represented by the Pythagorean comma, is kept in check by the pentagram-like power of the circle of fifths. As we have seen, however, this protective operation introduces irrationalities of its own—among them not only the aforementioned ambiguity of pitches, but also the fact that the chords of the Western harmonic system become subject to an internal hierarchy based on their relationship to the major triad.

Leverkühn's grand ambition over the course of the novel will be to replace these compromises and hierarchies of the past two hundred years of classical music with a new and mathematically more perfect system: his "strict style." Wittingly or unwittingly, however, he makes himself the servant of the devil in these attempts. For to smash the circle of fifths also means to break open the pentagram, with potentially devastating consequences.

Polyphony and Political Culture

In order to understand these consequences, and thus also the larger allegorical stakes of *Doctor Faustus*, we need to talk about the ways in which Mann connects music to politics. Chapter XXVIII, devoted to a description of the Munich salon society in which Leverkühn and Zeitblom move prior to the outbreak of the First World War, can be particularly helpful in this regard. There, the cultural philosopher Chaim Breisacher, whom we have already encountered on several previous occasions in this guide, gets into a debate about musical history with the dull-witted and easily swayed Baron von Riedesel. The larger context for this debate concerns the true nature of political conservatism. Riedesel, besides being an amateur music-lover who likes to plonk around on the piano and gaze up the skirts of ballerinas, is a royalist and classical nationalist. His basic political position, to the extent that we can discern it, is very similar to that of a member of the German National People's Party, or of one of the

10 Bekker, *The Story of Music*, 88.

other conservative parties that would dominate the political discourse in the early years of the Weimar Republic, but which then increasingly lost out to Nazism. Musically speaking, he loves everything that has been hallowed by tradition, and he hates music that he conceives as being too modern.

Breisacher, on the other hand, is a very different animal. He conceives of conservatism not as a passive resistance to all that is new, but rather as an active force with which to oppose "progress," a word that he hates more than any other. Zeitblom informs us that "he had a scathing way of saying it, and one indeed sensed that he understood the conservative scorn he devoted to progress to be [...] the badge of his presentability" (295/406). Breisacher opposes progress because he actually understands it as a form of retrogression, a process by which deeper values—specifically the ability to derive contentment and inner rest from willful ignorance—become lost. Tellingly, while Riedesel will vanish into the maelstrom of history that grabs hold of Germany following the First World War, Breisacher will reappear as a member of the proto-fascist Kridwiss Circle in chapter XXXIV.

Over the course of their conversation in chapter XXVIII, Riedesel shows himself no match for Breisacher. Instead, the philosopher ties ropes around him politically, with the help of an extended segue into the musical history of the Roman Empire. The defining musical event of late antiquity, so Breisacher claims, was the displacement of the monophonic musical textures that the Romans had inherited from the Greeks by polyphonic textures that had been pioneered by so-called "barbarians" at the fringes of the Empire, in what is now France and England. (This, too, is an idea taken straight from Bekker). The term "monophony" refers to music in which there is only a single melodic line, with neither any form of counterpoint nor a chordal accompaniment. On the other hand, "polyphony," as we already learned in earlier chapters, refers to the simultaneous layering of multiple independent melodic lines. Breisacher's purpose in turning to such a musical example is twofold. First, he wants to ridicule the notion of teleological progress, stressing instead that "so-called higher development, musical complexity, progress—sometimes those are the achievement of barbarism" (295/407). Secondly, he applies dialectical logic to argue that "polyphonic vocal music, that invention of progressive barbarism, had become the object of conservative protection as soon as the historical transition from it to the principle of harmonic chords [...] had taken place" (296/408).

Breisacher is, in other words, using a musical allegory to dismiss the efforts of conventional conservatives who oppose the modern in the name of tradition, as Riedesel does when he privileges nineteenth-century operas and ballets over the fruits of modern music. For to attack modernism as mere "barbarism," as conservatives like Riedesel are likely to do, is to ignore the fact that barbarism can be a productive cultural force in its own right. And to treat the harmonic traditions of the eighteenth and nineteenth centuries as an unalloyed good, in turn, means to already have succumbed to the progressive logic of modernity. Breisacher instead advocates for what he calls a "post- and counterrevolutionary" (294/405) cultural program, a program that would turn the clock back to a state before the victory march of the homophonic chordal logic set into motion in the eighteenth century. He calls, in other words, for a return to polyphony.

Twenty-first-century readers might be excused if they find the relevance of all this talk about ancient music elusive. For Mann's contemporaries, however, or at least for those who like him had lived through the German culture wars of the early twentieth century, the allegorical resonance would have been clear. The clue is that Breisacher repeatedly stresses the origins of polyphonic music in the "raw-throated north" (295/407). Bekker, in the corresponding section of *The Story of Music*, was actually thinking of the great monastic centers of Metz and St. Gallen, but in Breisacher's reformulation, it sounds as if the new music arose as the *vox populi* of the barbarian invaders who defeated Rome in late antiquity. For Breisacher is clearly meant to be an intellectual mouthpiece of *völkisch* nationalism, the movement that took hold of conservative German thought in the years prior to the First World War and extolled everything Germanic, declaring the "barbarism" of the Huns and the Goths to be immeasurably superior to the "decadence" of the Mediterranean world.[11]

Leverkühn, of course, is no *völkisch* nationalist. He is not motivated by adherence to any particular tribe, and as recent criticism has stressed, he is in some respects quite cosmopolitan in outlook.[12] He does, however, seem to pine for a scene of original wholeness as well. The primal moment of his musical education, we need to remember, is the barnyard scene at the end of chapter IV, during which the "floppy bosomed" (26/39) milkmaid Hanne led him in the singing of rounds, a genre of music that moves "on a comparatively high plane of musical culture, a branch of imitative polyphony" (32/49). Years later, in conversation with

11 For a still standard description of the rise of *völkisch* nationalism and of its infatuation with "Germanic barbarism," see Mosse's chapter on "Ancient Germans Rediscovered," in *The Crisis of German Ideology*, 69–88. It's probably not a coincidence that when Mann introduces Breisacher in chapter XXVIII, he describes him with the adjective *rassig* (294/405). John E. Woods correctly translates this as *thoroughbred*, but the term literally means "racially pure," the words for "race" and "breed" being the same in German. The description becomes all the more ironic, of course, by virtue of the fact that Breisacher is the quintessential literary archetype of a self-hating Jew.

12 See in this context Vaget, "Kaiseraschern als geistige Lebensform"; Goebel, *Esmeralda*; and Todd Kontje, "Saul Fitelberg's Failed Seduction: Worldliness in *Doktor Faustus*," *German Life and Letters* 75, no. 1 (2022): 78–97.

Zeitblom following Wendell Kretzschmar's lecture on the Ephrata brethren, Leverkühn will invoke the "bovine warmth" (76/105—the German original has *Stallwärme*, or "stable warmth") of vocal music, contrasting it with "inorganic instrumental sound" on one hand, and associating it with "genitalia" on the other.

What is the meaning of this strange final comparisons? And does it matter that the name of Hanne's immediate superior in the Buchel hierarchy, the dairy manager Frau Luder, translates as "Ms. Hussy"? Or that Hanne's equivalent on the farm of Pfeiffering is called "Waltpurgis," nominally linking her with the orgiastic rituals of Walpurgis Night, the witch's sabbath? Or that Leverkühn emerges from his barnyard experiences with a strange somatic response, a laugh that "did not suit his young years at all" while his eyes "registered a special look" with the "dusk of their metallic flecks" retreating "deeper into shadow" (32/49)? Does it matter that this retreat of the pupils into shadow is a symptom also of syphilis that Leverkühn himself will display during the final years of his life, starting with the disastrous performance of *The Lamentation of Doctor Faustus* in chapter XLVII?

The question of what, precisely, happened in that barnyard at Buchel is not one that can be resolved in the present context. What is clear, however, is that this early encounter with vocal polyphony deeply imprints itself upon Leverkühn, to the point that his conscious decision to contract syphilis might even be interpreted as a willful attempt to repeat this primal moment. The hours spent with Hanne in the barnyard form the state of innocence to which Mann's protagonist will long to return for the rest of his musical life, the treasure for which he is willing to overthrow centuries' worth of musical tradition. In this, they correspond to the tribal and *völkisch* ideals advocated by Breisacher, the state of barbarism for which the cultural philosopher, in turn, is willing to sacrifice the values of the Enlightenment and the achievements of political liberalism.

Leverkühn's increasingly audacious experiments with polyphonic form, along with his interest in seemingly outdated genres and instruments such as the oratorio or the *corno di bassetto*, span the entirety of what we might call his compositional "middle period," from the devil's pact to the outbreak of tertiary syphilis in 1918. The grand summation of this period is the oratorio *Apocalypsis cum figuris*, one of the defining characteristics of which is the heavy use of choral *glissandi*, or slides between pitches. Such slides, in turn, highlight the "untampered" nature of early modern music, in which pitches also needed to be constantly readjusted. Leverkühn's compositions, much like Breisacher's *völkisch* rhetoric, can therefore be read as attempts to break out of the pentagram-like regime of compromises by which Western civilization assured several centuries of musical and political harmony.

Ludwig van Beethoven and Homophony

Leverkühn's composition of the *Apocalipsis* in 1918 and 1919 coincides with a fundamental turning point not just for German history, but for modernity more generally. For Mann's protagonist, 1918 represents the halfway point of his pact with the devil, which was sealed in 1906 and which guaranteed him a productive period of twenty-four years. Fittingly, this fateful year also marks his progression from latent secondary to tertiary neurosyphilis, a transition most recognizable in the insistent migraines that afflict him during the compositional process. (I explore Leverkühn's syphilitic infection and its allegorical potential in more detail in the next chapter, "Illness and Redemption.") As we have already seen, for Germany, these same years were the time of an abortive communist revolution, which tried to overturn the social foundations of a dying imperialist state.

Zeitblom, in one of his most lucid moments in the novel, gives an even grander interpretation of these events, however. Writing at the beginning of chapter XXXIV, Mann's narrator describes his uneasy feeling that:

> an epoch was coming to an end, an epoch that embraced not just the nineteenth century, but also reached back to the end of the Middle Ages, to the shattering of scholastic ties, to the emancipation of the individual and the birth of freedom, an epoch that I quite rightly had to view as that of my extended intellectual home, in short, the epoch of bourgeois humanism—the feeling, I saw, that its last hour had come, that a mutation of life was about to happen, that the world was trying to enter into a new, still unnamed sign of the zodiac—this feeling, then, which demanded one pay it closest heed, had first arisen not with the end of the war, but with its outbreak, fourteen years after the turn of the century and had formed the basis of the shock, the sense of being seized by destiny, that people like myself felt at the time. No wonder, then, that the disintegration that came with defeat brought this feeling to its peak, and no wonder, either, that in an overthrown nation like Germany it occupied people's minds more than it did those of the victors, whose average emotional state was, as the result of victory, far more conservative. (372/512–13)

Zeitblom's feeling reiterates one of the main points that I have been trying to make throughout this introductory guide, namely that the novel should be read as the diagnosis of a general change in the modern condition ("the world was trying to enter into a new, still unnamed sign of the zodiac"), which was nevertheless felt most clearly in postwar Germany, the nation where "the disintegration that came with defeat" heightened the historical senses.

In the chapter called "Five Masters from Germany," I already pointed out how *Doctor Faustus* is structured as an extended typological allegory in which Adrian Leverkühn takes on aspects of earlier figures from German history. In the present context, the most important such figure is Ludwig van Beethoven, not only because his life overlapped with the beginning of an important new phase in the history of "bourgeois humanism" (the French Revolution and its aftermath) but also because his compositions represent everything that Leverkühn will ultimately rebel against in his own musical struggles. Mann once again took a great deal of what he has to say about Beethoven from Paul Bekker, but an even more important influence on his thinking about the great composer was his musical advisor Theodor W. Adorno.[13] We first detect this influence in Wendell Kretzschmar's two Beethoven lectures in chapter VIII.

Leverkühn's future music teacher devotes his opening lecture to the question "Why didn't Beethoven write a third movement for his last piano sonata Opus 111?" (55/78) The answer to this turns out to be deceptively simple. Kretzschmar essentially affirms that Beethoven was too great an artist to be bound by traditional strictures on the sonata form, which would have required him to compose a third movement. This thought is already present in Bekker, who declared Beethoven's essential novelty to lie in the fact that "dependent upon himself alone, growing only from within, he interprets life through his own vision and his own feeling."[14] But Mann takes the matter considerably further, in sentences that are greatly influenced by Adorno's 1937 essay "Late Style in Beethoven."[15] There, Adorno gives a dialectical interpretation to Beethoven's musical development. Instead of merely viewing him as

---

13 Adorno's relationship with Mann has always been a topic of keen interest for literary scholarship, especially in America, where the Frankfurt School cast an outsized shadow on the development of German Studies. Important publications in English include Evelyn Cobley, "Avant-Garde Aesthetics and Fascist Politics: Thomas Mann's *Doctor Faustus* and Theodor Adorno's *Philosophy of New Music*," *New German Critique* 86 (2002): 43–70; Eberhard Bahr, *Weimar on the Pacific: Exile Culture in Los Angeles and the Crisis of Modernism* (Berkeley: University of California Press, 2008), 242–64; Justice Kraus, "Expression and Adorno's Avant-Garde: The Composer in *Doktor Faustus*," *The German Quarterly* 81, no. 2 (2008): 170–84.

14 Bekker, *The Story of Music*, 183–84.

15 It's not known whether Mann ever discussed Bekker with Adorno. If he did, Adorno's reaction would almost certainly have been less than charitable, for he was fairly skeptical about Bekkers socio-historical approach. For an examination of the relationship between the two music theorists, see Nanette Nielsen, *Paul Bekker's Musical Ethics* (London: Routledge, 2018), 63–67.

a Romantic genius who "interprets life through his own vision," Adorno identifies three distinctive periods in the composer's musical development. He further links these to a corresponding argument about cultural advance more generally, thus turning Beethoven into a cipher for the modern condition. In the first period, Beethoven's compositions more or less accord with established formal patterns. Kretzschmar, summarizing Adorno, talks about "snug regions of tradition" (56/81). In the middle period, which more than any other is responsible for shaping the image of Beethoven that most of us have today and which produced works such as the *Eroica* and the Fifth Symphony, individual genius liberates itself from social convention. "Beethoven's own artistry," so Kretzschmar claims, "had outgrown itself [...] and, as humanity gazed on in horror, climbed to spheres of the totally personal, the exclusively personal (56–57/80–81). Adorno similarly talks about the middle-period Beethoven as the "purported representative of a radically personal stance" who "transformed [musical conventions] through his intentions."[16]

Adorno's radical innovation comes with his description of Beethoven's late period, however. In these works, so he argues, "even where [they] avail themselves of such a singular syntax as in the last five piano sonatas, one finds formulas and phrases of convention scattered about [...]. Often convention appears in a form that is bald, undisguised, untransformed."[17] Mann quotes these lines almost verbatim: "Beethoven's late work—the five last piano sonatas for instance—had a quite different, much more forgiving and amenable relation to convention. Untouched, untransformed by the subjective, the conventional often emerged in the late works with a baldness [...] that, in turn, had an effect more terrifyingly majestic than any personal indiscretion" (57/81–82).

Mann's use of the word "subjective" (rather than simply "personal"), which he also takes from Adorno, points us to what is ultimately at stake in this analysis. For Adorno, Beethoven's various stylistic periods illustrate not only a biographical narrative but rather the larger shape of historical development in the West. A pre-modern "objective" stage, in which individual lives are largely subordinated to, and in harmony with, social circumstances is followed by a modern "subjective" stage in which individual freedom is prized above all else. The fruits of this subjective stage are humanist education, political liberalism, and bourgeois self-development. Where other music historians see Beethoven simply as the Romantic apotheosis of this subjective tendency, however, Adorno instead detects in his late work a dialectic synthesis, a return of conventions. And

---

16 Theodor W. Adorno, "Late Style in Beethoven," in *Essays on Music*, ed. Richard Leppert, trans. Susan H. Gillespie (Berkeley: University of California Press, 2002), 565.

17 Adorno, "Late Style in Beethoven," 565.

his assessment of what this portends is less than rosy: Adorno speaks of a tendency towards the "primitive" in the late sonatas, declares that the "formal law" of the late works "is revealed precisely in the thought of death," and finishes his essays with the magisterial (if slightly mysterious) pronouncement, "in the history of art late works are the catastrophes."[18]

When Mann read Adorno's essay, he was undoubtedly struck by the fact that the philosopher's description of this dialectic employed some of the same terms and concepts with which he was already familiar from Bekker, but put them to unorthodox ends. Although Beethoven's late sonatas are unquestionably homophonic in texture, Adorno speaks of them as a field of battle between a "polyphonically objective construction" and the "monophony" of a "subjectivity that [...] fills the dense polyphony with its tensions."[19] What he means by this is never made entirely clear in the essay, though, as we will see shortly, Adorno provided a more satisfactory account in his later *Philosophy of New Music*. What is undeniable, however, is that Adorno reinterprets the terms "monophony," "polyphony," and "homophony," which Bekker treated simply as the characteristic musical textures of successive periods in Western musical history, dialectically. He approaches them as expressive tendencies that never entirely vanish but recur in sublated form.

For Mann, the encounter with Adorno provided an opportunity for a far deeper engagement with modern music than would ever have been possible through Bekker alone. It also shaped his depiction of Leverkühn's career, which, like Beethoven's, can be divided into three main stages. The first, which encompasses the years prior to the devil's pact and culminates with the symphonic fantasy *Phosphorescence of the Sea*, is, much like Beethoven's early period, characterized by an adherence to "objective" conventions, which in Leverkühn's case means to the chromaticism of the 1890s. Following the devil's pact, Leverkühn during his middle period embarks upon an intensely personal quest for a repeat of his primal scene, the barnyard lessons with Hanne. The ultimate product of this "subjective" phase, the *Apocalipsis cum figuris*, is unquestionably his most daring work to date, but it is also his most eccentric. Zeitblom, in his extended description of the *Apocalipsis* in chapter XXXIV mentions "choruses [...] that move through all the shades of graduated whispering, antiphonal speech, and quasi-chant on up to the most polyphonic song" (393/543) along with "loudspeakers [...] whose use the composer specified at various points to produce directional and acoustic gradations that had never been achieved before" (396/547) and with "jazz sounds for purely infernal purposes" (296/547). It is almost as though the *Apoalipsis* combines musical advances that in real life were carried out by composers as diverse

---

18 Adorno, "Late Style in Beethoven," 565, 566, 567.
19 Adorno, "Late Style in Beethoven," 566–67.

as Igor Stravinsky, Paul Hindemith, and Darius Milhaud. Perhaps it is no wonder, then, that the oratorio fails to win over a devoted audience when it premieres under the baton of Otto Klemperer. Tellingly, even Zeitblom accuses his friend of succumbing to "aestheticism," that is, to an exaggeratedly subjective stance (392/541).

After the Apocalypse: Strict Style

A way out of this subjectivist dead end is provided in chapter XXV of *Doctor Faustus*, in which the devil appears to Adrian Leverkühn in the guise of Theodor W. Adorno.[20] The devil begins his disquisition about musical matters by sketching out why exactly the subjective phase in cultural history must lead to an impasse. Music, we learn, like all other art ultimately depends for its commercial and public success on a certain proximity to convention, to the "objective" relations in society. Absent such a proximity, it labors under the "threat that production will cease" and risks a "lack of demand—so that, as in the preliberal era, the possibility of production greatly depends on the accident of a patron's favor" (254/349). Subjective innovation, however, is defined precisely by the departure from convention, and by its own internal nature is forced to become ever more extreme. "The diminished seventh [chord] is right and eloquent at the opening of Opus 111," the devil argues, thereby drawing a connection with the Kretzschmar lectures back in chapter VIII. But once it has been used, it loses this eloquence and becomes "defunct" through a "historical process no one can reverse" (255/349). In other words, it becomes a cliché. The only possible solution for the subjective composer is to continually push the boundaries of what is permissible in harmonic theory, adding dissonance, chromaticism, and ever more complex exceptions to the established rules of voice leading. The result are compositions that only experts can comprehend and that no longer present themselves as self-evident masterworks to the ordinary listener. "I am against works on the whole," declares the devil rather cynically, and: "the prohibitive difficulties of the work lie deep within the [modern] work itself" (256/351).

These lines recall Mann's lamentations about Joyce in *The Story of a Novel*. There, Mann argues that "neither *A Portrait of the Artist* nor

---

20 Somewhat amusingly, Adorno didn't recognize himself in Mann's description of a "gentleman" with "white collar and a bow-tie, spectacles rimmed in horn atop his hooked nose, behind which somewhat reddened eyes shine moist and dark; the face a mingling of sharpness and softness; the nose sharp, the lips sharp, but the chin soft, with a dimple in it, and yet another dimple in the cheek above; pale and vaulted the brow, from which the hair indeed retreats upwards, whereas that to the sides stands thick, black, and woolly" (253/347).

Finnegans Wake is a novel, strictly speaking, and *Ulysses* is a novel to end all novels." He also suggests that *Ulysses* should be considered an epic, rather than a novel, and thus a return to premodern forms just like the fictional *Apocalipsis cum figuris*.[21] Far from merely making an argument about music history, the devil in *Doctor Faustus* should therefore be understood as formulating a critique of modern art, and indeed modern intellectual labor more generally. As modernity advances, innovative art and thought by necessity become increasingly specialized, subject to their own jargon, disciplinary conventions, and historical references. This, in turn, estranges avant-garde intellectuals from the general population. "The claim to presume the general as harmonically contained within the particular is a self-contradiction [in modern art]," says the devil. "It is all up with conventions once considered prerequisite and compulsory, the guarantors of the game's freedom" (257/352–53).

In chapter XXV, Leverkühn and the devil discuss two possible ways out of this social dilemma, both of which Mann's protagonist will pursue during his musical compositions of the 1920s. The first is parody, that is, an art or thought that embraces cliché but does so knowingly, with a wink and a certain self-conscious cleverness. This would allow the intellectual to win the affection of the masses while simultaneously remaining on good terms with other initiates of his craft, who alone would recognize all the parodic elements. Leverkühn proposes such an approach: "One could raise the game to a yet higher power by playing with forms from which, as one knows, life has vanished" (257/353). His first truly major composition following the *Apocalipsis*, the violin concerto that he writes for Rudi Schwerdtfeger, represents an attempt to put this ambition into practice. Its most obvious purpose is to appease Schwerdtfeger, the innocent and somewhat simpleminded violinist who despite his talents is never quite capable of keeping pace with Leverkühn intellectually. But as we learn in the discussions surrounding the concerto that Zeitblom relates in chapter XXXVIII, Leverkühn is actually secretly contemptuous of all the musical platitudes that he has woven into it. Unsurprisingly, his relationship with Schwerdtfeger will take a dark turn soon after as well.

Mann, too, at various points of his life expressed the conviction that parody was the only remaining recourse for the modern artist. In *Doctor Faustus*, however, he takes a more expansive vision. The devil already reacts dismissively to Leverkühn's thought experiment: "I know, I know. Parody. It might be merry if in its aristocratic nihilism it were not so very woebegone" (257/353). Instead, he promises a very different kind of intellectual achievement to Leverkühn, one that will allow him to "break through the laming difficulties of the age" (259/355). In chapter XXV, the devil does not further expound what this new kind of intellectual

---

21 Mann, *The Story of a Novel*, 91.

achievement might look like but attentive readers have already encountered a basic description of it in chapter XXII, where Leverkühn, four years into his pact with the devil, first explains his idea for a "strict style" to Zeitblom.[22] It is this "strict style" that two decades later will become the basis for his final and most advanced composition, the symphonic cantata *The Lamentation of Doctor Faustus*.

Leverkühn's definition of the strict style is worth quoting at length:

> "Just once, in the Brentano cycle," he said, "in the song 'Oh sweet maiden' [did I achieve my vision of a strict style]. It all comes from one basic figure, from a row of intervals capable of multiple variation, taken from the five notes B–E–A–E–E-flat, both the horizontal and vertical lines are determined and governed by it, to the extent that is possible in a basic motif with such a limited number of notes. It is like a word, a key word that leaves its signature everywhere in the song and would like to determine it entirely. It is, however, too short a word, with too little flexibility. The tonal space it provides is too limited. One would have to proceed from here and build longer words from the twelve steps of the tempered semitone alphabet, words of twelve letters, specific combinations and interrelations of the twelve semitones, rows of notes—from which, then, the piece, a given movement, or a whole work of several movements would be strictly derived. Each tone in the entire composition, melodic and harmonic, would have to demonstrate its relation to this predetermined basic row. None would dare recur until all have first occurred. No note would dare appear that did not fulfill its motif function within the structure as a whole. Free notes would no longer exist. That is what I would call a strict style." (205/279–80)

As readers of *Doctor Faustus* recognized even before the novel was actually published, the system of composition described in the second part of this paragraph—in which the twelve notes of "tempered semitone alphabet" are no longer arranged in scales but rather in "tone rows" or "words of twelve letters"—was actually pioneered by Arnold Schoenberg and is generally known not as "strict style" but as "twelve-tone" or "dodecaphonic" music. This particularly egregious act of montage led to a quarrel between the two émigrés and ultimately resulted in the "Author's Note" printed at the end of all subsequent editions of the novel.

In truth, however, Mann took most of what he had to say about dodecaphonic music not from Schoenberg directly, but from Theodor W. Adorno. In his *Philosophy of New Music* Adorno returns to the problems

---

22 In music history, the term "strict style" refers to a particular form of polyphonic composition that was practiced in the early eighteenth century. The name is thus another indicator of Leverkühn's affinity for pre-homophonic forms.

of subjectivism he had already raised in his writings on Beethoven. There, he claims that, "subjective disposition over the material compels conventional language to speak anew."[23] This return of the conventional, so Adorno explains, can already be seen in Wagner's deployment of leitmotifs, which reinsert the eighteenth century's affinity for musical motifs into a fundamentally Romantic and thus "subjective" musical texture. But it was Schoenberg who "was the first to detect the principles of universal unity and economy in the new, subjective, emancipated Wagnerian material."[24] It was Schoenberg, in other words, who through the invention of twelve-tone music brought music history into the "late phase" that Adorno had already described in the Beethoven essay, a late phase in which the "objective" returns in sublated form amidst the "subjective." And as in the Beethoven essay, Adorno once again describes this as an eruption of a polyphonic disposition amidst a fundamentally homophonic texture, claiming that "polyphony is the appropriate means for the organization of emancipated music [...]. Schoenberg [...] asserted the principle of polyphony as no longer heteronomous to an emancipated harmony but as, instead, a principle at every point awaiting reconciliation with it. He revealed polyphony as the essence of harmony."[25]

Leverkühn's turn towards the "strict style" in his own personal "late period" must similarly be seen as a new approach to polyphony, an approach that would treat its usage in twentieth-century music no longer as a mere subjective fancy, but rather as something grounded in historical development, something more "objective." Adorno, lecturing on dodecaphonic music, offers the following explanation for this: "[In twelve-tone music] the individual chord, which in the classical-romantic tradition—as a bearer of subjective expression—represents the antipode to polyphonic objectivity, is understood in its own polyphony. The means for this is none other than the extreme of romantic subjectivization: dissonance. The more a chord is dissonant [...] the more it is polyphonic."[26] In twelve-tone music, we need to remember, chords are liberated from the internal hierarchies imposed by the harmonic system that governed earlier classical music. Tonic and dominant are no longer tonal centers, and the other scale degrees are freed from their gravitational pull. Instead, each tone in a dodecaphonic chord is of equal value to all the others.

Unlike Leverkühn's prior experimentation with polyphonic techniques in pieces such as the *Apocalypsis*, this emergence of polyphony in the midst of the strict style does not represent a mere subjective

---

23 Theodor W. Adorno, *Philosophy of New Music*, trans. Robert Hullot-Kentor (Minneapolis: University of Minnesota Press, 2006), 48.
24 Adorno, *Philosophy of New Music*, 48.
25 Adorno, *Philosophy of New Music*, 48.
26 Adorno, *Philosophy of New Music*, 48–49.

affectation, a return to antiquated forms out of disgust with modernity. It is, rather, the logical fulfillment of modernity itself, the "revelation of the essence of harmony," as Adorno puts it, and thus also of homophony. For the subjective tendency in homophonic music expressed itself in the erosion of traditional tonality, and thus in an ever-greater move towards dissonance. Composers, seeking to avoid the kinds of clichés that Adorno castigates in his analysis of the diminished seventh chord in Beethoven, throughout the nineteenth century experimented with ever more daring exceptions and additions to the established rules of harmony, introducing chords that would have seemed unnecessary or impermissible to earlier generations into their tonal vocabulary. Schoenberg radicalizes this tendency, abandoning tonality categorically rather than incrementally, and thereby also preparing the way for the return of polyphony from within the midst of a homophonic era.

Adorno refers to the music created by Schoenberg as "emancipated." By this he means the emancipation of music from the subjective stage of its development, but also its liberation from the fetters of harmony altogether. Because it is atonal, twelve-tone music no longer needs to care about Pythagorean commas or about the major thirds and perfect fifths of traditional harmony. It is mathematically perfect in a way that harmonic music never was. Mann seems to have also believed that dodecaphony introduced simplicity to a period of music history that sorely needed it.[27] The rules of the strict style as Leverkühn describes it are indeed quite simple: the nascent composer is instructed take the twelve notes of the chromatic scale and arrange them in any order, thereby forming what Leverkühn calls a "key word." These twelve notes may now be sounded successively (thus forming a melody) or simultaneously (thus forming dodecaphonic chords). To increase complexity, key words may also be read upside down (as an "inversion") front-to-back (as a "retrograde") or as a combination of both ("retrograde-inversion"). The only rule is that a note may not be repeated until the entire tone row has been used up.

This combination of mathematical perfection and radical simplicity fulfills Leverkühn's resolution, in chapter VIII, to submit the laws of music to a "chilling effect" (76/104) brought about by a compositional system based not on emotions but on intellectual "interest," or "a love that has been deprived of its animal warmth" (77/106). It also moves his music into the vicinity of that of Georg Conrad Beissel, whose Ephrata compositions are discussed in Kretzschmar's final lecture in chapter VIII.

When Zeitblom attacks Beissel's works as "absurdly decreed order, a piece of childish rationalism," Leverkühn is dismissive, responding that

---

27 This is marked misunderstanding of Adorno, who in *Philosophy of New Music* explicitly states that "Schoenberg's procedure has indeed made composition more difficult, not easier" (50).

"even foolish order is always better than none at all" (75/105). The devil, in chapter XXV, is somewhat more direct when he explains to Leverkühn the ultimate outcome of an eventual turn towards dodecaphonic composition: "You will lead, you will set the march for the future, lads will swear by your name, who thanks to your madness will no longer need to be mad" (258/355). The German original of the first phrase, *du wirst führen*, makes even clearer that Mann was drawing a not-so-subtle analogy between his syphilitic composer and the supreme leader of the German people, between Leverkühn and Hitler.

This is not to imply, of course, as Schoenberg falsely surmised in the 1940s, that Mann wants us to see an equivalence between the two. Leverkühn is not Hitler, and dodecaphony, which always remained a part of elite culture and never won any mass appeal, bears no self-evident relationship to the history of the Nazi movement. Mann's reflections on the history of twentieth-century music, however, allowed him to develop a sophisticated commentary on problems that also afflict modern politics. Adorno's notion of "romantic subjectivization," so crucial to Mann's narrative, refers not only to music but rather to any intellectual formation that is in the grip of overspecialization and that worships "progress" without any thought about those whom it leaves behind. The result of this tendency is the violent return of what Adorno calls "objectivity" and what Snyder would call the "politics of eternity." Twelve-tone music as Leverkühn describes it is characterized by predetermination (the key word is chosen before the actual act of composition begins, and may not be altered) and endless recurrence (it starts anew every twelve notes). Contemporary authoritarian politics are similarly characterized by the appeal to seemingly eternal categories (ethnic identity, patriarchal gender norms, the precedence of biological sex over socially constructed gender, to name just a few) and by the repetition of ever-identical outrage cycles to keep the populace distracted. When Leverkühn, upon the completion of the *Lamentation of Doctor Faustus*, describes his aim to take back the Ninth Symphony, he is therefore describing not only an artistic ambition to undo homophony, but also a spiritual and political program to reverse the progressive and universalist aspirations that Beethoven's choral symphony expresses. Leverkühn's ambition is esoteric indeed, but our contemporary tragedy is that it manifests itself in tangible forms the world over.

11: Illness and Redemption: Leverkühn as Christ

IN HER 1977 study "Illness as Metaphor," Susan Sontag famously argued that "the most truthful way of regarding illness—and the healthiest way of being ill—is the one most purified of, most resistant to, metaphoric thinking."[1] As Sontag was well aware, Thomas Mann would not have agreed with this statement.[2] Mann was the twentieth-century's great poet of illness: typhoid fever in *Buddenbrooks*, cholera in *Death in Venice*, tuberculosis in *The Magic Mountain*, syphilis and meningitis in *Doctor Faustus*, uterine cancer in the late story "The Black Swan." In most of these works, disease serves a metaphorical function and is usually used to indicate a fundamental inner unsoundness of the characters whom it afflicts.

The syphilitic infection at the heart of *Doctor Faustus* is slightly different in this regard. "The syphilitic personality type [is] someone who ha[s] the disease," Sontag wrote, "not someone who [is] likely to get it. In its role as scourge, syphilis implie[s] a moral judgment (about off-limits sex, about prostitution) but not a psychological one."[3] This insight is central to the novel. Leverkühn is not predisposed towards syphilis but *chooses* to contract it. The moral indictment that this choice precipitates is triggered not by the literal action of having had sex with a prostitute, however, but rather by the allegorical significance of this act. And allegory in *Doctor Faustus* is, as we have already seen, always a highly complicated matter. In chapter 9, "Five Masters from Germany," I introduced the four-fold allegorical schema pioneered by early Christian thinkers as a framework through which to interpret *Doctor Faustus*. I also offered a "typological"

---

1 Susan Sontag, "Illness as Metaphor," in *Illness as Metaphor and AIDS and Its Metaphors* (New York: Anchor Books, 1990), 3.

2 Sontag was a big Thomas Mann fan and refers to his works throughout "Illness as a Metaphor." She also chronicled her youthful infatuation with the writer, which led her to pay a visit to his house in Pacific Palisades shortly after *Doctor Faustus* was finished, in her essay "Pilgrimage," *The New Yorker*, December 14, 1987, https://www.newyorker.com/magazine/1987/12/21/pilgrimage-susan-sontag. The relationship between the two figures is plotted in Kai Sina, *Susan Sontag und Thomas Mann* (Göttingen: Wallstein Verlag, 2017).

3 Sontag, "Illness as Metaphor," 39. The proximity of Mann's thought on this matter to Sontag's is demonstrated by the fact that he, too, makes a great deal of syphilis's historical reputation as a punishment or "scourge" (247/338).

reading of the novel that stressed the similarities between Leverkühn and a number of prior figures from German intellectual life. In chapter 10, "Music Theory and Political Allegory," I added to this a "moral" layer, according to which Leverkühn's musical project allegorizes the slide into unreason and anti-democratic reaction that took place in the early twentieth century. In a final layer of allegory, one which early Christian theorists would have called "anagogical," Leverkühn's life can also be read theologically, as a commentary on the ultimate outcome of the struggle between good and evil in modern times.

Syphilis and the Devils' Pact

To get at better grip on Mann's metaphorical use of illness, it is helpful to first know a little bit more about syphilis.[4] Syphilis is a sexually transmitted disease caused by the bacterium *treponema pallidum* (in Mann's day known as *spirochaete pallida*). As we already saw in chapter 9, it arrived in Europe in the late fifteenth century, during the time of Albrecht Dürer, who produced the first known pictorial representation of the disease in the West, and who may have himself contracted it. Syphilis progresses in three distinct stages: primary, secondary, and tertiary. While primary and secondary stages occur in quick succession, years can pass between the remission of the secondary stage and the outbreak of the tertiary, during which time the disease remains latent in the body.

Leverkühn contracts syphilis in May 1906 during a visit to the town of Pressburg in the Kingdom of Hungary (now Bratislava in Slovakia), where he reunites with the prostitute Esmeralda, whom he first met during his Leipzig student days. As Zeitblom tells us in chapter XIX, five weeks later he decides "to seek medical treatment for a localized infection" (166/228). This localized infection would almost certainly have been a chancre, a skin ulceration that is the most distinctive symptom of primary syphilis. Leverkühn consults with two different dermatologists to determine a plan of treatment, but the former meets an untimely end and the latter is arrested during a follow-up visit. At this point, Leverkühn "let the matter rest." However, Zeitblom also tells us, "the localized infection healed quickly" and "no secondary symptoms whatever were manifest" (168/231).

Secondary syphilis, the onset of which usually coincides with the healing of the initial chancre, can indeed occur without any specific symptoms, in which case the disease enters straight into its latent phase. Zeitblom may, however, simply be underestimating Leverkühn's condition, for he repeatedly tells us about the migraine headaches that afflict his friend and

---

4   The following description is largely guided by Hemil Gonzalez, Igor J. Koralnik, and Christina M. Marra, "Neurosyphilis," in *Seminars in Neurology* 39, no. 4 (2019): 448–55.

also mentions a fever that he contracts while in Palestrina. While it is true that Leverkühn had been struggling with migraines ever since he was a child, these are common symptoms of secondary syphilis as well.

A little more than twelve years after the initial infection, during the fall of 1918, Leverkühn develops the first symptoms of tertiary neurosyphilis, probably of the meningovascular kind. Neurosyphilis frequently manifests as paresis, also known as "general paralysis of the insane" (GPI). GPI affects the frontal and temporal lobes of the patient's brain; its early symptoms are once again debilitating headaches, like the ones that Zeitblom suffers from in 1918. As the illness develops further, it leads to degenerative changes, to hallucinations, suicidal ideation, and to the eventual collapse of all mental faculties. In its meningovascular manifestations, the disease also spreads to the arterial system, in some cases triggering a stroke. Leverkühn seems to succumb to all of these factors simultaneously when he collapses in spectacular fashion during his demonstration of excerpts from *The Lamentation of Doctor Faustus* in chapter XLVII.

So far, I have provided a depiction of syphilis as it is to be found in the modern medical literature. *Doctor Faustus* contains its own description of the disease, of course, in the first third of chapter XXV, where the devil provides it when he appears to Leverkühn in the guise of the redheaded porter who introduced him to the prostitute Esmeralda. Mann based this passage on medical reference works as well as on a descriptive letter sent to him by a doctor friend, Martin Gumpert. Nevertheless, metaphorical elements predominate in it, such as when the devil compares the "flagellates" that cause the disease to medieval penitents known as "flagellants" (247/338) or when he invokes the Latin names of the membranes that surround the brain, *dura mater* and *pia mater* (249/340), with clear knowledge of the religious tinge of these terms. The overall thrust of the metaphors is clear: the devil stresses the early modern origins of the disease, aligns it with cultic excess through the comparison with the flagellants, and uses the ability of the syphilis bacteria to penetrate the blood-brain barrier as a figurative equivalent to the process of artistic inspiration.

The larger significance of this has already become clear a few pages earlier, when the devil announces to Leverkühn that he would like to "come to an understanding with you" about the fact that "the hour-glass has been turned, [...] the sand has begun to run" (243/332). For in *Doctor Faustus*, syphilis ultimately serves as a physiological correlative to the written devil's pact of pre-modern legends. By deliberately contracting the disease, Leverkühn has given the devil permission to alter his neurological state, providing musical inspiration as the side result of a pathological trajectory that will ultimately also claim Leverkühn's soul. The total length of the process is to be twenty-four years, the same time span also found in the Chapbook and in other sources. As the devil makes clear, there is one other price to which Leverkühn must submit in addition to the painful symptoms of his disease: he may not love, in either the sexual or the Platonic sense. This is another update to the early modern sources, in which Faustus was prohibited from Christian marriage.

Whether the devil actually exists or not is an open question, of course. Zeitblom is conflicted about the matter, and in the opening paragraphs of chapter XXV does his best to convince himself that Leverkühn's interlocutor might just have been the product of a fever dream. Indeed, hallucinations and delusions of grandeur are classical manifestations of syphilis, though rarely encountered a mere six years into the progression of the disease. The question of whether the devil is real or not has a crucial bearing on the political dimensions of the novel. Are Adrian Leverkühn's musical ideas truly his own, or are they rather the result of a demonic influence? And by extension, should the course towards fascism that they figuratively chart be seen as the inherent fault of the German people, or do structural factors and outside agents bear at least part of the blame? In Thomas Mann's day, these were hotly contested questions, and as scholarly debates such as the so-called "Goldhagen Controversy" of the 1990s show, they have not been fully settled even today.[5] As historians gain greater distance to the tragedies of the early twenty-first century, similar questions about collective culpability will undoubtedly be raised regarding our present moment.

Leverkühn as Christ Figure

Political readings of the devil's pact thus provide one answer to the question of how Mann employs illness as a metaphor in his novel. Syphilis, in such a reading, is the metaphorical expression of the German "devil's pact" that led to Nazism and to total annihilation in the Second World War. An even wider-ranging interpretation is possible, however. In the epilogue to the novel, Serenus Zeitblom describes Leverkühn, who at this stage of his life has succumbed completely to GPI and seems incapable of formulating any rational thought, as possessing a "hunched posture" and "a shrunken face, an *Ecce homo* countenance, that despite a healthy country tan revealed a mouth opened in pain and unseeing eyes" (533/736–37). The reference here, of course, is not only to Nietzsche (who wrote a book called *Ecce Homo*) but also to Jesus Christ, to whom the words *ecce homo* ("behold the man," see John 19:5) originally referred. Indeed, comparisons between Adrian Leverkühn and Christ are hidden all over

---

5   Daniel Goldhagen, *Hitler's Willing Executioners* (New York: Alfred A. Knopf, 1996). For an introduction to the Goldhagen Controversy, see the chapter "The Past Distorted: The Goldhagen Controversy," in Fritz Stern, *Einstein's German World* (Princeton, NJ: Princeton University Press, 2016), 272–88.

the novel, as are many Biblical quotations. Already in chapter, XV, for example, Zeitblom describes a tableau he observed at Buchel that clearly alludes to early modern depictions of the pietà: "[Leverkühn's mother] looped her arm around him, so to speak, not around his shoulders, but around his head, her hand resting on his brow, and then with her black eyes directed at Kretzschmar and still speaking to him in her sweet, resonant voice, she rested Adrian's head on her breast" (137/188). These allusions multiply as the story nears its conclusion. In chapter XLVI, for example, Zeitblom points out that Leverkühn's newly grown beard "lent his countenance a kind of spiritualized suffering, indeed, something Christlike" (507/699–700), while the opening line of chapter XLVII, spoken by Leverkühn himself, is "Watch with me!"—Jesus's words in the Garden of Gethsemane, as reported in Matthew 26:40.

Needless to say, this comparison of a Faustus figure to Christ is more than a little unusual within literary history. Ever since the time of Johannes Manlius in the 1560s, Faustus has been linked to themes of apostasy. He sells his soul to the devil, after all. And indeed, there are passages within Mann's novel that suggest that he should be read as an Antichrist, rather than a Christ figure. Zeitblom makes repeated note of Leverkühn's tendency towards paroxysmic fits of mocking laughter, for example. Mann's protagonist also derives the inspiration for his most important composition from Albrecht Dürer's woodcuts of the Apocalypse, the series of events that portend the coming of the Antichrist. Then there is the fact that Kretzschmar establishes Ludwig van Beethoven as a kind of Christ figure in chapter VIII, when he describes the compositional process that led to the *Missa solemnis* in terms that clearly recall the final days of Jesus. Leverkühn explicitly declares his intention to undo the legacy of Beethoven and seems to reenact the same Biblical episode when he premieres the *Lamentation of Doctor Faustus* in chapter XLVII. Should he therefore not be seen as the diabolical antithesis to Beethoven's redemptive struggle to bring joy and spiritual unity to all of humanity?

It's hard to reconcile such a reading with the image of Leverkühn cradling his face on his mother's bosom, however, or with Zeitblom's description of his behavior following his return to Buchel at the very end of the novel: "he readily joined her with demonstrations of love and joy, dogged her every step once they were home, and was the most docile of children, whom she tended with that total dedication of which only a mother is capable" (532/736). Indeed, throughout the novel, Zeitblom continuously stresses the human and mortal aspects of Leverkühn's allegorical relationship to Christ. Mann's protagonist never appears in any guise that would even remotely resemble the *Christus Imperator Maximus* so ardently extolled by the pseudo-fascist poet Daniel Zur Höhe in chapter XXXIV. As a result, he also never becomes a compelling Antichrist figure, come to execute the devil's victory on earth. During his ostensible moment of triumph, in chapter XLVII, where he presents the compositional fruits of his devil's pact, Leverkühn appears wracked by guilt and remorse. His story thereby repeats that of Christ, who sacrificed his mortal body for the benefit of humankind but did so while experiencing feelings of fear and doubt.

There is, thus, a third allegorical layer in the novel that we might add to the political and typological reading described in previous chapters. It is a theological layer, an interpretation of the novel in which Leverkühn becomes the ultimate redeemer of a sinful humanity who, thanks to his compositional efforts, strives to liberate us from the paradoxes of the modern condition. It is fitting, surely, that this grandest of all interpretive schemes also comes into clearest focus in the final chapters of the novel.

Lament and Redemption

The theological interpretation that I have just sketched out seems to stand in blatant opposition to the political reading that was the subject of the previous chapter. There, I argued that Leverkühn's final symphonic cantata, which is governed by the "strict style" and its enforced subservience to pre-determined "musical words," should be understood as an allegory of fascism. How, then, can it simultaneously serve as the culmination of a Christological redemption story?

The answer, as with so many other things pertaining to the musical aesthetics of *Doctor Faustus*, is to be found in Adorno. As Dieter Borchmeyer has pointed out, Adorno's *Philosophy of Music* makes the attempt to think beyond twelve-tone music, arguing very strongly that "if it is to hope to make it through the winter, music must emancipate itself from twelve-tone technique."[6] It does this, so Adorno argues, when it "casts away the dignity of the judge and abdicates, stepping down to take the side of the plaintiff who can be reconciled only by reality."[7] What Adorno presumably means by these words is that music must take a step back from the ambition to reconcile the objective and the subjective aspects of historical reality, in the same way in which a judge reconciles the "subjective" nature of an individual case with the "objective" reality

---

6 Adorno, *Philosophy of New Music*, 89. Borchmeyer's "'Musik-Dämonie'—Saturn und Melancholie" offers by far the most complex analysis of the question of redemption that I am pondering here, even if he takes the rather surprising position that Leverkühn is not a Christ figure at all (1244). For another recent treatment of the same subject, see Tim Lörke's chapter on "Kultur der Trauer und Klage" in his *Die Verteidigung der Kultur: Mythos und Musik als Medien der Gegenmoderne: Thomas Mann, Ferrucio Busoni, Hans Pfitzner, Hanns Eisler* (Würzburg: Königshausen & Neumann, 2010), 261–72.

7 Adorno, *Philosophy of New Music*, 97.

of the law. Instead, music must openly decry the broken nature of the modern condition in the manner of a legal plaintiff who demands, but cannot himself provide, justice and reconciliation.

The German word that Adorno uses for "plaintiff," however, is *Klage*, a term that can also mean "lamentation" and that resurfaces both in the title of Leverkühn's very last composition, *The Lamentation of Doctor Faustus* (*Doktor Fausti Weheklage*) and in Zeitblom's descriptions of it as a "single immense variation on lamentation" (511/705; *ein ungeheueres Variationenwerk der Klage*). The strong implication, then, is that the very same composition that ostensibly documents the triumph of the devil through its stringent use of the pseudo-fascist "strict style" also points the way towards a possible redemption from this triumph. This redemption is triggered by Leverkühn's persistent lamentations, through which he emancipates himself from the devil's influence and becomes a truly Christ-like figure.

The terms "lament" or "lamentation" occur more than forty times over the course of the novel and are first applied to one of Leverkühn's compositions in Zeitblom's description of the puppet opera *Gesta Romanorum* on 335/463. About a hundred pages later, the aria (actually a duet) "Mon coeur s'ouvre à ta voix" (Softly Awakes My Heart) from Camille de Saint-Saëns's 1877 opera *Samson and Delilah*. is described as a "dark lament for happiness" (*dunkle Glückesklage*) (434/599). At this point of his life, Leverkühn still mocks the emotional content of the French piece, which he denigrates as "not intellectual, but exemplarily sensual."[8]

This attitude changes completely in chapter XLV, however, which describes the painful death from meningitis of Leverkühn's nephew Nepomuk "Echo" Schneidewein. Echo's decline is accompanied by the child's "heart-rending laments and shrill cries" (498/688). Of all of Mann's "literary murders" and ethically questionable applications of the montage technique, the "Echo" chapters are probably the most infamous. Earlier in the story, Mann had already copied the suicide note of his own sister Carla into the novel word-for-word. The character of Echo, however, was based on his six-year-old grandson Frido, whom the author dearly loved and whose literary counterpart he nevertheless condemned to a slow and agonizing demise. Clearly Mann felt that the literary payoff of such an action would be worth it. And indeed, it is Echo's death—brought about by Leverkühn's transgression of the devil's pact when he shows fatherly affection for the young boy and caused by an inflammation of the same brain membranes the devil mentioned in chapter XXV—that leads the composer to renounce his pact with the devil. Towards the end

---

8   The importance of the Saint-Saëns episode for the novel as a whole is analyzed in great detail by Hans Rudolf Vaget in "'Blödsinnig schön!' Französische Musik im *Doktor Faustus*."

of the chapter, he rages: "Take his body, over which You have dominion. But You will have to be content to leave his sweet soul to me—and that is Your impotence and Your absurdity, for which I shall laugh You to scorn for eons. And may eternities be rolled twixt my place and his, I will yet know that he is in the place from whence You, foul filth, were cast out" (500/691). A little earlier than this, he had already begun one of his final musical projects, a song cycle setting to music Ariel's songs from Shakespeare's *The Tempest*. At the end of Shakespeare's play, the childlike spirit Ariel is released from his bondage to the sorcerer Prospero, suggesting that an escape from the confines of black magic is indeed possible.

Of course, it is precisely Echo's death that causes Leverkühn to sink to his lowest depths, when he grimly announces: "I have discovered that it ought not be. [...] The good and the noble, [...] what people call human, even though it is good and noble. What people have fought for, have stormed citadels for, and what people filled to overflowing have announced with jubilation—it ought not be. It will be taken back. I shall take it back. [...] The Ninth Symphony" (501/692-93). *The Lamentation of Doctor Faustus*—described as a "symphonic cantata" and thus the musical inverse of the Ninth Symphony, which is a choral symphony—clearly represents such a negation. But Mann's thoughts about music, which follow Adorno's, are ultimately dialectical and do not obey the zero-sum game of traditional philosophical logic. The *Lamentation* can negate the optimism and progressivism of the Ninth Symphony and the homophonic era more generally without thereby emerging as the final word on the matter.

Zeitblom acknowledges as much when he claims at the end of chapter XXXVI, that "there were years when we children of the dungeon dreamt of a song of joy—*Fidelio*, the Ninth Symphony—with which to celebrate Germany's liberation, its liberation of itself. But now only this work can be of any use, and it will be sung from our soul: the lamentation of the son of hell, the most awful lament of man and God ever intoned on this earth" (509/702). The original German word for "liberation of itself," *Selbstbefreiung*, makes clear that Zeitblom is here talking in allegorical terms about the German people casting off the yoke of Nazism. Such a liberation, as Zeitblom writing in 1945 realizes, never came. But he also holds out hope that Germany will not be confined to hell (or, in Snyder's terms, to the "politics of eternity") forevermore. For as he adds in the next paragraph:

> But from a creative viewpoint, from the viewpoint both of music history and personal fulfillment, is there not something jubilant, some high triumph in this terrible gift for redress and compensation? Does it not imply the kind of "breakthrough," which, whenever we contemplated and discussed the destiny of art, its state and crisis, had so often been a topic for us, as a problem, as a paradoxical possibility?

Does it not imply the recovery, or, though I would rather not use the word, for the sake of precision I shall, the reconstruction of expression, of emotion's highest and deepest response to a level of intellectuality and formal rigor that must first be achieved in order for such an event—the reversal, that is, of calculated coldness into an expressive cry of the soul, into the heartfelt unbosoming of the creature—to occur? (509–10/702–3).

The term "breakthrough" has a rich a conceptual prehistory in *Doctor Faustus* and was earlier used by Zeitblom to discuss both the German war aims in the First World War and Leverkühn's invention of the "strict style." Here it refers to something altogether different, however, namely to "emotion's highest and deepest response to [...] intellectuality and formal rigor."

Zeitblom's hope, in other words, is that the cold and ultra-rational style that Leverkühn applies in his symphonic cantata might bear within itself the seeds for its own negation, and therefore also for Germany's redemption. The tools for such a negation are lamentation and Christian *contritio*, or the sincere regret at one's own sinful nature—a concept first discussed during Leverkühn's theological studies in chapter XV.

The important question with which *Doctor Faustus* concludes is whether Zeitblom's redemptive hopes are justified or not. The novel is full of ambiguous gestures in this regard: the final "high G of a cello" at the end of the *Lamentation*, for example, which can be interpreted as either "the dying note of sorrow" or as its opposite, "a light in the night" (515/711). Or Leverkühn's attempt to walk into the Klammer Pool (the German name *Klammerweiher* means "clinging pond"), which can be read as either a final expression of madness and an attempt to extinguish the sinful self, or as an attempt at a redemptive baptism.

Ultimately, only the reader can decide on an answer to this question. Philologists tell us that Mann's manuscript for *Doctor Faustus* came down much more firmly on the side of redemption, and that the author changed his text only at the insistence of the ever-pessimistic Adorno. But the change was made, and the novel now stands before us in all of its glorious ambiguity. Which is, perhaps, as it should be, for even eighty years after the end of Nazism the question whether Germany can ever be forgiven still stirs up debate, and other historical cataclysms cast a similarly long shadow.[9] Zeitblom concludes his novel in the optative mood with the words: "may God have mercy on your poor soul, my friend, my fatherland" (534/738). The mixture of desperation and hope that speaks through these lines has lost nothing of its relevance in the twenty-first century.

---

9   For an excellent demonstration of the ambivalence surrounding the question of German redemption, see Susan Neiman, *Learning from the Germans: Race and the Memory of Evil* (New York: Picador, 2019) as well as the essays that Neiman has published since then, partially retracting her earlier more optimistic position.

Part Four: Materials for Consultation

12: Chapter Summaries and Page-by-Page Commentaries

IN THE HEADING for each chapter, "time of composition" refers to the dates on which Thomas Mann wrote these pages, "time of narration" refers to the dates on which the fictional Zeitblom writes them, and "narrated time" refers to the time at which the action narrated in the chapter takes place.

For the sake of concision, I have glossed terms that the reader could elucidate with a simple internet search only if those terms are central to *Doctor Faustus* (e.g., "polyphony"). Foreign phrases are translated only if their meaning will not be immediately deducible from context.

Thomas Mann used Luther's Bible translation for his many scriptural references throughout *Doctor Faustus*. James Woods chose the King James Version for his English edition, and I have done the same for this commentary.

Descriptive character names are an important feature of the text and a useful interpretive aid for the first-time reader. Because characters sometimes resurface many chapters after which they were initially introduced, I have moved the appropriate entries to a separate "Cast of Characters." A number of historical figures make cameo appearances in *Doctor Faustus* as well; these are glossed in the commentary.

The following abbreviations are used: L.= Leverkühn; Z. = Zeitblom; *DF* = *Doktor Faustus*; TM = Thomas Mann

Epigraph

Lo giorno se n'andava	The epigraph consists of the first nine lines of Canto II from *Inferno* (ca. 1315) by Dante Alighieri (1265–1321). Dante's poetic labors take place in a world that is transitioning from day into night, something that is symbolically true also for Z. in *DF*. And like Z., Dante confronts both contemporary woes and the agony of recollection. In Henry Wadsworth Longfellow's translation of 1867:

Day was departing, and the browned air
Released the animals that are on earth
From their fatigues; and I the only one

Made myself ready to sustain the war,
Both of the way and likewise of the woe,
Which memory that errs not shall retrace.

O Muses, O high genius, now assist me!
O memory, that didst write down what I saw,
Here thy nobility shall be manifest!

I

In the opening chapter, we are introduced to Z.'s distinctive voice and first apprehend some of the difficulties (both compositional and political) with which he is struggling.

Time of composition: May 23–31, 1943. Time of narration: May 1943. Narrated time: n/a.

5/11	raised him up & cast him down	Z.'s description of L. as *erhobener und gestürzter Mann* anticipates L.'s later self-identification as a "wicked and good Christian" (511/705).
5/11	Fortress Europe	Term borrowed from Nazi propaganda. Z. is perhaps not as immune to the influence of Nazism as he himself would like to believe.
5/11	labored breathing	Z.'s metaphor parodies the proems of classical epics and serves as an early indicator that something is amiss with his compositional process.
5/11	23 May 1943	The day on which TM, too, began with the composition of *DF*. Owing to an oversight on TM's part, early editions of *DF* have "27 May 1943" here. The GKFA follows this tradition.
6/12	thoroughly even-tempered [...] humanely tempered	A metaphor that not only alludes to Z.'s humanism, but also compares him to a musical instrument.
6/12	viola d'amore	A six- or seven-stringed instrument popular in the Baroque period and distinguished by its use of sympathetic strings, which are not themselves bowed but resonate with the main strings. The relationship between the two sets of strings metaphorically recalls that between L. and Z, although it is left ambiguous whether it is Z. who lives his life in the shadow of L., or rather L. who exists in the novel only in the shape given to him by Z.'s unreliable narration.

6/12	*Letters of the Obscure Men*	The *Letters of Obscure Men* was written by Crotus Rubianus of Dornheim (ca. 1480–ca. 1539) and published anonymously in 1515. It is a satirical attack on the theologian Johannes Pfefferkorn (ca. 1469–ca. 1522), who had called for the public burning of Jewish books. The names that follow are of German humanists who lived between 1455 and 1540 and castigated the excesses of the Lutheran Reformation.
6/12	attitude has meant sacrifices	Ironically, Z.'s lifelong attempts to resist the temptations of the demonic have been sustained only through "sacrifices," i.e., precisely the kind of actions one ordinarily performs to placate dark powers.
6/12	prematurely to retire	Z. voluntarily retired from his teaching position at a public university when the Nazis came to power in 1933.
6/13	my late friend	The German adjective used here and in several later passages is *verewigt* (lit. "eternalized"), a term that might refer both to posthumous reputation and to the sufferings of eternal damnation.
6/13	*divinis influxibus ex alto*	Latin: "divine inspiration from above."
6/13	demonic and irrational	Z. alludes to the fact that the Latin *genius* and the Greek *daimon* both originally described minor guardian spirits. The words acquired their modern associations with good and evil only during the early Christian period.
7/13	announced such a theme	Z. draws a connection between literary and musical composition, reminding us that the biography that we are reading is an artistic, rather than purely factual, construct.
8/15	around him lay coldness	The thematic motif of "coldness" (usually in the sense of "aloof," "disinterested") will play a major role in *DF*. The phrase used here recalls descriptions of the devil in Dante's *Inferno*, where he is portrayed as surrounded by an icy chill even amidst the fires of hell. Another possible reference point is chapter 6 of the Chapbook, where Faust needs to heat the blood he will use to sign the infernal contract in a crucible over hot coals.

II

We learn more about Z., and especially about his predilection for classical literature. Other important themes introduced include the vexed opposition between the "cultic" and the "cultural" as well as the contrast between Z.'s "jovial" and L.'s "saturnine" (that is, melancholic) temperament.

Time of composition: June 1–6, 1943. Time of narration: Summer 1943. Narrated time: n/a

9/16	literary current [...] held me back	Another indication that Z. is not in full control of his narrative.
9/16	Kaisersaschern an der Saale	Fictional town, whose name translates as "emperor's ashes." The Saale River, a tributary of the Elbe, runs through modern-day Bavaria, Thuringia, and Saxony-Anhalt in central Germany.
9/16	Merseburg	Small town in Saxony-Anhalt, roughly twenty miles west of Leipzig. Most famous as the home of the Merseburg Charms, two incantations written in Old High German and generally dated to the tenth century CE.
9/16	*meister*	In nineteenth-century German, *Meister* was a common appellation used to address distinguished musicians. The term possibly also alludes to another reverential epithet, that of *Führer*.
10/17	unsympathetic character	Z. clearly has a conflicted relationship with Judaism. The question whether there are latent anti-Semitic currents running through *DF* (and TM's thought more generally) has preoccupied scholars ever since the novel was published.
10/18	heart of Luther country	The names that follow are all of towns in central Germany that are closely associated with the life of Martin Luther (1483–1543).
10/18	*Jovis alma parens*	Latin: "the nurturing mother of Jupiter." Throughout *DF*, Z. self-associates with Jupiter and a "jovial" disposition, while associating L. with Saturn and a "saturnine" temper.

10/18	Brethren of the Common Life	Early modern religious order that operated in the Netherlands and Northern Germany. Thomas à Kempis (1380–1471) and Erasmus of Rotterdam (14766–1536) were both trained by the Brethren.
11/19	*bonae litterae*	Latin: "good letters" (i.e., classical literature).
12/20	Sacred Way	Road that leads from Athens to Eleusis, site of an important ancient Greek sanctuary where annual initiation rites into the cults of Demeter and Persephone took place.
12/20	Iacchus	Minor Greek deity worshipped at Eleusis. Often associated (but not to be confused) with Bacchus/Dionysus.
12/20	Eubouleus	Minor Greek deity worshipped at Eleusis.
12/20	Culture [...] propitiory inclusion	Our first exposure to a main theme of *DF*, namely the nature of culture and its relationship to several ostensible opposites, such as the cultic or the barbaric.
12/20	At age twenty-six	The German original has "at age twenty-five." Woods corrects an obvious inconsistency in TM's chronology.
12/20	fourteenth year of the century	The German original has "twelfth year of the century," another inconsistency corrected by Woods.
12/21	Helene, née Ölhafen	Reference to Helen of Troy, whom the Faust of the Chapbook (as well as of many subsequent versions of the story) summons from the netherworld and takes as his consort. The fact that the legendary beauty is here paired with the rather unprepossessing Z. is an obvious parody, as is the maiden name *Ölhafen*, which means "oil harbor." Z.'s somewhat vexed marital relations will be a running joke throughout *DF*.

13/21	ties of these young men	Z.'s estrangement from his sons and the "void" created by their devotion to the Nazis is a possible reference to chapter fifty-nine of the Chapbook, which tells us that Faust's wife and son vanished into thin air after his damnation. Because of references like this, some critics have speculated that Z. might be the true Faust figure of the novel.

III

This chapter introduces the Leverkühn family and especially L.'s father Jonathan, whose physical appearance is modeled on a Dürer portrait and who loves to perform physical and chemical experiments. Important passages include the one dedicated to the butterfly "Hetaera Esmeralda" and the description of mathematical acoustics by way of Chladni sound figures.

Time of composition: June 8–24, 1943. Time of narration: Summer 1943. Narrated time: n/a

14/22	Buchel [...] Weissenfels	Buchel is a fictional toponym, which TM took from the *Malleus Maleficarum*, a treatise on witchcraft published in 1486 by the theologian and inquisitor Henricus Institoris (ca. 1420–1505). Weissenfels is a real town in modern Saxony-Anhalt, about fifteen miles southwest of Leipzig.
14/22	linden tree	TM regarded linden trees, the subject of a famous song by Franz Schubert (1797–1828), as a quintessential symbol of Germanic inwardness. The Schubert song already features in his earlier novel *The Magic Mountain* (1924).
14/22	young man [...] only later	An early example of the theme of mythic repetition and the Nietzschean "eternal recurrence of the same."
15/23	ash-blond hair in need of a comb	Jonathan L.'s features were inspired by the portrait of Philip Melanchthon painted by Albrecht Dürer (1471–1528) (Fig. 1).

16/24	migraine headaches		Friedrich Nietzsche (1844–1900) is supposed to have suffered from this condition, but migraines are also one of the symptoms of syphilis and associated with the early modern topos of melancholia.
16/24	mammoth family Bible		The L. bible is modeled on that of the Mann family, an early example of TM harnessing autobiographical experience for the composition of *DF*.
16/25	speculate the elements		A phrase from the Faust Chapbook.
17/26	papilios and morphos		"Papilio" is the Latin for "butterfly"; "morpho" is the name of a genus of butterflies found mostly in South and Central America.
17/27	*Hetaera esmeralda*		Butterfly from the Nymphalidae family, indigenous to the Amazon. (Greek: *Hetaera* = "prostitute", Spanish/Portuguese: *Esmeralda* = "emerald"). TM copied this and the other descriptions of butterflies from the 1935 book *Falterschönheit* by Adolf Portmann, though he made minor changes such as adding the reference to "transparent nakedness"—presumably to strengthen the association with prostitution, which will become relevant later in *DF*.
18/27	the butterfly's purpose		The German term *Zweckmäßigkeit* (often translated as "purposiveness") alludes to Kantian aesthetics, and thus introduces the question whether aesthetic production presupposes the existence of culture or can take place in its absence as well.
18/29	would make Adrian laugh		L.'s uncanny laughter is another important motif in *DF*. Critics have linked it to, among other things, the early modern topos of melancholia, to Nietzsche's *Zarathustra* (1883–1885), to the character of Kundry in *Parsifal* (1882) by Richard Wagner (1813–1883), and to the medieval folk belief that Christ never laughed.

19/29	demiurge	In Platonic and Gnostic teaching, a subsidiary divinity responsible for the shaping and maintenance of the physical universe. The demiurge of Gnostic thought is frequently portrayed as antagonistic to the will of the Supreme Being, thus related to the devil.
19/31	hieroglyphics	The German word *Charaktere* is rare in this sense but used in the Chapbook to denote magical symbols.
21/32	man from Wittenberg	The "father of acoustics," Ernst Chladni (1756–1827), who first described these visual correlatives of sound waves. The close relationship between music and mathematics will be another important theme of *DF*. Wittenberg was not only the home of Martin Luther, but also the city in which Faust lived in the Chapbook and many subsequent versions of the myth.
23/35	osmotic pressure	References to the physical principle of osmosis recur in *DF* and will become associated with the devil's pact and with L.'s syphilitic infection, in which the bacterial "flagellates" penetrate the brain membrane, the *dura mater*.

IV

Chapter IV gives us a description of the Buchel farm and its inhabitants, especially L.'s mother Elsbeth. We are further introduced to a number of other suspicious characters, such as the hunchbacked stableboy Thomas, the "floppy-bosomed" milkmaid Hanne, and the smiling dog Suso, all of whom will have counterparts at L.'s later abode in Pfeiffering. We also learn about L.'s first encounters with music and with "imitative polyphony" in the form of the rounds that Hanne teaches the Buchel children.

Time of composition: June 25–July 7, 1943. Time of narration: Summer 1943. Narrated time: n/a

24/36	swelled to excess as it is	Another reminder that Z. is having tangible trouble controlling the shape of his narrative—either out of incompetence or because of dark forces conspiring against him.

24/37	handsome old German head	Elsbeth L.'s features were inspired by Albrecht Dürer's *Portrait of a Young Venetian Woman* (Fig. 2).
24/37	an Italian	The German term *welsch* refers to speakers of any romance language. The term thus also implies an association with France, a country that is repeatedly associated with cosmopolitanism in *DF*.
26/39	that very off-putting imperial	A *Knebelbart* combines a twirled mustache and goatee with clean-shaven cheeks.
26/39	blue-gray-green irises	Z. will repeatedly allude to the color of L.'s eyes over the course of the novel.
26/39	afflicted with a humpback	A possible reference to the devil, as well as to *The Hunchback of Notre Dame* (1831) by Victor Hugo (1802–1885), which features an important character named Esmeralda.
26/40	wanton last name	"Luder" means "hussy" in German.
28/42	antithesis […] artist and bourgeois	An important aspect also of TM's aesthetics.
28/43	hated and scorned the word	An early example of L.'s persistent anti-Romanticism and mistrust of the concept of genius.
29/42	Pfeiffering near Waldshut	Fictive toponym modeled on the village of Polling in Upper Bavaria, about 30 miles southwest of Munich. The equally fictive Waldshut is modeled on the nearby town of Weilheim.
31/47	here was a temporal intertwining	Hanne's early music lessons introduce L. to the principles of polyphony and again illustrate the theme of mythic repetition.

V

A lengthy excursus gives us better insight into Z.'s state of mind and his complex relationship to national socialism. We also learn about L.'s early education at the hands of schoolmaster Michelsen, who gives him his first lessons in imitative counterpoint.

Time of composition: July 8–July 13, 1943. Time of narration: Summer 1943. Narrated time: 1893–1895.

32/50	our prison … stale air	An allusion to *Fidelio* (1805), the only opera by Ludwig van Beethoven (1770–1827).

33/50	fate has squeezed the German	More evidence of Z.'s conflicted nature as a narrator. He clearly longs for the defeat of his country but is unable to articulate why it is necessary, attributing the current "awful straits" to "fate" rather than to German crimes.
34/51	those who have brought such good people	Z. blames the Nazi elite for the downtrodden condition of the German people, but not the ordinary citizens even though they, after all, enthusiastically supported the Nazis. He even speaks of the Germans as "hopelessly [estranged] from themselves." In this, he echoes the views of many émigré intellectuals (especially from the Marxist left) but notably not those of TM, who had to endure significant abuse from Bertolt Brecht (1898–1956) and others because of his public insistence that all Germans bore responsibility for the crimes of the Third Reich.
36/54	*ingenium*	Latin: "innate quality, intrinsic intelligence."
37/55	nine bars of horizontal melody	An early lesson in counterpoint that also establishes a link between Hanne's musical rounds and the "magic square," which will later inspire L.'s invention of the twelve-tone technique.
37/55	first grade of higher education	The *Quinta* would actually have been the second grade in a *Gymnasium*, equivalent to sixth grade in the U.S. educational system.

VI

Zeitblom's recollection of late-nineteenth-century Kaisersaschern was heavily influenced by descriptions of early modern Nuremberg, the town of Albrecht Dürer. This is an important example of "typological allegory" in DF, a technique whereby people and places are superimposed onto earlier figures from German history to illustrate continuities. Here, Z. explicitly suggests a resemblance between quotidian life under the Nazis and medieval religious fanaticism.

Time of composition: July 13–17, 1943. Time of narration: Summer 1943. Narrated time: 1895–1903.

38/56	he who sows the wind	See Hosea 8:7. In this chapter, Z. shows a greater degree of introspection than in the previous one.	
38/56	alliterative magic charms	The "Merseburg Charms," generally dated to the tenth century CE.	
39/56	Kaiser Otto III	Otto III (980–1002) became Holy Roman Emperor in 996. His actual grave is in Aachen (Aix-la-Chapelle). Otto III was famous for his love of Italy, and for moving the capital of the Empire to Rome. By relocating his grave to the fictive Kaisersaschern, TM is possibly trying to establish a link between the protestant German world and the Catholic Latin sphere.	
39/57	*nunc stans*	Latin: standing now. In scholastic philosophy, a description of the temporal nature of God, in whom all of eternity is equally present. Kaisersaschern, much like Buchel and Pfeiffering, seems to stand outside the general flow of history. TM knew the concept of *nunc stans* through the philosopher Arthur Schopenhauer (1788–1860) and drew extensively on it in *The Magic Mountain*.	
39/58	some utopian [...] lunatic	The German original refers specifically to Hans Böhm (ca. 1458–1476), the "Drummer of Niklashausen," who was put to death because he preached the equality of all men regardless of the estate they were born into.	
40/58	burning books	Z. here draws an explicit connection between medieval times and the Third Reich, thereby alerting us to the fact that his description of Kaisersaschern should be read also as a commentary on Germany under the Nazis.	
40/58	neurotic descent into the depths	The German has *Unterteuftheit*, an extremely rare term from miner's jargon that means "undermined," but phonetically also alludes to *Teufel* = devil.	
40/59	*Volk*	The term *Volk* (adjectival form *völkisch*), referring to a culturally, ethnically, and linguistically homogenous large group of people, was of central relevance to nineteenth- and twentieth-century conservative thought, including that of the Nazis.	

41/60		compelled to perform [...] jerky dance	A possible reference to the maniacal passion with which German crowds performed the Hitler salute, or to the goose-stepping of German soldiers.
41/60		*fladus [...] flute douce*	Z. (or TM) is incorrect. *Fladus* is actually a north German dialectal word for a specific kind of headdress. A *flute-douce* (French) is a type of organ stop.
41/60		eight years of [...] young life	The German original has "nine years." John. E. Woods is trying to correct for obvious inconsistencies in the chronology.

VII

Following on the description of Kaisersaschern, chapter VII gives us the second descriptive tour-de-force in DF. Nikolaus L.'s musical instrument shop takes on characteristics of an alchemist's kitchen or a witch's cellar, yet at the same time is described in an extremely detailed realist style. TM achieved this effect through his montage technique, relying on a 1921 textbook by Fritz Volbach for all his information about musical instruments. We also watch L. master the circle of fifths, which confers upon him the powers of musical modulation.

Time of composition: July 19–August 2, 1943. Time of narration: Summer 1943. Narrated time: 1895–1899 or 1900.

43/61		among its houses	The description of Nikolaus L.'s house is modeled on the still extant residence of Albrecht Dürer (1471–1528) in Nuremberg.
43/62		straight-hanging [...] unkempt hair	Nikolaus L.'s features were inspired by Dürer's *The Master-Builder Jerome of Augsburg* (Fig. 3).
44/62		room and board	The German employs the antiquated term *Losament*, which TM took from the Chapbook.

CHAPTER SUMMARIES AND PAGE-BY-PAGE COMMENTARIES ♦ 137

44/63	the warehouse [...] mezzanine	TM composed the ensuing bravura passage describing Nikolaus L.'s warehouse with the help of Fritz Volbach's 1921 reference work *Das moderne Orchester*, frequently excerpting passages directly into his manuscript. Like the description of Jonathan L.'s laboratory, the musical instrument store recalls a witch's kitchen or alchemist's workshop. TM also wove allusions to several musical compositions with a Faustian, macabre, or melancholic character into his description.
45/64	adept at mournful airs	Allusion to the opening of the third act of Wagner's *Tristan and Isolde* (1865), an influential depiction of melancholy.
45/65	will-o'-the-wisps	Allusion to the opera *La Damnation de Faust* (1864) by Hector Berlioz (1803–1869).
46/66	graveyard dance of skeletons	Allusion to the *Danse macabre* (1874) by Camille Saint-Saëns (1835–1921).
47/67	no matter what material	Cimabue's disquisitions can be read as a sly commentary on modern literature. Like the "sage authorities" discussed by Cimabue, TM was convinced that what ultimately mattered in a literary work was the form and not the nature of the raw materials, which he frequently (as in this passage) copied word-for-word from mundane sources in an act of literary montage.
49/70	just how immaterial and secondary	L. displays the cardinal sin of pride, closely associated with the Faust myth.
50/72	Order is everything	A central pillar of L.'s musical aesthetics and also of the political allegory that lurks behind them.
50/72	"For what is of God [...]"	A somewhat free translation of Romans 13:1 that Mann took directly from the *Malleus Maleficarum*.

50/72	circle of fifths	A graphematic way of organizing the twelve pitches of an evenly tempered scale into a closed circle of perfect fifths. In *DF*, the circle of fifths functions as an elementary expression of musical "magic," much like the pentagram (another grapheme that revolves around the number five and that, when traced, returns to its starting point) is a symbol of black magic.
51/73	he struck a chord	L. has taught himself how to modulate from one key to another by adding a minor seventh to a tonic chord, thereby changing it to the dominant of the key signature that is located one step further in counterclockwise direction along the circle of fifths. Woods introduces an error in this paragraph: the phrase "yielding the modulation from B major to A major" should read "from B major to E major." The GKFA isn't faultless either, however. Following the lead of the 1948 Vienna edition, it prints what Mann meant as key-signatures in lower-case letters and omits hyphens in the phrase: "*und so kam er über a, d, und g nach C-Dur*," thereby confusing the names of notes with those of key signatures.
51/73	tertian harmony [...] Neapolitan Sixth	"Tertian harmony" refers to the harmonic system that characterizes Western music from the late Renaissance to the late nineteenth century, in which chords are based on the interval of the third. A Neapolitan Sixth is a chord built on the subdominant of a major or (more usually) minor scale in which the fifth has been replaced with a minor sixth; it is an especially useful tool for modulation. L. is discovering some of the theoretical fundamentals that distinguish post-Renaissance music from that of the polyphonic era.
51/74	ambiguity as a system	This definition of music already figures in *The Magic Mountain* (1924), where it is voiced with some distaste by the arch-rationalist Settembrini.

| 51/74 | enharmonic transposition | The practice of reading a tone in two different ways (for instance as C♯ and D♭), thereby enabling modulation into a different key. Enharmonic transposition is a direct consequence of even temperament. In perfect tuning, C♯ and D♭ would be different pitches. |
| 51/74 | cheeks had taken on a flush | The German reads *Er hatte erhitzte Wangen* and thereby draws attention to bodily heat rather than color. See also 8/15. |

VIII

Kretzschmar's four lectures on music introduce some of the most important themes in DF and set up many later passages in the novel. The first lecture, heavily influenced by Mann's discussions with Theodor W. Adorno, deals with Beethoven's sonata Op. 111 and the distinctions between Beethoven's early ("polyphonically objective"), middle ("harmonically subjective"), and late (synthetic) periods. It also establishes Beethoven as an artist who overcame the classical sonata form, much like later passages will characterize the Ninth (or "Choral") Symphony as a work that overcomes the form of the classical symphony. The second lecture, influenced both by Adorno and by the music historian Paul Bekker, deals with Beethoven's inability to compose a fugue. It establishes Beethoven as the quintessential artist of the homophonic era and also describes him as a Christ figure. The third lecture on "Music and the Eye" expands on Pythagorean themes, proposing that music is better apprehended by means of the intellect than by aural stimulation, and also alluding to the notion of a "music of the spheres" that unifies the cosmos. The final lecture on "The Elemental in Music" introduces us to Johann Conrad Beissel and the Ephrata Brethren. Beissel's attempts to overthrow five centuries of musical development foreshadow L.'s own efforts at a "strict style," while his dictatorial influence over the Ephrata Brethren move him in the vicinity of Adolf Hitler and other autocratic leaders.

Time of composition: August 4–September 22, 1943, with subsequent revisions. Time of narration: Summer 1943. Narrated time: 1900–1901.

| 53/76 | *The Marble Statue* | *The Marble Statue* is an 1818 novella by the German romantic poet Joseph von Eichendorff (1788–1857). Significantly, its protagonist has to choose between art and a pious life. |

53/76	Schütz	Heinrich Schütz (1585–1672) did not actually write for the organ. When TM became aware of this, he substituted the name of Michael Praetorius (1571–1621). This change is reflected in the GKFA, but not in the GW or the Woods translation.
54/67	our community had no use for lectures	In the years prior to the composition of *DF*, TM made his money as an itinerant lecturer in the United States and was continuously amazed by the eagerness and patience of his American audiences.
55/78	Op. 111	Beethoven's Piano Sonata No. 32 in C minor, Op. 111 was written in 1821 or 1822. Kretzschmar's lecture was heavily influenced by Theodor Adorno's 1937 essay "Late Style in Beethoven." Adorno, a neighbor of TM in Pacific Palisades, also provided feedback on the entire chapter.
56/79	famulus	An assistant, especially one working for a scholar or magician. In the Chapbook, both Faust's servant Wagner and Mephistopheles are referred to by this term. The "famulus" in question here is Anton Schindler (1795–1864), an acquaintance of Beethoven's who wrote a salacious biography of him that became another major source for this chapter. Z. is to some extent modeled on Schindler.
56/80	works of the last period	Beethoven's life is often divided into "early," "middle," and "late" periods, with the late period frequently said to begin around 1812, after the composition of the Eighth Symphony. The late period is characterized by increasingly forceful attacks on classical forms and conventions—a development that we now recognize as the beginning of musical Romanticism, but which disturbed many of Beethoven's contemporaries.

57/81	so far so good		Kretzschmar's theory that Beethoven was at his most "subjective" during the middle period, and that the musical works of the late period pivot back to a new "objectivity" in which musical conventions are invoked at arm's length, as if in parody, was heavily influenced by Adorno's dialectical approach to music history.
57/81	harmonic subjectivity [...] polyphonic detachment		"Polyphony" refers to a musical texture in which two or more independent melodies occur simultaneously; "harmony" refers to the way in which multiple pitches combine to form a chordal structure. While polyphony and harmony are not mutually exclusive, Kretzschmar's reference to a "radical will to harmonic expression" associates Beethoven's middle period with homophony—i.e., with musical textures in which chordal structures supersede the independent musical lines of polyphony.
58/83	the arietta theme		Kretzschmar's comments on the second movement draw heavily on detailed written feedback that Adorno provided in response to questions TM had submitted to him.
58/83	meadowland		*Wiesengrund* in the original, a sly reference to Adorno's birth name.
58/83	counterpoint		Relationship between two or more musical lines that are harmonically (vertically) interdependent, but rhythmically and melodically (horizontally) independent. Rounds and fugues are forms of counterpoint.
59/84	weight of the chord's joints		TM copied this phrase from a letter by Adorno, who had written to him about the *Eigengewicht der Akkorde* (inherent weight of the chords). However, because of TM's musical ignorance and Adorno's bad handwriting, TM initially read the phrase as *Fugengewicht der Akkorde* (fugal weight of the chords), a construction that makes no technical sense but has a certain metaphorical charm given what follows. The error was quickly pointed out to TM, though the mistake remained in all versions printed during his lifetime. Both Woods and the GKFA opt to silently "correct" the phrasing.

60/86	dazedly hummed	The listeners have literally been enchanted by the music, drawing a connection to the black magic of the Faustus myth.
60/86	Beethoven and the Fugue	A "fugue" is a compositional technique in which two or more voices repeat the same theme at different pitches. It represents a formal evolution of the round, with which L. began his apprenticeship in music.
60/86	Prince Esterházy	Nikolaus II, Prince Esterházy (1765–1833) was a Hungarian prince and a patron of Beethoven's. His Hungarian origin moves him into the vicinity of L.'s own later benefactress, Frau von Tolna.
61/87	strict style	Compositional style of the eighteenth century, characterized among other things by the prevalence of polyphonic textures. L. will later (204/279) adopt this name to describe his invention of the twelve-tone technique.
62/88	a terrifying tale	The following anecdote, like so much else in this chapter, is taken from Schindler's Beethoven biography, although TM rewrote it to stress the Christological parallels to Christ's agonies in the Garden of Gethsemane.
62/89	could ye not watch with me	Words taken from Matthew 26:40, thus emphasizing the Christological parallel.
62/89	deaf man sang, howled, and stomped	An allusion to chapter 68 of the Chapbook, in which Faust's students overhear their master's final struggle with the devil through the closed door of his study.
63/915	Nor were we familiar	TM excised the next three paragraphs following the publication of the 1947 first edition, as he did many other passages, especially in chapters VIII and IX. For concision, I have not flagged subsequent elisions in this commentary.
63/915	"Monster of all Quartets"	Beethoven's String Quartet No. 13 (1826).
63–64/917	in a freer style	German original has *im freien Stil* in italics, marking it as a technical term to be contrasted with the "strict style" mentioned on 61/87.

64/917	*Well-Tempered Clavier*	The *Well-Tempered Clavier* by Johann Sebastian Bach (1685–1750) was finished in 1722 and not only represents a milestone of classical music but also led to the eventual codification of the even temperament so central to the aesthetic discussions in *DF*.
64/918	cultic to the cultural	The opposition between cultic/liturgical and cultural/profane epochs is of central importance to the debates about history between L. and Z. and should be seen also as a metonym for larger debates about pre-modernity and enlightenment.
64/918	*Parsifal*	Wagner's *Parsifal* carries the subtitle *Ein Bühnenweihfestspiel* (A Stage Consecration Play); it thus mixes cultic and cultural elements.
64/918	*a cappella*	Italian for "in the church style" (meaning "without instrumental accompaniment"). The linkage between cultic and vocal music was extremely important to Paul Bekker (1882–1937), whose *The Story of Music* (1927) greatly influenced Kretzschmar's second lecture as well as *DF* as a whole
65/91	art's apparently imminent retreat	A probable allusion to the ways in which art was put to use by the Nazis in their assemblies and cultic celebrations.
66/91	alternative to culture	The idea articulated here can be traced back all the way to TM's essay "Thoughts in Time of War" (1914), but it also alludes to the central thesis of *Dialectic of Enlightenment* (1944) by Theodor Adorno and Max Horkheimer.
66/91	homophonic-melodic	"Homophony" refers to a musical texture in which a primary voice is supported by one or more other voices that are subordinated to it and provide the harmony. In "polyphony," multiple voices act independently. See also the contrast on 57/81.
67/94	Pythagorean	Pythagoras (sixth century BCE) held that numbers structure the cosmos. His thinking is a central influence on L. and alluded to at various points throughout the book.

68/94	Kundry		The central female character of Wagner's *Parsifal*, tied to themes of the cultic and of redemption, but also to incantation.
70/96	*Ring of the Nibelung*		A cycle consisting of the operas *Das Rheingold, Die Walküre, Siegfried,* and *Götterdämmerung* by Richard Wagner; the complete cycle premiered in 1876 and was later hugely influential on TM both through its content and its formal innovations. The equation of "the basic elements of music" with "those of the world itself" is especially apropos to the opening bars of *Das Rheingold*.
70/925	monodic isolation		"Monody" is a musical texture consisting of a single vocal line with instrumental accompaniment. TM is more specifically referring to "mono*phony*," a musical texture in which there is a vocal line with *no* (or only percussive) accompaniment.
71/97	Beissel		TM learned about Beissel (1691–1768) and the Solitary Brothers and Sisters through an article in *The American-German Review* by Hans Theodore David, from which he quotes extensively in the following paragraphs. He later had the opportunity to examine Beissel's manuscripts in the Library of Congress. Beissel will provide L. with an obvious model in his strivings to overcome the modern "cultural" epoch and return music to a "cultic" condition.
72/99–100	Music […] his spiritual kingdom		A likely allusion to the ways in which art and popular entertainment were harnessed for propagandistic purposes by the Nazis. In the German original, the word for "kingdom" is *Reich*.
73/100	froze out the singing teacher		The German *kaltstellen* is more drastic and carries connotations of "to eliminate, to kill."
74/102	driven by an irresistible longing		Another instance of music being connected to incantation.
75/104	even a foolish order is better		A dictum that, though its literal referent is musical composition, has significant allegorical implications for the political realm.

76/104	music has so much warmth		Another example of the theme of bodily heat already raised on 51/74. The term "bovine warmth" (*Stallwärme* or "stable warmth" in the original) links this passage to the encounter with Hanne in chapter IV.
76/105	I felt I was the older		Z. *is* older of course, though his relationship with L. rarely conveys this.
77/106	interest		The German *Interesse* has a somewhat stronger association with intellectual interest than its English equivalent. L. is talking about intellectual curiosity rather than romantic or sexual interest.

IX

L. begins to take English and music lessons from Wendell Kretzschmar. The former introduce him to Shakespeare, who will provide him with a lifelong source of inspiration; the latter deepen his appreciation of Beethoven and spark his awareness of the interdependence of harmony and melody, the vertical and the horizontal aspects of music. This recognition, in turn, leads him to postulate the interdependence of polyphony and homophony, and to thereby stress the continuity of early modern musical textures with nineteenth-century music. Like the last one, this chapter was heavily influenced by both Adorno and Bekker, and passages from both are pasted directly into the novel.

Time of composition: September 23, 1943–January 14, 1944, with breaks and later revisions. Time of narration: Summer 1943. Narrated time: 1902–1903.

79/107	Laurence Sterne	The reference that follows is to *Tristram Shandy* by the Irish novelist Laurence Sterne (1713–1768), a novel that TM had read in 1941–42.
79/107	humanistic curriculum	In the German educational system of the Wilhelmine period, elite "humanistic" high schools (*Gymnasien*) focused on ancient languages, not on modern ones. TM criticized this tendency in his 1936 lecture "Humaniora und Humanismus."
79/107	Shakespeare and Beethoven [...] binary star	These two men were the self-avowed lodestars also of Richard Wagner.

81/111		all the notes of the chromatic scale	L.'s attempts to incorporate all twelve notes of the chromatic scale into an ordered progression foreshadow his later discovery of the twelve-tone system.
81/111		identity of the horizontal and vertical	Another foreshadowing of twelve-tone composition, in which the tone row governs both the melodic (horizontal) and harmonic (vertical) structure of a composition.
82/112		each note [...] itself a chord	Every real-world tone contains within itself resonant frequencies at a higher pitch level. Played sequentially, these so-called "overtones" can be rearranged to form a scale.
82/931		chord is the result of polyphonic	L. is developing a theory of voice leading that de-emphasizes harmony and emphasizes the roots of classical and post-classical music in early modern polyphony.
82/112		Dissonance [...] polyphonic merit	L. linking of polyphony and dissonance would surely astonish any Renaissance composer but is crucial for the overall argument of *DF* that twelve-tone music is not so much a modernist advance as a regression to a pre-modern ("cultic") mindset. TM took this idea (like much else in this chapter) from Adorno's *Philosophy of New Music* (1949).
84/115		old church mode	The church modes were systems of pitch organization in use from the early Middle Ages to roughly the sixteenth century, when they were displaced by the major and minor scales. The tone rows that L. will eventually invent are a system of pitch organization as well.
85/116		al fresco chords	TM took the somewhat odd term "al fresco chord" from Paul Bekker's *The Story of Music* (German original 1926), which provided another important source for this chapter.

86/118	Michaelmas [...] *Der Freischütz*		The Feast Day of Saint Michael on September 29. Saint Michael (also called the Archangel Michael) is principally known for his role in suppressing the devil. Having his protagonist travel on Michaelmas to hear *Der Freischütz*, an opera about a devil's pact by Carl Maria von Weber (1786–1826), is a good example of the irony with which TM heavily laces his text.
86/118	Hans Heiling [...] Dutchman		Demonic protagonists, respectively, of the Romantic operas *Hans Heiling* (premiered 1833) by Heinrich Marschner (1795–1861) and *The Flying Dutchman* (premiered 1843) by Richard Wagner.
87/118	*Fidelio*		The only opera by Beethoven, premiered in 1805. A major theme of *Fidelio* is the overcoming of injustice and arbitrary power through human solidarity. Within the thematic structure of *DF*, this lifts it into the vicinity of the Ninth Symphony. See also 22/50.
87/118	great overture in C		Also known as the "Leonore Overture No. 3" and frequently performed as a solo work. The fact that it is in C major not only signals purity but, within *DF*, also moves it into the vicinity of the *Freischütz* overture.
87/119	peculiar about your music		The pronoun in the original German is in the plural. L. is speaking as though he were not a part of humanity.
87/119	*per se*		The German original has *an sich*—a reference to the Kantian concept of the *Ding an sich* or "thing-in-itself."

X

L. announces his intention to study theology—much to the displeasure of Z., who sees in it an expression of sinful pride.

Time of composition: January 16–26, 1944. Time of narration: Summer 1943. Narrated time: 1902–1903.

90/121	arrogance		The German term here is *Hochmut*, an overt reference to the cardinal sin of pride.

90/122	superiority		The German term *Superiorität* is rarely used and probably represents another allusion to the cardinal sin of pride (Latin *superbia*).
91/123	certain discussions we had		See, e.g., 64/918.
91/124	his desire [...] had contributed		Another implication of Z.'s realization is that L. is studying theology not out of any inherent piety, but out of the desire to intellectually return to an age in which music had not yet become separated from other spheres of human activity.
93/125	he makes a wicked guest		From *Simplicissimus* (1669) by Hans Jakob Christoffel von Grimmelshausen (1622–1676).
93/126	innate merits		The German term *angeborene Verdienste* is probably better translated as "innate achievements." The paradoxical phrase derives from Goethe's autobiographical work *Poetry and Truth* (1811–1833); Mann had already commented on it in his essay "Goethe and Tolstoi" (1925).
93/126	"Only scoundrels are modest"		From Goethe's poem "Rechenschaft" ("Accountability," 1810).

XI

Chapter XI offers a general description of Halle an der Saale, the town where L. will study theology for two years. We learn of the varied history of the town and of the theological faculty, which has hosted Catholics, Lutherans and Pietists, humanists and dogmatic reformers, scientifically-minded theologians and more mystical figures

Time of composition: January 31–February 8, 1944. Time of narration: Summer 1943. Narrated time: 1903–1905.

95/129	at whose feet [...] wanted to sit		Although this phrase has obvious Christological implications, it is actually taken from Goethe's *Poetry and Truth*.
95/129	University of Wittenberg		The University of Wittenberg is where Faust studies in the Chapbook.

96/130	Crotus Rubianus		A sixteenth-century humanist, to whom Z. has already expressed intellectual fealty on 6/12, where he appears as "Crotus of Dornheim."
96/130	"Dr. Kröte, the toad [...]"		*Kröte* means toad in German and was Luther's favorite insult for Crotus (whose given name actually derived from the Greek satyr Krotos). The quotation is taken from David Friedrich Strauß's biography of the German humanist Ulrich von Hutten (1488–1523).
97/131	Holy Communion under both kinds		At Pietist services the faithful receive Communion through both bread and wine.
97/131	subjective arbitrariness [...] objective ties		This opposition recalls very similar terms in Kretzschmar's Beethoven lectures in chapter VIII.
97/132	should actually be welcomed		The ideas expressed here derive from Nietzsche's *Ecce Homo* (1888), but probably also allude to the so-called Conservative Revolution in Germany during the 1920s.
98/132–33	Would it not have been better?		Z.'s critique of scientific theology was heavily inspired by an exchange of letters between TM and his friend Paul Tillich, who also provided TM with a description of Halle around the turn of the century and an overview of the state of theological instruction in Germany at that time. Z.'s mistrust of extreme rationalism and preference for intuition once again stresses his contrast with L.
100/136	Winfried		The fictional fraternity "Winfried" is modeled on the actual fraternity "Wingolf," of which Paul Tillich was a member when he studied theology at Halle in the early years of the century.

XII

At Halle, two of the most influential professors are Kolonat Nonnenmacher, who lectures on the pre-Socratics, and the systematic theologian Ehrenfried Kumpf. Nonnenmacher expands L.'s knowledge of Pythagoras and thereby shapes the way the young man thinks about music. Kumpf is a parody of Martin Luther and highlights the vulgar, anti-intellectualist, and downright xenophobic tendencies that TM believed Luther bequeathed to German culture.

Time of composition: February 8–20 (?), 1944. Time of narration: Summer 1943. Narrated time: 1903–1905.

101/946	Otto II		Otto II (955–983) was the father of Otto III, whose grave TM relocated to Kaisersaschern in chapter VI. This strengthens the impression that L. has not entirely left his hometown behind by moving to Halle.
102/138	a so-called magic square		A "magic square" is a square array of positive integers from 1 to n arranged in such a way that the rows, columns, and main diagonals all add up to the same sum. This equivalence, as well as the fact that each number can occur only once, symbolically links the magic square to the tone rows that L. will eventually make the basis of his music.
102/138	Dürer's *Melencolia*		Dürer's copper etching *Melencolia I* (1514) is one of the most important visual reference points in *DF* (see the cover of this *Reader's Guide*). It depicts a brooding angel surrounded by various symbols related not only to alchemy, but also to the early modern trope of melancholia. Among these is a magic square with four numbers to each side.
103/139	*Autòs épha*		Greek: "he himself has said it." A common phrase amongst the disciples of Pythagoras, but also a likely nod to the blind obedience that characterized Nazism.
103/140	entelechy		Greek.: "that which carries its goal (*telos*) within itself." A central concept of Aristotelian philosophy; here possibly also another wink to Nazism, with its rhetoric of destiny and its emphasis on blind obedience.
104/142	Instead of "gradually" he said		Kumpf expresses himself in an archaic idiom that more closely resembles sixteenth-century rather than twentieth-century German. TM took many of his phrases directly from the writings of Martin Luther, Grimmelshausen's *Simplicissimus,* and other early modern sources.
106/144	*Si Diabolus non esset...*		Latin: "If only the devil weren't a liar and murderer!" A quotation from the Chapbook.

106/145	*Dicis-et-non-facis*	Latin: "You say and do not act." A quotation from *Simplicissimus*.
106/145	Black Caspar	A common name for the devil, which we already encountered in chapter IV, where we are introduced to the farm dog Kaschperl.
107/146	*Apage!*	Greek: "Away with you!" See Matthew 4:10.
107/146	grabbed a hard roll	A parody of the famous anecdote about Luther hurling an inkwell at Satan, who tried to tempt Luther while he was translating the Bible into German.

XIII

Another memorable presence at Halle is the private lecturer Schleppfuss, who instructs L. and Z. in "The Philosophy of Religion." Schleppfuss means "drag-foot" and this name, along with several other clues, marks the lecturer as a probable incarnation of the devil. Schleppfuss offers his eager students a rather tenuous definition of spiritual freedom and titillates them with stories that TM took from the inquisitor's manual Malleus Maleficarum. *The point of these stories is to illuminate the psychological disposition of an "integrated" (111/151) culture that did not know the individual freedoms pioneered by the Enlightenment.*

Time of composition: February 20(?)–March 8, 1944. Time of narration: Summer 1943. Narrated time: 1903–1905.

108/146	XIII	The numbering is, of course, significant, as Z. himself will point out at the start of the next chapter.
108/146	*venia legendi*	Latin: "authorization to teach." As a "private lecturer" (*Privatdozent*), Schleppfuss has the state's permission to teach courses at the University of Halle but does not hold a formal professorship.
109/147–48	forked beard [...] splinter-sharp teeth	These serpentine attributes reinforce Schleppfuss's diabolical nature.
109/148	empyrean	Heaven. However, the term derives from the Greek πῦρ ("fire") and thus encapsulates Schleppfuss's intertwining of the diabolical with the divine.

109/148	"classical epoch"	Throughout his lectures, Schleppfuss repeatedly refers to the age of the Inquisition as the "classical epoch," a term applied in music history to the eighteenth century and to the period which Beethoven would eventually come to transcend.
109/148	"The Fat Lady"	TM took this epithet from the *Malleus Maleficarum*, a 1486 treatise on witchcraft by the theologian and inquisitor Henricus Institoris that served as the main source for most of this chapter.
111/150	we have the word as well	The opposition between a theological conception of freedom and a political one is central to TM's thought of the 1940s. In the 1945 lecture "Germany and the Germans," for example, he explicitly faults Luther for having developed the former but not the latter.
111/151	incubus	A demon who seeks to have sexual intercourse with a sleeping woman; the female equivalent would be a succubus. TM took the following story from the *Malleus Maleficarum*.
112/152	*flagellum haereticorum fascinariorum*	Latin: "the scourge of heretical betwitchers." Title of a 1458 treatise by the inquisitor Nicolas Jacquier (1410–1472). The term "flagellum" will recur in chapter XXV in conjunction with L.'s syphilitic infection.
112/152	*illusiones daemonum*	Latin: "the illusions of evil spirits." Title of a treatise by Bishop Bertramus Teuto (ca. 1356–1387).
115/156	*femina [...] minus*	This derivation of Latin *femina* ("woman") from *fides* ("faith") and *minus* ("less") is etymological humbug, but can also be found in the *Malleus Maleficarum*.
115/157	Heinz Klöpfgeissel	Another story from the *Malleus Maleficarum*.
115/158	a low dive for women	The German uses the antiquated term *Schlupfbude*, which will recur in XVI, when L. visits the brothel in Leipzig.
116/158	Hungarian female	Another foreshadowing of Esmeralda/Frau Tolna.

117/160	*specificum*		Church Latin: "remedy for a specific disease."

XIV

While studying at Halle an der Saale, L. and Z. join the student fraternity Winfried and participate in excursions into the Thuringian countryside. Z.'s detailed description of the students' idealistic nighttime conversations gives us a sense of the intellectual atmosphere in Germany prior to the First World War and to the growing self-consciousness of what would later come to be known as the "Generation of 1914."

Time of composition: March 9–April 17, 1944. Time of narration: Summer 1943. Narrated time: 1903–1905.

121/165	Christian fraternity Winfried	TM's main source for his description of the student fraternity was his correspondence with Paul Tillich, who had been member of a Christian fraternity named "Wingolf" during his years at Halle.
121/166	*frère-et-cochon*	French: "brother and pig." Idiomatic expression meaning "close friends" in Swiss French.
121/165	informal pronouns	German has both formal and informal pronouns of address. In early-twentieth-century university settings, virtually all people would have used formal pronouns to address one another, except within the confines of student fraternities, where informal pronouns would have been customary. In keeping with his "cold" and distanced character, L. naturally gravitates towards formal modes of address.
122/167	walk straight to the piano	L. habit of avoiding interpersonal contact by busying himself with a musical instrument foreshadows his later behavior in Chapter XVI.
122/167	bursting up with fever	The German verb for "to improvise" (*phantasieren*) can also mean "to hallucinate." TM is foreshadowing the conversation with the devil in XXV.
123/169	*in corpore*	Latin: "in the flesh."
124/169	on Shank's mare	An old-fashioned expression meaning "on foot."

124/170	voluntary cutting-back and simplification	The enthusiastic return to "simpler" forms of life described by Z. with some ironic distance in this paragraph spoofs the national-conservative and proto-fascist tendencies within German youth culture in the early twentieth century. Z.'s willfully archaic idiom contributes to this impression.
124/170	discussion launched in a barn	The following discussions have become known in German as the *Schlafstrohgespräche* ("sleeping straw discussions"). TM's main source, from which he often quotes verbatim in the following pages, was the Winter 1931 edition of the magazine *Die Freideutsche Position: Rundbriefe der Freideutschen Kameradschaft*, a student newsletter. Hans-Joachim Schoeps (1909–1980), who wrote most of the relevant passages and sent the issue to TM in 1931 as a token of appreciation, later criticized the author's decision to employ phrases written in the 1930s for a portrait of the early twentieth century; he also characterized his original writings as entirely unpolitical in nature.
125/171	one's specific form of life	In Germany, the early twentieth century in general, and the Weimar years in particular, were characterized by an explicit clash of generations, something TM already thematized in his short story "Disorder and Early Sorrow" (1925). The students are debating the validity of generational consciousness, as well as the question of how new collective identities come into the world.
125/172	the gentlemen started	In the German original, L. gets his pronouns of address confused, reluctantly moving from the third person plural (which serves as a formal address but also signifies total separation of subject and object) to the first person plural.
126/173	*quod demonstramus*	Latin: "what we are proving."
126/173	Eisenach and the Wartburg	Sites associated with Martin Luther, wo went to school in Eisenach and later translated the Bible while hiding at the Wartburg Castle.

126/173	privilege of our nation	In keeping with his name, Deutschlin represents the German nationalist position throughout these discussions.
127/174	our having been a little late	A reference to Germany's status as a "belated nation"—thus the title of a 1935 book by Helmuth Plessner (1892–1985), which TM almost certainly knew. Germany unified only in 1871, long after most other nation-states in Western Europe.
127/174	the eternally striving student	In this paragraph TM fuses ideas from Goethe's *Faust* with direct allusions to the study *Nietzsche: Attempt at a Mythology* (1918) by his erstwhile friend Ernst Bertram (1884–1957).
128/175	Kierkegaard has […] made us aware	TM had originally planned to include many more allusions to Søren Kierkegaard (1813–1855) in the Halle chapters, but refrained from doing so after Paul Tillich informed him the Danish philosopher was almost unknown amongst German theologians at the time.
128/175	ride between death and the Devil	An allusion to Dürer's engraving *Knight, Death, and Devil* (1513), which exerted a lifelong fascination on TM, who viewed the image as a visual manifestation of Nietzsche's philosophy (Fig. 4).
128/176	France has been chosen	L. significantly does not concur with Deutschlin's nationalist condemnation of all things French; French music will come to exert an important influence on him later in *DF*.
129/178	there is no direct access	Deutschlin's argument in this paragraph is heavily influenced by Max Weber (1864–1920). He and Arzt are articulating alternative visions of how deeper meaning might still be found in modern society with their conflicting spheres of interest; Deutschlin appealing to collective national consciousness, Arzt to religion and social values.
130/179	von Teutleben said	In the German, Teutleben conducts his argument in terms of the *völkisch* ("folkish") rather than the "national," which differentiates his particular brand of chauvinism from that of Deutschlin.

130/179	Ruhr	River in Western Germany and center of German heavy industry.
134/185	Venusburg	This should be *Venusberg* (Mountain of Venus), a reference to the Hörselberg, which supposedly hid an entryway to the underground realm of Venus, and which plays a central role in Wagner's opera *Tannhäuser* (premiered 1845). Another devil's reference as well as a sly indictment of the perhaps somewhat impractical nature of the students' nighttime conversations.

XV

Sometime in the first half of 1905, L., in consultation with his old teacher Wendell Kretzschmar, decides to abandon theology and instead devote himself to the study of composition. In justifying the choice, he draws explicit comparisons between music and the black arts.

Time of composition: April 19–May 9, 1944. Time of narration: Summer 1943. Narrated time: 1903–1905.

136/187	in Germany music […] literature in France	A common prejudice in the nineteenth and early twentieth centuries, in which TM frequently indulged as well.
137/188	she looped her arm around him	Elsbeth L.'s posture recalls the iconographical tradition of the pietà, i.e., of the Virgin Mary cradling the mortal body of her son Jesus after the crucifixion, thereby strengthening the Christological dimensions of the narrative.
137/189	Hase's Private Conservatory	A fictional school.
139/191	as weary […] with iron ladles	This turn of phrase is indeed "Baroque," since TM copied it from *Simplicissimus*.
139/191	gentle sir	In the German original, L. addresses Kretzschmar in the second person plural, an antiquated and courtly form of address.
139/191	misericord	Mercy, compassion. Woods's translation for the antiquated term *Erbärmde*, which TM again took from *Simplicissimus*.

CHAPTER SUMMARIES AND PAGE-BY-PAGE COMMENTARIES ♦ 157

139/191	neither cold nor hot	See Revelations 3:15–16. This passage is another example of L.'s recurring association with coldness.	
140/192	*contritio*	Contrition. Theologically speaking, the act of regretting a sin out of sincere penitence, as opposed to *attritio*, which describes regret motivated by a fear of punishment. According to Luther, only *contritio* leads to the forgiveness of sins, whereas in Catholic teaching both *contritio* and *attritio* can lead to salvation. The distinction will be further developed in chapters XXV and XLVI.	
140/192	Holy Writ under the bench	An expression from the Chapbook.	
140/193	"step outside the path"	Though this phrase may sound Biblical, *Der Schritt vom Wege* is actually the title of a 1939 film by Gustav Gründgens (1899–1963). The reference seems incongruous with the rest of this chapter although it is perhaps worth noting that Gründgens, an erstwhile friend of the Manns who put his considerable talents as an actor and director at the service of the Nazis, appears in thinly disguised form as the protagonist of the novel *Mephisto* (1936) by TM's son Klaus (1906–1949).	
140/193	laboratory work of the Alchemist and sorcerer	Although L. begins by comparing music to theology, he then moves it into the vicinity of alchemy and the Black Arts (the German speaks explicitly of *Schwarzkünstler*).	
140/193	Apostasy is an act of faith	See Schleppfuss's lectures in chapter XIII.	
140/193	"No use killing nettles"	A verbatim quotation from Prof. Kumpf. See 104/142.	
141/194	Albertus Magnus	Dominican monk and theologian (1193–1280) who also practiced alchemy and was therefore sometimes suspected of being a Black magician.	
141/194	*prima materia* […] *magisterium*	Med. Latin: "primal matter" and "sorcerer's stone," both basic ingredients in many alchemical formulas.	

141/195	*O homo fuge*	Latin: "Fly away, man!" A quotation from the Chapbook, where the words appear in blood on Faust's hand immediately after he cuts it open to seal the devil's pact. The phrase alludes to 1 Tim. 6:11.
141/195	making promises to art	The German phrase *Promission zu machen* is antiquated and used in the Chapbook specifically to indicate promises made to the devil.
142/195	how beauty happens	The paragraph that follows offers a description of the prelude to Act III of Wagner's *Die Meistersinger von Nürnberg* (1868). TM sent the passage to his musical advisor Theodor W. Adorno in order to determine whether the allusion was too obvious and expressed surprise when Adorno didn't recognize it.
143/197	a desperate heart	Another phrase from the Chapbook.
144/199	Art's vital need	Kretzschmar here develops ideas he already advanced in his lectures on Beethoven in chapter VIII.
145/200	Cherubini's *Wayfarer*	*The Cherubinic Wanderer* (1657), Baroque compendium of mystical writings by Angelus Silesius (Johann Scheffler; 1624–1677).

XVI

Having decided to study music, L. moves to Leipzig in order to begin his private studies with Wendell Kretzschmar. Leipzig is the city of Johann Sebastian Bach, whom nationalists have always loved to claim as one of the most canonically "German" composers, but also of Felix Mendelssohn (1809–1847), the Jewish composer who reintroduced Bach to the German public after a century of near oblivion. This productive tension will cast a long shadow over L.'s career: his preoccupation with premodern musical forms will allude to Bach, while his final work will be a symphonic cantata, a genre practically invented by Mendelssohn. Leipzig is also where L. first meets Esmeralda, the succubus-like prostitute who will infect him with syphilis and thereby initiate the devil's pact. Esmeralda has already been foreshadowed by the butterfly of the same name in chapter III and will reappear later in the novel as the mysterious Frau von Tolna. L. recounts their meeting in a letter to Z. written in a mockingly archaic idiom.

Time of composition: May 10–24, 1944. Time of narration: Summer 1943. Narrated time: 1905.

146/201	a pronounced taste for quotes	L.'s taste for parody, pastiche, and quotations has been shaped by Kretzschmar's lectures on Beethoven in VIII, and will later also come to characterize his musical compositions. TM thought about his own works (and specifically *DF*) along similar lines.
147/202	"shoving Holy Writ"	See 140/192.
148/204	Friday after The Purification, 1905	Candlemas, celebrated annually on February 2. The dating makes no sense; L. did not arrive in Leipzig until the fall of 1905. Perhaps TM intended to write "1906," although this would mean that roughly four months passed between the incident in the brothel and the composition of the letter, not "weeks" as Z. will claim on 156/214.
148/204	Ballistier	Someone who operates a siege weapon; a reference to Z.'s service in the artillery. The German *ballisticus* has an even more mocking ring to it.
148/204	feet and *morae*	In the study of poetry, a "foot" is a metrical unit that in turn is comprised of one or more *morae*. For instance, an Iambic foot is comprised of an unstressed and a stressed *mora*.
148/204	"In God shalt thou believe"	A folk saying that dates back to the seventeenth century.
148/204	Pleisse, Parthe, and Elster	The description of the city in the following paragraphs, like that of Halle in the previous chapters, was heavily influenced by the relevant entry in the *Encyclopedia Britannica*.
148/204	"That great city"	John 4:11.
148/204–5	its fairs, the autumnal variety	The great fair of Leipzig does indeed take place in the autumn, which cements the dating of L.'s arrival.
149/205	my Leipzig	A quotation from the "Auerbach's Cellar" scene in Goethe's *Faust I*, which takes place in Leipzig.
149/205	*centrum musicae*	Latin: "center of music." Leipzig is famous, among other things, for being the city of Johann Sebastian Bach.

149/205	Gewandhaus	The Gewandhaus is a famous concert hall in Leipzig. The Jewish composer and conductor Felix Mendelssohn, who among other things was responsible for the Bach revival of the nineteenth century, directed it from 1835 to 1841.
149/205	clavicymbal	Cembalo (an ancestor of the piano).
149/206	*punctum contra punctum*	Latin: "counterpoint."
150/206	*Gradus ad Parnassum*	1725 textbook on counterpoint by Johann Joseph Fux (1660–1741).
150/207	somewhat like our Schleppfuss	The porter's external appearance, his pronunciation, and his servile demeanor all mark him as another devil figure.
151/208	Auerbach's Inn	Famous tavern in Leipzig; the setting for one of the scenes in Goethe's *Faust*.
151/208	Lantern [...] the very red	Red lanterns are a traditional identifying mark of brothels.
151/208	through the entry a dame	L.'s adventures in the brothel were heavily influenced by a similar episode that TM found in a 1901 biography of Friedrich Nietzsche by Paul Deussen (1845–1919).
151/209	morphos, clearwings, esmeraldas	The comparison of the prostitutes to butterflies links this chapter to chapter III.
152/209	behold opposite me a piano	L. has already displayed similar behavior on 122/167.
152/209	hermit's prayer [...] *Freischütz*	The "hermit's prayer" concludes Carl Maria von Weber's opera about a devil's pact, *Der Freischütz*, and functions as a kind of musical exorcism, in which demonic influences are dissolved by the musical purity of C major.
152/209	*ars metrificandi*	Latin: "the art of meter."
152/209	"comprehensive worldview"	TM appears to have invented this quote as a way of setting up the subsequent discussion of Romanticism.
152/210	later Beethoven and his polyphony	This phrase owes a lot to Adorno's unconventional use of the term "polyphony" in both "Late Style in Beethoven" and *Philosophy of New Music*. The idea will be developed more fully in chapter XXV.
153/958	Beethoven never achieved	See Kretzschmar's second lecture in VIII, which L. is here combining with some of his own reflections from 82/931.

153/958	elves and nixies		A reference to *A Midsummer Night's Dream* (1842) by Felix Mendelssohn.
153/210	*J'espère vous voir ce soir*		French: "I hope to see you tonight, although that moment might possibly drive me mad." The hint of queer longing that we can detect in this phrase possibly alludes to the quite similar desires Z. seems to project onto L.
153/211	*Ecce epistola!*		Latin: "Look at the letter [I have written]!" A reference both Nietzsche, who wrote a book called *Ecce Homo*, and to Jesus Christ, to whom these words traditionally refer.

XVII

Z.'s analysis of the letter from chapter XVI reveals much about L.'s sexuality and even more about Z.'s own.

Time of composition: May 30–June 6, 1944. Time of narration: Summer 1943. Narrated time: 1905.

157/215	not so much out of hot-bloodedness	Z.'s attitude towards heterosexual relationships is consistently characterized by coldness and analytical distance—a reminder that he is perhaps not entirely dissimilar to L.
157/215	cool irony [...] suit of armor	A probable reference to Dürer's *Knight, Death, and Devil*.

XVIII

In Leipzig, L. begins composing, although he dismisses the fruits of his labor as "root-canal work" (162/221).

Time of composition: June 9–15, 1944. Time of narration: Summer 1943. Narrated time: 1905–?.

160/218	strangely cabalistic	The Kabbalah is a Jewish mystical tradition with a strong numerological element.
160/219	he went so far as to commission	TM's description of L.'s apprenticeship is heavily influenced by Igor Stravinsky's (1882–1971) recollections of his studies with Nikolai Rimsky-Korsakov (1844–1908) in *Chronicle of My Life* (1935).

160/219	Grétry or Cherubini	André Grétry (1741–1813) and Luigi Cherubini (1760–1842) were composers of the Classical period, who lived a hundred years earlier than Berlioz, Clause Debussy (1862–1918), and the late Romantics from whom L. is deriving inspiration.
160/219	*particella* scores	Preliminary sketches of a musical score.
161/220	oratorio as a genre	Z. here implies that *The Lamentation of Doctor Faustus* is an oratorio. Later, he will consistently refer to it as a "symphonic cantata," a hybrid genre pioneered by Felix Mendelssohn.
161/220	even if one no longer considers it essential	Another echo of Kretzschmar's lectures in VIII on outworn conventions in late Beethoven.
161/221	*Phosphorescence of the Sea*	The most obvious model for this composition is Debussy's *La Mer* (1905), which carries the subtitle "Three Symphonic Sketches." Critics have also identified the string sextet *Transfigured Night* (1899) by Arnold Schoenberg (1874–1951), the *Firebird Suite* (1908) by Igor Stravinsky, and Mendelssohn's *Calm Sea and Prosperous Voyage* (1828) as possible models.

XIX

A little more than six months after his initial encounter with Esmeralda, L. travels to Pressburg to see her again. Although she warns him that she is infected with syphilis, he sleeps with her, contracting the disease and initiating the devil's pact. In subsequent months, L. consults two dermatologist to cure the initial symptoms of his infection, but both meet uncanny fates and he abandons any further attempts to seek treatment.

Time of composition: June 16–July 4, 1944. Time of narration: Summer 1943. Narrated time: 1906.

163/223	a little more than a year	Another inconsistency in the chronology; it would actually have been less than a year. See 148/208.

CHAPTER SUMMARIES AND PAGE-BY-PAGE COMMENTARIES ♦ 163

163/223	pierced by the arrow of fate		In addition to fate, the arrow is also a symbol of pestilence (via the Greek god Apollo and various Biblical passages) and of love (via the Greek god Eros)—both plausible reference points in relation to Esmeralda. Another possible referent is the Christian martyr Saint Sebastian, whose image plays an important role in TM's novella *Death in Venice* (1912), where it is associated both with homoeroticism and with art.
163/223	Apollo and the Muses		Not for the first time, Z. invokes the aid of the Muses for his epic task. In doing so, he puts the Greco-Roman world in opposition to the medieval one of the Faust story, but he also calls up irrational powers.
163/223	impudent porter		The German has *frecher Sendbote* (impudent emissary), which highlights that the porter is in the service of demonic powers.
164/224	the same man he was		That is, a virgin, since Z. told us on 158/217 that L. had "never 'touched' a female" prior to his first visit to the brothel.
164/224	first Austrian performance of *Salome*		The first Austrian performance of the opera *Salome* (1905) by Richard Strauss (1864–1949) took place in Graz, the provincial capital of Styria, on May 16, 1906. It was attended by many leading composers of the day as well as (supposedly) Adolf Hitler. Aggressively dissonant, *Salome* was instantly recognized as a foundational work of modern music and a definitive break with the nineteenth century.
164/225	Pressburg		Contemporary Bratislava, the capital of Slovakia. In 1906 it was a part of the Kingdom of Hungary (itself a part of the Austro-Hungarian Empire).
165/226	without a religious shudder		Z.'s "religious shudder" moves Esmeralda into the vicinity of Wagner's Kundry from the opera *Parsifal*; his line about one party forfeiting salvation while another finds it also recalls Senta and the Dutchman from Wagner's *The Flying Dutchman*.

165/226	nor will he have been the last	The most famous composer to employ "logograms" of this type is Johann Sebastian Bach (B♭–A–C–B♮, or B–A–C–H in the German notation system).
166/227	which Anglo-Saxons call a B	In the German system of musical notation, B♮ is known as "H," B♭ simply as "B." Other flats are designated by adding an "-es" or "-s" to the name of the note, making E♭ "Es," pronounced exactly like the letter "s." While Mann was busy working on *DF*, his contemporary Dmitri Shostakovich (1906–1975) integrated the logogram D–E♭–C–B (or D–Es–C–H, alluding to the German spelling "**D**mitri **Sch**ostakowitsch") into his Violin Concerto No. 1 (1947).
166/227	thirteen Brentano lieder	The number thirteen is presumably not an accident. Clemens Brentano (1778–1842) was a major figure of German Romanticism, known especially for his fantastical tales.
166/227	talented shipmate	The German is *Kegelbruder* or "bowling partner." There are many German folktales about foolhardy young men who challenge the devil to a bowling match.
166/228	a local infection	Presumably a genital chancre, the distinctive symptom of primary syphilis.
168/230	hallmark of a face in world history	A reference to Adolf Hitler.
168/230	"falls on the Rhine"	In German a play on the homophones *Rheinfall* ("the falls on the Rhine") and *Reinfall* ("failure, defeat").

XX

In Leipzig, L. strikes up a friendship with Rüdiger Schildknapp, whose description TM patterned on his own friend Hans Reisiger. Schildknapp is the first of many real-world acquaintances of TM to find their way into the novel, usually in unflattering form. L. starts to produce his first major compositions, favoring vocal music. He makes plans for an opera based on Shakespeare's Love's Labour's Lost, *hoping that Schildknapp will adapt the libretto.*

Time of composition: July 6–24, 1944. Time of narration: Summer 1943. Narrated time: 1906–1910.

169/232	I called out his name		As was the case at their moment of parting, Z. addresses L. by name, while L. refuses to reciprocate.
170/232	Schaffgosch Quartet		Unlike most other conductors, virtuosos, and musical ensembles mentioned in *DF*, the Schaffgosch Quartet is fictional.
170/232	Lydian movement		The Lydian is one of the church modes already mentioned on 84/115.
170/233	"I drain that cup at every feast"		An allusion to Gretchen's song in Goethe's *Faust I*. L. is clearly telling the truth, for when he later composes a violin concerto of his own, he will quote from Beethoven's Op. 132.
170/233	tempered [...] "pure" scales		"Pure scales" are ones in which the intervals between notes are determined by the ratios of whole numbers. Tempered scales divide the octave into a certain number of equivalent intervals. While many musicians and theoreticians have argued for the superiority of pure scales, L.'s justification doesn't make much sense, as tempered scales were invented precisely to simplify modulation.
171/233	Pythagoras' theory of cosmic harmony		See 67/94.
171/233	Paganini		Because of his wild appearance and preternatural playing, the violin virtuoso Niccolò Paganini (1782–1840) was sometimes rumored to have made a pact with the devil.
171/235	Schildknapp		Schildknapp's last name translates as "shield bearer," and thereby alludes to Dürer's engraving *Knight, Death, and Devil*. In all other regards, however, the character was inspired by TM's friend Hans Reisiger (1884–1968), who was not amused by the less-than-flattering portrait (*TM* privately called the depiction a "literary murder"). The introduction of Schildknapp marks an important turning point in *DF*: henceforth, many more characters inspired by real people will appear, as L.'s life becomes more intertwined with the events and the social circles of the early twentieth century.

171/235	*Love's Labour's Lost*	Comedy (1598) by William Shakespeare (1564–1616). Early editions of *DF* have *Love's Labour Lost*, and this spelling is adopted in the GKFA. The play revolves around a pact between the main characters, who swear an oath to renounce all contact with women to focus on their studies of philosophy. The theme foreshadows the conditions outlined by the devil in XXV.
172/236	*Purgatorio* and *Paradiso*	Two of the three main divisions of Dante's *Divine Comedy*. The one not mentioned here is, of course, the *Inferno*.
173/237	man in a parable from the *Purgatorio*	The reference is to the Roman poet Virgil (70–19 BCE). The theme of the artist whose achievements benefit only those who come after him will recur in *DF*.
174/238	music and speech, he insisted	Besides Kierkegaard, the following reflections are obviously influenced by Kretzschmar's lecture on Johann Conrad Beissel.
174/239	absolute music	"Absolute" music is music that is non-representational, i.e., not explicitly "about" anything. In nineteenth-century German music, there were long-standing theoretical disputes about whether the future of the art form lay with "programmatic" or absolute music. Richard Wagner and Johannes Brahms (1833–1897) were commonly seen as the figureheads of the respective camps.
174/239	*opera buffa*	Italian: "comic opera." More specifically, a genre of opera most closely associated with Italian music of the eighteenth century.
174–75/239	Don Armado [...] Berowne	Characters from *Love's Labour's Lost*.
179/246	"View yonder sight!"	The humor in German rests on the distinction between the formal demonstrative pronoun *jenes* and the informal demonstrative *das*. As such, Schildknapp's joke points back to L.'s struggles with formal and informal personal pronouns.

CHAPTER SUMMARIES AND PAGE-BY-PAGE COMMENTARIES ♦ 167

180/247	Any luck they had with him	The description of Schildknapp is suffused with subtle suggestions that he might be gay (as was his real-life model Hans Reisiger). This perhaps explains Z.'s obvious jealousy of him.
180/247	(German for "squire")	"Squire" is indeed the most literal translation of *Schildknapp*; I've chosen "shield bearer" instead to draw attention to the "shield" in Rüdiger's name, which parallels the "sword" in Rudi Schwerdtfeger. In the German, TM builds a further pun into this sentence by incorporating the rarely used term *reisig* ("errant"): a subtle reference to Schwerdtfeger's real-life model Hans Reisiger. Reisiger was not pleased by the allusion and convinced TM to change it in later printings.
181/248	something of a sponge	The German is *Krippenreiter*, a term for an impoverished knight, which continues the semantic games of the previous lines.
182/250	His eyes were exactly the same color as Adrian's	See 26/391

XXI

Several months have now passed since Z. began writing his biography of L., and we have arrived in October 1943. Z. reflects on several crucial battles in a war that is increasingly turning against Germany. Returning to the life of L., we learn about several of his compositions from his Leipzig period and get a detailed description of the Brentano Songs, the cycle in which L. first employed the Hetaera Esmeralda "logogram." We also learn about the first public performance of one of L.'s works.

Time of composition: July–August 30, 1944, with later revisions. Time of narration: October 1943. Narrated time: 1906–1910.

| 183/251 | Helene [...] breakfast beverage | A likely parody of Book IV of *The Odyssey* by Homer (ca. eighth century BCE), in which Helen serves her husband Menelaus a drink of nepenthe—the drug that alone makes their fraught marriage bearable. |

183/251	auspicious revival of our submarine war	The information that follows allows us to date Z.'s reflections to October 2, 1943. As in chapter I, Z.'s tone seems to waver between ironic distance to the Nazi regime and begrudging admiration of it.
183/251	a European Germany	The distinction between the cosmopolitan ideal of a "European Germany" and the Nazi vision of a "German Europe" recurs in several of TM's essays and lectures of the time period.
183/251	kidnapping the fallen Italian	Italian dictator Benito Mussolini (1883–1945) was deposed on July 25, 1943 and "rescued" (or kidnapped) by German paratroopers on September 12.
183/252	passionate scholar	Kurt Huber (1893–1943), a professor of psychology at the University of Munich and one of the members of the anti-Nazi resistance organization "The White Rose."
184/252	*va banque*	French: "all or nothing." Z.'s use of this phrase possibly alludes to an apocryphal exchange between Hermann Göring (1893–1946) and Hitler. Discussing plans for the invasion of Poland, Göring is supposed to have said, "we'd better not play *va banque*," to which Hitler supposedly replied, "I have played *va banque* all my life."
184/252	agitated state	Z. reminds us of a main compositional principle of *DF*: time of narration and narrated time constantly fuse with one another. This device will become increasingly central in the coming chapters.
184/253	King Claudius	In Shakespeare's *Hamlet* (ca. 1600).
184/253	City of Dürer	Nuremberg, which was bombed by the Allies on August 28, 1943. Willibald Pirckheimer (1470–1530) was a humanist and contemporary of Dürer.
185/253	had done away with its great man	Benito Mussolini, already alluded to on 183/251.
185/254	The price [...] has been paid	An estimated 100,000 German soldiers died at the Dnieper, another 350,000 were wounded. Soviet casualties are believed to be almost three times as high.

CHAPTER SUMMARIES AND PAGE-BY-PAGE COMMENTARIES ♦ 169

185/255	our European *lebensraum*		*Lebensraum* was the Nazi term for the conquered territories in the East, which were to be the subject of a giant project of settler colonialism. Z.'s use of the term represents one more example of his ambiguous embrace of Nazi terminology.
186/256	old and genuine, faithful and familiar		The German *des Alt- und Echten, des Treulich-Traulichen* parodies lines from Wagner's *Die Meistersinger von Nürnberg* and *Das Rheingold*. Z. is drawing a connection between German culture and the crimes of the Nazis.
188/258	eye-people and ear-people [...] the latter		TM himself frequently made this distinction, counting himself, like L., among the "ear-people" (*Ohrenmenschen*).
188/259	the magic of eyes		Z.'s tangent may indeed seem random, but the color of L.'s eyes was already highlighted on 26/39.
189/259	a trip to Basel		Friedrich Nietzsche spent much of his life in Basel and held a professorship there. The description of the concert that L. attends was heavily influenced by a newspaper article on an actual performance that took place there in 1943.
189/259	*musica riservata*		A particularly expressive style of music characteristic of the late sixteenth and early seventeenth centuries. With the exception of Dieterich Buxtehude (1637–1707), the composers mentioned in this paragraph all lived during this period.
189/260	a certain Someone		An allusion to folktales according to which the devil supplied the blueprints for Cologne cathedral.
189/260	Orchestre de la Suisse Romande		A real orchestra, though not founded until 1918.
190/261	"root-canal work"		See 162/221.
191/262	*corno di bassetto*		Italian: "basset horn." A member of the bassoon family, rarely used in music written after about 1840.

192/263	artistic sense	The German for "sense" here is *Verstand*, a term central to post-Kantian philosophy and more commonly translated as "mind." At stake here and throughout the rest of the paragraph is the question to what extent a modern artwork can still be considered a product of spontaneous inspiration rather than conscious intellectual labor. These reflections were heavily inspired by Adorno's *Philosophy of New Music*.
192/264	he himself aspired to a work	Z.'s worries are not exactly selfless, given that he has been commissioned to arrange the libretto for L.'s opera.
194/972	Through the night that now envelops	The final two lines of the poem "Abendständchen" (Evening Song) by Clemens Brentano.
194/266	with its lettered symbol	The logogram H-E-A-E-Es (or B-E-A-E-E♭) already mentioned on 166/227. The titles of the songs in this paragraph are all drawn from poems by Brentano.
196/269	Dr. Volkmar Andreae	Swiss conductor (1879–1962); an acquaintance of TM from his Zurich years.
196/269	used a crutch to walk	Another possible devil figure.

XXII

Z. reunites with L. on Buchel Farm to celebrate the wedding of L.'s sister Ursula to the optician Johannes Schneidewein. Z. informs L. that he, too, intends to get married. After some gentle mockery involving Shakespearean quotations, L. shifts the conversation to music and outlines his idea of a new "strict style" for Z. The system that he describes is that of dodecaphonic music as invented in real life by Arnold Schoenberg. Z. compares this system to the "magic square" that L. hung over his piano in Leipzig.

Time of composition: September 14–October 4, 1944. Time of narration: After October 1943. Narrated time: 1910.

198/270	vestiges of an older German	The German uses the compound adjective *stehen geblieben-altdeutsch* ("a static old German") aligning Schneidewein's speech more closely with the *nunc stans*, or "static now" of Kaisersaschern.

199/271	Tieck and Hertzberg	Ludwig Tieck (1773–1853) and Wilhelm Hertzberg (1813–1879) both translated Shakespeare into German. TM owned the Hertzberg edition of *Love's Labour's Lost*.
199/271	feast of the sacrifice	An unusual way to describe marriage, but congruent with a theme in Z.'s narration that we first observed on 6/12.
200/272	"Good eyes"	Another occurrence of the motif of eyes. Schneidewein's "good eyes" contrast with the "veiled cast" of L.'s own eyes mentioned in the previous paragraph. Eyes, of course, are traditionally regarded as windows to the soul.
200/272	smuggled the Devil out	The original uses the archaic term *wegpaschen*, an allusion to the scene "Entombment" in Goethe's *Faust II* (1832). L.'s thoughts about marriage as a Christian sacrament that wards off the devil also allude to the Chapbook.
200/273	"And shall be one flesh."	Matthew 19:5. L.'s subsequent commentary on this passage is heavily influenced by both Nietzsche and Kierkegaard.
201/274	"Well roared, lion!"	Z., currently at work condensing *Love's Labour's Lost*, uses a Shakespearean phrase, from *A Midsummer Night's Dream*. There may also be an ironic allusion to 1 Pet. 5:8, where the devil is referred to as a "roaring lion."
202/275	"But if thou [...] greasily"	Quotes from *Love's Labour's Lost* (IV.1).
203/277	freedom that has begun to coat talent	L.'s arguments in favor of an "archaic restorative" revolution that would seek to counteract an excess of "freedom" do not seem confined to the realm of music. The passage anticipates the so-called Conservative Revolution of the Weimar Republic.
203/277	Freedom [...] dialectic reversal	A central idea of *DF*, and one that TM would have found explicated in great detail in the works of his musical advisor Theodor W. Adorno.

203/278	moreover, that's a political song	A quotation from the "Auerbach's Cellar" scene in Goethe's *Faust I*. Woods translates the German *übrigens* as "moreover"; a more literal translation would be "however": L. is trying to distance art from politics. This rhetorical move will recur in the coming chapters, where L. will repeatedly claim to speak only about art, but will do so in vague terms that permit a much broader interpretation.
204/278	You're thinking of Beethoven	The following paragraphs recap and develop Kretzschmar's Beethoven lectures in VIII, but also summarize Adorno. The gist of L.'s argument is that once freedom (typified here by the development section of the sonata form) becomes absolute, it will inevitably revert into its opposite.
204/279	It does so in Brahms	By reading Brahms as an even more extreme exponent of Beethoven, L. is preparing the way for TM's argument that all of nineteenth-century German music stands in the shadow of Beethoven's Op. 111.
204/279	strict style	See 61/87.
205/279	both the horizontal and vertical	By "horizontal" L. means the melody, which in the logic of *DF* is associated with polyphony and the fugue. By "vertical" he refers to harmony, associated with homophony and the sonata. TM's manuscript shows that he initially even used the terms "melody" and "harmony" here. The substitution of "vertical" and "horizontal" strengthens the link to the magic square.

205/280	twelve steps of the tempered semitone alphabet	In the remainder of this paragraph and the next few, L. describes the twelve-tone technique that in real life was developed by Arnold Schoenberg in 1923, and which TM knew via Adorno's *Philosophy of New Music*. This arguable act of plagiarism caused a public rift between Mann and Schoenberg (who were basically neighbors in Pacific Palisades) and caused TM to add an acknowledgment of Schoenberg's "intellectual property" to all editions of the novel beginning with the third in 1948. Also noteworthy here is L.'s equation of tone rows with words, and of the chromatic scale with the alphabet. This continues his general tendency to fuse musical with lexical expression.
206/280	old contrapuntal devices	Schoenberg did indeed borrow contrapuntal devices to add flexibility and variation to his tone rows. In an "inversion," the tone row occurs back-to-front. In a "crab canon," the intervals are inverted. An inverted crab canon combines the two techniques.

XXIII

Upon completion of his studies in Leipzig, L. moves to Munich where he quickly wins the affections of Inez and Clarissa Rodde, the daughters of his landlady Frau Senatorin Rodde. The product of a bourgeois culture that no longer feels quite timely in the early twentieth century, Inez and Clarissa deepen TM's portrait of the "Generation of 1914," as do many of the other figures who visit the Rodde household. On a bicycle excursion into the Bavarian countryside, L. discovers the Schweigestill Farm in the village of Pfeiffering (Fig. 11), a location that bears an uncanny resemblance to Buchel Farm on which he grew up.

Time of composition: October 6–November 1, 1944. Time of narration: After October 1943. Narrated time: 1910–1911.

208/270	He needed an overview [...]	The compositional problems created by the invariable interaction of part and whole would have been much on TM's mind, since his American translator, Helen Tracy Lowe-Porter, was working on the English-language version of *DF* even while its author was still writing the novel.
209/285	Ramberg Strasse	Street near the Academy of Fine Arts in Munich's university district Schwabing. TM's mother, on whom Frau Senatorin Rodde is modeled, moved here in 1893; TM lived in the vicinity during the 1890s.
209/285	Giacomo Meyerbeer	Prolific composer of Grand Operas in the French style, and thus regarded as a less-than-serious musician by many German intellectuals of the early twentieth century. This disdain was only increased by the fact that Meyerbeer (1791–1864) was Jewish.
212/289	*Sezession*	The term *Sezession* can refer to any number of artistic movements in the German-speaking world of the late nineteenth century that rebelled against the academic art of their time. The Munich Secession was founded in 1892.
213/290	Zapfenstösser-Orchestra	Fictional orchestra, modeled on the "Kaim Orchestra" which developed into the Munich Philharmonic. "Zapfenstösser" translates as "cone thruster"—in conjunction with Schwerdtfeger's name an unmistakably phallic reference.
213/291	steel-blue eyes	Schwerdtfeger's steel-blue eyes offer another variation on the theme established on 26/39 and 182/250.
214/291	Saw away at his cello	The German has *sein Cello zu fegen*, which draws a connection to Schwerdtfeger's name with its possibly phallic implications.
214–15/292	"View yonder sight!"	See 179/246.
215/293	*bel étage*	The second floor of a stately residence, usually with higher ceilings than the other floors.

215/294	Felix Mottl		A historical figure. In 1910, Mottl (1856–1911) was general music director at the Bavarian court and director of the Royal Opera.
215/294	Herr von Gleichen-Russwurm		Carl Alexander Freiherr von Gleichen-Rußwurm (1865–1947) was an acquaintance of TM's and an actual great-grandson of Friedrich Schiller (1759–1805).
216/295	*sit venia verbo*		Latin idiom meaning "excuse me for saying this!"
216/295	Capua		Italian town proverbial as a place of wealth and lax morals.
217/295	Regency		The regency of Prince Regent Luitpold, necessitated by the mental illness of his nephew, King Otto of Bavaria, lasted from 1886 to 1912.
217/296	fusty Wagnerism		Mann had already attacked Munich's Wagner cult in his 1933 lecture "Suffering and Greatness of Richard Wagner," which led to a "Protest of the Wagner City Munich" signed by more than a hundred cultural dignitaries, mostly from the ultra-nationalist and Nazi camps.
218/298	bleating laughter		Another example of uncanny laughter in the novel. Spengler's double, Zink, had already been compared to a faun on 213/289.
219/299	Pfeiffering near Waldshut		Fictional toponyms, but closely modeled on the actual villages of Polling and Weilheim, twenty-five miles southwest of Munich. TM's mother, Julia Mann (1851–1923), moved to Polling in old age, where her son frequently visited her.
219/299	the Schweigestill farm		Modeled on the Schweighart farm (Fig. 11), in close proximity to Julia Mann's apartment in Polling.
219/299	Klammer Pool […] Rohmbühel		*Klammerweiher* (Clinging Pool) is the name of a small pond in Bad Tölz, twenty-five miles east of Polling, where TM owned a vacation home in the early twentieth century. The real-life model for Rohmbühel Hill can be found just outside Polling.

219/300	an elm, I admit	See 14/22, with its description of the linden tree at Buchel.
220/300	Winged Victory of Samothrace [...] abbot's study	The Greek goddess of victory, Nike. Both the "Nike parlor" (Fig. 12) and the abbot's study, which will become central locations in the novel, are based on actual rooms at the Schweighart farm.
220/301	Painters were like daisies	Polling was indeed a popular destination for painters from the Munich Secession.
221/302	understanding [...] most important thing in life	This attitude will become characteristic of Else Schweigestill, symbolically associating her with the Virgin Mary in the Christological scheme of *DF*.
224/306	glance at the pigsty	Pigs never seem to be very far away from the places where the devil appears in *DF*. In Matthew 8:32, Jesus drives the demons that have possessed two Gadarene supplicants into a herd of these animals.

XXIV

L. spends most of 1911 and 1912 in the company of Rüdiger Schildknapp in Palestrina, a small Italian town that TM had also frequented as a young man. There he composes his first major work, the opera Love's Labour's Lost, *in the same place where TM wrote his first novel* Buddenbrooks *(1901). Z. visits L. in 1912 and uses the bawdy nature of Shakespeare's text to engage in speculations about sex and marriage that strongly suggest his jealousy of Schildknapp.*

Time of composition: November 24–December 12, 1944. Time of narration: After October 1943. Narrated time: 1911–1912.

226/308	Palestrina	TM himself lived in Palestrina with his brother Heinrich (1871–1950) for part of the summer 1895, and again for several visits between 1896 and 1898. As Z. already indicates, the town is most famous as the birthplace of the composer Giovanni Pierluigi da Palestrina (1525–1594), a master of polyphonic composition. In choosing his vacation spot, L. is signaling his intention to devote himself to the study of early modern music.

226/308	breed of little black pigs	See 224/306.
227/309	stately matron	Signora Manardi's physical description resembles that of L.'s mother and of Elsa Schweigestill. Together, these three mother-types are symbolically associated with the Virgin Mary in the Christological scheme of *DF*.
227/310	of somewhat simple wits	The feeble-minded Amelia possibly foreshadows L.'s later syphilitic madness.
228/311	*quest'uomo*	Italian: "what a man!"
228/311	*distinti forestieri*	Italian: "distinguished foreigners."
228/311	*contadino*	Italian: "farmer."
228/311	*libero pensatore*	Italian: "freethinker."
229/312	*regie*-cigarettes	Cigarettes that have been properly taxed by the Italian state. Here as throughout these pages Z. is using superfluous Italian terms to show off his cosmopolitanism and erudition.
229/312	*Fa sangue il vino*	Italian: "wine fortifies the blood."
229/313	demonic Pan-like head	As is usually the case (see e.g., 6/12 or 12/20) Z.'s encomia to classical antiquity seemingly unintentionally conclude on a demonic note.
230/313	"View yonder sight!"	Another reference to 179/246.
230/314	scene set in Armado's house	*Love's Labour's Lost* I, 2
231/315	to take poetic revenge	Z. projects onto Shakespeare's play notions of jealousy and romantic rivalry, which may be indicative of his own feelings about Schildknapp, but also foreshadows the latter love triangle involving L., Schwerdtfeger, and Marie Godeau.
231/315	dark lady of the second sonnet series	The "Dark Lady" (so-called because of her hair color, not because of any association with the "dark arts") is a poetic persona that occurs in Shakespeare's sonnets 127–52. As Z. already notes, she too is part of a love triangle.

232/316	begot in the ventricle [...] womb of *pia mater*	Shakespeare's anatomical correlative to the creative process anticipates the devil's description of L.'s syphilitic infection in XXV. The *pia mater* (Latin: "tender mother"—an epithet also commonly applied to the Virgin Mary) is the innermost of three membranes that envelop the brain and spinal cord. Meningeal syphilis causes the formation of swollen masses of tissue ("gumma") on the *pia mater*.
232/987	"He who seeketh hard things [...]"	Not from the Letter to the Hebrews but actually Luther's translation of the second half of Proverbs 25:27.
232/317	"study" and "barbarism"	Another example of the thematic opposition between "culture" and "barbarism." TM translates the Shakespearean term "study" as *Bildung* (= humanist education), making this connection even more evident.
232/317	Even Berowne [...] admits	In *Love's Labour's Lost* I, 1.
233/318	weary of Romantic democracy	The link between Romanticism and democracy is somewhat unorthodox, though very characteristic of TM ever since his 1922 lecture "On the German Republic."
232/318	esoteric spirit [...] exaggerated itself as parody	This formulation touches on both Wendell Kretzschmar's thoughts about Beethoven's late style and TM's own opinions about modernist literature.
233/318	*Pranzo*	Italian: "lunch."
234/318	*Bevi! Bevi!*	Italian: "Drink! Drink!"
234/319	Via Torre Argentina	TM's own address during his stays in Rome in 1895 and 1896–98.
235/320	that neither had ever touched a woman	Another instance of the theme of homosexuality and homosociality that pervades the novel.
236/321	roué of potentialities	A "roué" is a rake, a man devoted to sensual pleasure.
236/322	*noli me tangere*	Latin: "do not touch me." See John 20:17.

XXV

During a night alone in his residence in Palestrina, L. is visited by a shape-shifting stranger. The question whether it is the actual devil or a figment of L.'s feverish imagination remains unresolved and causes Z. much anguish. The visitor first converses with L. about the nature of syphilis, describing the disease and how it can precipitate artistic inspiration while also making clear that L.'s infection should be understood as a pact in which he is granted twenty-four years of superlative creativity in exchange for his soul. Shifting his external appearance, the visitor then talks about the crises of music in the early twentieth century, before changing form yet again and offering a description of a hell in which sinners are constantly tossed back and forth between extreme heat and extreme cold.

Time of composition: December 12, 1944–February 20, 1945. Time of narration: After October 1943. Narrated time: Summer 1911 or 1912.

237/323	The Document to which repeated reference has been made [...]	The narrative device of the found document allows Z. to assume a position of skeptical distance to L.'s conversation, but it also recalls a similar found text in chapter 25 (!) of the Chapbook.
238/324	He apparently used music paper because [...]	Plausible, but L.'s choice of writing material also reminds us how closely intertwined musical and textual composition are in *DF* (compare L.'s description of twelve-tone rows as "words" on 174/238). It also moves L. and Z., the composer and the author, closer together. In German, the word for musical notes (*Noten*) is not the same as the one for textual notes (*Notizen*), but they are nevertheless related, a fact that TM's musical advisor Theodor W. Adorno would later also exploit in his essay collection *Noten zur Literatur* (Notes to Literature, 1958).
238/324	Mum, Mum's the Word	The German *Weistu was so schweig* is a quotation from chapter 65 of the Chapbook, which in turn quotes a phrase allegedly used by Martin Luther. There are several other quotations from the Chapbook scattered throughout the following paragraphs.
238/325	by the bitter cold	See 8/15
238/325	*in eremo*	Latin: "in the desert." Another phrase used by Luther.

239/325		Kierkegaard on Mozart's *Don Juan*	Part I, chapter 2 of *Either—Or* (1843) by Søren Kierkegaard. *Don Juan*, of course, is another story about a character doomed to hell. Kierkegaard explicitly contrasts it with the Faust myth.
239/326		seated upon the horsehair couch	L.'s vision is closely patterned on Ivan Karamazov's conversation with the devil in Book XI, chapter 9 of *The Brothers Karamazov* (1880) by Fyodor Dostoevsky (1821–1881).
239/326		*Chi è costà*	Italian: "Who is there?"
239/326		Who speaks familiarly with me?	In the original, the devil uses informal pronouns, a form of address that would have been grossly insulting in this context. A similar exchange takes place in *The Brothers Karamazov*.
240/327		a more spindled figure	The external appearance of the devil in this first part of the vision is partly inspired by *The Brothers Karamazov*, but also recalls the porter in XVI.
240/327		*strizzi*	Bavarian dialect for "pimp."
240/327		tramontane	A cold wind "from beyond the mountains."
240/328		giving forth cold	See 8/15.
241/328		You say only such things as are in me	The question whether L.'s interlocutor is real or only a product of a fevered imagination is central to *The Brothers Karamazov* as well.
241/329		shoved Holy Writ under the door	Expression from the Chapbook, already used on 140/192.
242/330		Master *Dicis-et-non-facis*	See 106/145.
242/330		*Dicis et non es*	Latin: "You say it and [yet] don't exist."
242/330		Where I am, there is Kaisersaschern	An ironic self-quotation by TM, who, when he arrived in the United States in 1938, had self-confidently announced "Where I am, there is Germany" in response to the question whether he missed his home country when he arrived in the United States in 1938.
242/330		German to the core [...] cosmopolitan at heart	The idea that true German identity implied a cosmopolitan component was central to many of Mann's political writings of the 1930s and 1940s.

242/331	in good Dürer fashion, freeze to pursue the sun	Albrecht Dürer, like many other great German writers and artists, spent time in Italy. The phrase "freeze to pursue the sun" is taken from one of his letters.
243/331	*Carcer* [...] *condemnatio*	Terms taken from chapter 16 of the Chapbook, in which the devil explains the nature of hell to Faustus.
243/332	hour-glass [...] square of numbers	See 102/138.
243/332	Black Kesperlin [...] Samiel	See 106/145 and 86/118. Samiel is the name of the demonic figure in *Der Freischütz*.
244/333	Johann Balhorn of Lübeck	A sixteenth-century printer infamous for the many mistakes he introduced into his books. The German verb *verballhornen* (= to corrupt a text) derives from his name.
244/333	Sammael [...] Angel of poison	In Hebrew.
244/333	Conformation [...] leaf butterfly	See 17/27 and the surrounding discussion.
244/333	song with its alphabetical symbol	L.'s "Oh Sweet Maiden" from his Brentano song cycle. See 166/227.
245/334	*salva venia*	Latin: "with all due respect."
245/334	the French measles	A common euphemism for syphilis.
245/334	Hold your tongue!	In the original, L. first uses the informal address with the devil, then switches to formal address after being mocked for it.
245/334	silence soon these five years	Evidence that the conversation takes place in 1911, not 1912.
245/335	*Respice finem*	Latin: "Consider the end." The phrase occurs in the apocryphal Sir. 7:40, but also in the medieval collection of tales *Gesta Romanorum*, which will come to play a main role in *DF*.
245/335	upon your local Zion	See the conversation between L. and Z. on 202/275 and surrounding.
245/335	twenty-four years, shall we say	The traditional timespan already accorded to Faustus in the Chapbook.
246/336	he may plainly and honestly deem himself a god	The mood swings described in this paragraph are indeed characteristic of syphilitic infection, but may also point to two of Mann's specific references, the composer Hugo Wolf (1860–1903) and Friedrich Nietzsche.

246/337	pains as one knows from a fairy tale	Reference to "The Little Mermaid" by Hans Christian Andersen (1805–1875), another text that deals with themes of coldness vs. warmth as well as art vs. life. The mermaid's tail also anticipates the reference to flagellates on 247/338.
247/337	I am not of the family Schweigestill	A pun on the name Schweigestill ("say nothing in silence")
247/338	inkpot	See 107/146.
247/338	small delicate folk [...] the flagellants	Actually "flagellates." A flagellate is a bacterium with a whip-like tail. The devil is jokingly comparing these to the "flagellants" of the Middle Ages, who mortified their flesh with whips and other instruments. In both German and English, the term *scourge* is similarly applied both literally to flails and metaphorically to deadly diseases.
247/338	*spirochaete pallida*	Now outdated Latin name for the bacterium that causes syphilis.
247/338	*flagellum haereticorum fascinariorum*	See 112/152.
247/338	*fascinarii*	Latin: "bewitchers." Derived from a name for bronze castings of a phallus, often worn around the neck as a token of divine protection.
248/339	*faunus ficarius*	Latin: "fig faun." A term used in the *Malleus Maleficarum* to designate incubi and other demonly creatures. Zink was already compared to a faun on 213/289.
248/340	was not of the brain	A reference to the fact that not all syphilitic infections penetrate the blood-brain barrier.
249/340	metaspirochaetosis	A term apparently of TM's invention.
249/340	meninges	A set of three membranes that envelop the brain and spinal cord.
249/340	dura mater [...] tentorium [...] pia	The dura mater (Latin: "tough mother") is the outermost of the meninges, the tentorium cerebelli (Latin: "brain tent") its extension into the brain. The pia mater (already mentioned on 232/316) is the innermost of the meninges.
249/340	parenchyma	Greek: Soft tissue on the inside of an organ.

249/341	The Philosopher	Aristotle (384–322 BCE).
250/342	feverish hearth	Woods's literal translation of the perfectly ordinary German term *Fieberherd* ("infected spot").
250/343	osmotic growths	See 23/35.
250/343	*sine pudore*	Latin: "without shame."
250/343	speculate the elements	See 16/25.
251/343	meninx	Singular of "meninges" (249/340).
251/344	If in a rapture a man [...]	A reference to a letter by Hugo Wolf dated February 22, 1888.
252/345	All they give, do the gods [...]	Lines of verse from a letter by Goethe, written in 1777.
252/345	*Si Diabolus non esset mendax* [...]	See 106/144.
252/345	*non datur*	Latin: "That is not given."
252/345	The artist is the brother of the felon	An idea taken from Nietzsche, but also characteristic of TM's own oeuvre, such as his novella *Tonio Kröger* (1903), in which a writer is briefly mistaken for a felon.
253/346	"fresh idea"	Another possible translation would be "inspiration." For this recurring motif see especially 192/263.
253/347	*meilleur*	French: "better." The question whether great art has to be an original creation or can instead "improve" upon found materials is central also to Mann's own modernist aesthetics.
253/347	spectacles rimmed in horn	The devil's second guise bears a marked resemblance to TM's musical advisor Theodor W. Adorno. When Adorno inquired about this, TM sent him a cheeky denial, asking "do you even wear glasses?" Somewhat incredibly, Adorno, who nearly always wore horn-rimmed glasses, seems to have been satisfied by this deflective maneuver.
254/348	folklorists and seekers of neoclassical asylum	This attack on musical neoclassicists (such as Igor Stravinsky) as well as on ethnologically minded modernists (such as Béla Bartók [1886–1945]) owes a lot to Adorno's *Philosophy of New Music*, which TM consulted extensively in manuscript form while he was writing this chapter.

254/349	Composition itself has grown too difficult	This paragraph, too, summarizes and quotes ideas from *Philosophy of New Music*. It furthermore refers back to Kretzschmar's Beethoven lectures in VIII, with their interpretation of "late style" as a return to musical convention, though under the sign of parody.
255/349	the diminished seventh [...] at the opening of Opus 111	Another reference that links this part of the conversation to Kretzschmar's Beethoven lecture in VIII. However, the devil is referring to the opening chord of the first movement, which Kretzschmar's lecture didn't cover.
255/349	lend the chord its specific weight	See 59/84.
255/350	In every bar he dares conceive, the general technical problem [...]	The devil is claiming (again summarizing and quoting from *Philosophy of New Music*) that modern music leaves no room for subjective expression, since the aesthetics of genius have themselves become a cliché by the end of the nineteenth century. Instead, composers in the twentieth century are reduced to solving mere technical puzzles placed upon them by their material—a return to the "objectivity" that also characterized early modern polyphony.
257/352	Criticism of ornament, of convention, of abstract generality [...] all one and the same.	According to the devil (and Adorno), musical Romanticism began as a revolt against the "ornament" and "convention" that characterized musical classicism,—that is, the prevalence of set motifs and musical forms, such as the rondo or minuet. But by the dawn of the twentieth century, the "abstract generality" to which its subjective aesthetics laid claim have become conventional as well.
257/353	Parody [...] so very woebegone	TM had begun to see his own art as a parody of nineteenth-century forms even before the First World War. This back-and-forth can thus also be read on the metaliterary level as an engagement with James Joyce (1882–1941), whose radical modernism TM both feared and admired as possibly superior to his own craft.

257/353	the Christian enamoured of aesthetics	Kierkegaard, whom L. was reading at the beginning of the chapter. This entire paragraph is saturated with allusions to Kierkegaard.
258/354	to intimate that you should break through it	The first mention of the important theme of "breaking through," which will henceforth recur multiple times in a threefold sense: in the aesthetic sense of a "breakthrough towards new music," in a military sense as a penetration of enemy lines, and in the socio-political sense of a departure from democracy and creation of a fascist state.
258/355	by homebaked bread alone	Matthew 4:4.
258/355	You will lead, you will set the march	The German for "lead" is *führen*, which connects L. to Hitler. The devil's promises here also raise questions about the narrative as a whole, for despite Z.'s assurances to the contrary, we never get any sense that L. does indeed set the tone for the future.
259/355	you will break through the laming difficulties of the age	Another reference to "breaking through," this time in an at least dual cultural and social sense. The term "laming difficulties" is possibly also a punning allusion to the devil, whose clubfoot is the subject of several jokes in *DF*.
259/356	Yet again the look of the fellow on the couch was changed	The devil's third iteration resembles Eberhard Schleppfuss from chapter XIII.
259/356	*légèrement*	French: "lightly."
260/357	*pernicies* [...] *confutatio*	Terms describing hell, which the devil previously used on 243/331.
260/357	that it lies hidden from language [...] "hopelessness"	In his diary entry for February 20, 1945, TM makes clear that his description of hell was inspired by the torture chambers of the Gestapo.
262/359–60	*attritio cordis* [...] *contritio*	Latin: "Attrition of the heart ... contrition." See 140/192.
262/360	choice between extreme cold and fire	This aspect of hell is already mentioned in chapter 16 of the Chapbook. It also relates to L.'s innate coldness and ironically to Rev. 3:16.
262/360	prideful remorse— that of Cain	In Genesis 4:13, also discussed in chapter 68 of the Chapbook.

263/361	*non plus ultra*	Latin: "no more beyond."
263/362	once again [...] as the male bawd	See 240/327.
263/362	*Ingenium* [...] *memoriam*	See 36/54.
263/362	*figuris, characteribus* [...] *incantationibus*	Latin: "figures, characters, and incantations." Traditional elements of black magic, here applied to music.
264/362	Spesser Forest	Forest in central Germany, about twenty miles east of Frankfurt, where Faust first encounters the devil in chapter 2 of the Chapbook.
264/362	no circles	Traditional figure of incantation, but also reference to the circle of fifths.
264/362	merely for confirmation	In most Christian denominations, the confirmation reinforces the covenant between the individual and God created by baptism—just like this second appearance of the devil reinforces the pact drawn up by L.'s pursuit of Hetaera Esmeralda.
264/362	*ab dato recessi*	Latin: "from the day of the contract."
264/363	you must renounce all who live [...]. You may not love	This clause is already mentioned in chapter 6 of the Chapbook. In *DF*, it is foreshadowed by L.'s obsession with *Love's Labour's Lost*.
264/363	*Caritas*	Latin: "charity." Theologically speaking, non-sensual love.
267/365	*giornali*	Italian: "newspapers." By withdrawing into his inner conversation with the devil, L. has missed out on traditional activities of the liberal nineteenth-century public sphere: debates about government and the study of newspapers.

XXVI

A year has passed since Z. began writing his biography, and German military defeats are multiplying. German cities are routinely being bombed and even a large-scale invasion across the English Channel by Allied forces no longer seems out of the question. Back in 1912, L. returns from his Italian journey and takes up residence at the Schweigestill farm.

CHAPTER SUMMARIES AND PAGE-BY-PAGE COMMENTARIES ♦ 187

Time of composition: April 12, 1945–May 16, 1945. Time of narration: April 1944. Narrated time: 1912–1913.

267/366	April 1944		While Z. has been working on his biography for a year, his real-life creator took two years for the same task. By April 1945 the Second World War was in its last days; Germany's unconditional surrender took place on May 8, 1945.
267/366	Pension Gisella		A real-life hotel in which TM lived from September to October 1902.
267/367	Fortress Europe		See 5/11.
268/368	attack on our European castello		The Normandy landings (D-Day) took place on June 6, 1944.
270/371	*semper idem*		Latin: "always the same." Compare Z.'s reference to the *nunc stans*, or "static now" of Kaisersaschern on 39/57.
271/373	a dialect form of the even more archaic		The original characterizes the dialect as having "stood still in the Old German," which emphasizes the general sense of stasis highlighted by this passage (the German term Waltpurgis uses is *stat*). Another example of the theme of mythic repetition.
272/374	eighteen years		Most German editions have "nineteen years." Woods corrects an inconsistency in TM's chronology.
273/376	a metal whistle whose tone was adjustable by a screw		Thus a primitive flute, which provides another example of the incantatory power of music. Compare also the story of Orpheus and Cerberus in the tenth book of the *Metamorphoses* (8 CE) by Ovid (43 BCE–17 CE).
274/378	the dramatist Richard Voss		The poet Richard Voss (1851–1918) does indeed relate such an episode in his memoirs.
276/381	easy communication with the capital		Freising is located roughly 10 miles northeast of Munich

XXVII

Now settled in Pfeiffering, L. composes a number of new works, including art songs on poems by William Blake (1757–1827) and John Keats (1795–1821) and the German sentimentalist poet Friedrich Gottlieb Klopstock (1724–1803). L.'s adaptation of Klopstock's "The Festival of Spring," as well as his orchestral fantasy Marvels of the Universe, *are both inspired by his study of works of deep sea exploration and of astronomy—or possibly, as L. insists, by actual travels to the bottoms of the ocean and into outer space in the company of a mysterious figure named Mr. Capercailzie. Z. reacts to these tales of exploratory travel with great unease, even if he does not yet realize that they bear a striking resemblance to an episode in the Faust Chapbook.*

Time of composition: May 21–August 6, 1945, with a long interruption in June and July. Time of narration: After April 1944. Narrated time: 1913–1914.

278/382	intended more to be read than heard	See Kretzschmar's third lecture in VIII.
278/383	"a god-witted man"	Epithet that Dürer applied to Martin Luther.
279/384	"Ode to a Nightingale" […] "Ode on Melancholy"	Both are famous poetic expressions of the theme of melancholy.
280/386	Klopstock's ode "The Festival of Spring"	Friedrich Gottlieb Klopstock (1724–1803) was one of the most important poets of the eighteenth century and an exponent of literary sentimentalism (*Empfindsamkeit*). The "drop in the bucket" mentioned in his poem is earth itself, which is described as but a tiny part of God's creation.
281/387	*attritio cordis*	See 140/192 and 262/359–60.
281/387	"speculate the elements"	See 16/25.
282/388	Needless to say, he had only read	In chapters 24 and 25 of the Chapbook, Faustus and Mephistopheles descend into hell and ascend to the stars during the eighth year of their pact. L.'s ostensible trip similarly takes place eight years after his first meeting with Hetaera Esmeralda, if one accepts TM's dating of 1905 rather than 1906 (see 148/204).
282/388	Mr. Capercailzie	A "capercaillie" is a large bird (a member of the grouse family) and one of the names given to the devil in chapter 61 of the Chapbook.

282/388	a spherical diving bell	TM's source for this description was the book *Half Mile Down* (1934) by the American ornithologist and marine biologist William Beebee (1877–1962), who explored the Atlantic Ocean in a bathysphere. Of possible relevance is the fact that Beebee was also an expert on pheasants, which are closely related to the capercaillie.
286/396	light-year […] some six trillion miles	The original has *9,5 Trillionen Kilometer*. TM, who consulted American astronomical sources, failed to realize that the English "trillion" corresponds not to German *Trillionen*, but rather to *Billionen*.
288/398	*une fleur du mal*	French: "a flower of evil." *Les Fleurs du mal* is the title of an 1857 poetry collection by Charles Baudelaire (1821–1867), which is often considered as an important forerunner of modernist poetry. The reference here serves as a reminder that the discussion between L. and Z. concerns not only humanism vs. anti-humanism, but also the nature and possibilities of modern art—or, as L. might put it, the question whether art can both produce new worlds and still be "moral."
288/398	*homo dei*	Latin: "man [as a creation] of God."
289/398	Your humanism is pure Middle Ages	This statement of L.'s inverts the more obvious way in which we might oppose L. and Z. and reminds us that L., despite his flirtations with polyphony and other aspects of early modernity, needs to be understood as a radically modern figure.
289/399	We once spoke about astrological conjuncture	On 207–8/283.
290/401	clockwork of the universe […] cosmos of tones	Recalls the discussion of Pythagoras on 103/139.

XXVIII

During the final years before the First World War, L. and Z. mingle in various Munich salons, especially that of the Schlaginhaufens, whose surname could be translated as "heap of punches" or "punch the rabble." As this little joke already implies, the Schlaginhaufens play host not only to artists and musicians, but also to some disturbingly reactionary figures. One of these is the philosopher Chaim Braisacher, who extols a völkisch *ideology and presents highly unusual interpretations of both music history and of the Bible, extolling primitivism and racial thought. His conversations with Baron von Riedesel showcase how traditional conservatism was overwhelmed by a new form of political reaction during the first third of the twentieth century.*

Time of composition: August 8–18, 1945. Time of narration: After April 1944. Narrated time: 1913–1914.

291/401	viola d'amore	See 6/12.
294/405	another kind of conservatism	The clash between Riedesel and Braisacher illustrates the opposition between national conservatism and nationalist reaction, which would find its fullest expression during the final years of the Weimar Republic, when the conservative German National People's Party became the unwitting handmaiden of the reactionary National Socialists.
294/406	we never got around to any detailed exchange	Like many a liberal of his generation, Z. instinctively despises the proto-fascism embodied by Breisacher, but takes no action to oppose him.
296/408	Perceive each note ambiguously [...] enharmonically	See 51/74 and 64/917.
296–97/409	moved on to matters of the Old Testament	The following lines draw heavily on *Die Wirklichkeit der Hebräer* (*The Truth of the Hebrews*; 1925), the main work by the philosopher Oskar Goldberg (1885–1953), who served as the main inspiration for Breisacher.
298/411	it has long since ceased to be *volk* and blood	Breisacher's lamentations about degeneration and emasculation remain, of course, a core feature of reactionary thinking to the present day.
298/411	The sons of Aaron had died because they had offered "strange fire"	In Leviticus 10:1–2. The German here is *artfremdes Feuer*, which might also be translated as "a fire foreign to the race."
300/413	At the very beginning of this account [...] annoying specimens of the race	See 10/17.

XXIX

In the final months before the outbreak of the First World War, Inez Rodde is courted by Dr. Helmut Institoris, an art historian who is the very epitome of a certain kind of post-Nietzschean intellectual, more devoted to concepts such as "life" and "beauty" than to questions of morality. Although Inez has a very different personality, and although she is secretly in love with Rudi Schwerdtfeger, she nevertheless encourages Institoris in his courtship, seeing in him a refuge from what she perceives as the "uprooted" (302/416) life her mother has bequeathed upon her

Time of composition: August 21–September 22, 1945. Time of narration: After April 1944. Narrated time: 1913–1914.

302/415	Twenty-two years have now passed	Woods silently corrects an error on Mann's part; German editions have "twenty-four years."
302/416	Both strove in different directions	Clarissa and Inez stand symptomatically for the fate of a generation for whom the fixed bourgeois certainties of the nineteenth century have become hollow. Both fail to find meaningful alternatives, and both pay for this with their lives.
302/418	"How strong and beautiful life is!"	In Mann's notebooks, he ascribes the same line to "a dreadful type of man cultivated by Nietzsche."
305/420	Dr. Institoris was […] man of the Renaissance	The contrast between Institoris and Inez is modeled on a recurring theme in Nietzsche, which finds expression, for example, in the opposition between "blond beasts" and "ascetic priests" in *On the Genealogy of Morals* (1887).
305/420	pessimistic moralism	A probable reference to the thought of Arthur Schopenhauer.
306/421	precarious balance between vitality and infirmity	Z. here is summarizing a lifelong artistic preoccupation of TM's that helps explain why the author was drawn to the depiction of disease over and over again throughout his career.
310/427	Cococello Club	A Munich artist's association and social club, named after a fictional musical instrument.
313/432	*in spe*	Latin: "full of hope"; in German, an idiomatic expression meaning "waiting in the wings."

XXX

The outbreak of the First World War represents a major turning point in German history. Most of L. and Z.'s acquaintances ardently support the war effort; in this, they are typical members of the "Generation of 1914." However, only Z. actually goes off to fight on the front lines. L. spends the early war years composing Gesta Romanorum, *a puppet opera inspired by the famous essay "On the Marionette Theater" (1810) by Heinrich von Kleist (1777–1811).*

Time of composition: September 25–October 7, 1945. Time of narration: After April 1944. Narrated time: 1914.

316/435	reserve staff sergeant		The German original is *Vize-Wachtmeister*, a Wilhelmine military rank that has a whiff of the ridiculous about it because it literally translates as "Assistant Policeman."
316/436	*Ah monsieur […] grand malheur!*		French: "Oh monsieur, the war, what great evil!"
317/436	And in general, I will not deny		Throughout the following paragraphs, Z. provides a summary of the so-called "Ideas of 1914," to which TM, then an ardent nationalist and defender of the monarchy, contributed several essays, as well as the book-length *Reflections of a Nonpolitical Man* (1918). TM liberally quotes from his earlier writings throughout this chapter.
317/437	quotidian morality is thereby superseded		Zeitblom's language here is very similar to that of Dr. Breisacher. Compare the latter's claim on 299/412 that "religion and ethics [are] related only insofar as the latter was the former in decay."
317/437	thoroughly unsoldierly playactor		The reference is to Kaiser Wilhelm II (1859–1941), whose proclivities for pompous military exercises were the source of ridicule even while he was still on the throne.
317/438	breaking through to a new form of life		See 258/354. In his wartime writings, TM advocated for the idea that state and culture, political and social/intellectual life should be one, but this notion is, of course, characteristic also of totalitarian societies.
318/438	(and we are always growing)		See 127/174.

318/438	a civil war		TM is likely thinking of the United States, for he greatly admired Walt Whitman (1819–1892), whose poems glorified the American Civil War as a crucible of democracy.
318/438	three fierce wars		The victorious wars against Denmark, Austria, and France fought between 1864 and 1871, which led to the proclamation of the Second Reich in 1871.
318/439	militaristic socialism yet to be defined		This phrase establishes a link between 1914 and 1933, when "militaristic socialism" would indeed take on a definite form.
320/442	*J'en ai assez* [...] *jours*		French: "I've had enough of that to last me till the end of my days!"
321/443	Frederick the Great's incursion into [...] Saxony		The subject also of one of TM's wartime essays, "Frederick the Great and the Grand Coalition" (1915).
322/445	Kleist [...] essay on marionettes		"On the Marionette Theater" by Heinrich von Kleist.
322/445	*Twelfth Night* [...] *Much Ado about Nothing* [...] *Two Gentlemen of Verona*		These three plays all contain courtship triangles and thus foreshadow the L.-Schwerdtfeger-Marie Godeau marriage plot that will take center stage in XLI and XLII.
322/445	*Gesta Romanorum*		A fourteenth- or fifteenth-century collection of exemplary tales that influenced Chaucer, Boccaccio, and Shakespeare among many other writers. The Latin title translates as *Deeds of the Romans*.
323/446	Monsieur Monteux		Pierre Monteux (1875–1964), the conductor of Diaghilev's *Ballets Russes* and a noted supporter of modern music. At the time of the composition of *DF*, Monteux was the chief conductor of the San Francisco Symphony Orchestra, where TM's son Michael was employed as a violist.
324/447	May God bless your *studia* [...] won't amount to much		L. is quoting one half of an old German student saying; Z. responds with the other half.

324/448	listening to you now it's as if I'm listening to them	An observation that strengthens the sense that TM wants us to read the student conversations of chapter XIV as precursors of the mindset that led to the "Ideas of 1914."
325/449	here too [...] the issue of breakthrough is dealt with	L. refers specifically to the last paragraph of Kleist's "On the Marionette Theater."
325/449	ultimately aesthetics is all things	Throughout this paragraph, Z. is channeling ideas from Nietzsche's *The Birth of Tragedy* (1872).
326/450	*kat exochen*	Greek: "pre-eminently."

XXXI

Z. records experiences from his brief time at the Western Front at the beginning of the First World War, where he witnessed scenes that make him question the naive patriotism of so many of his countrymen. Meanwhile, L. wins two disciples in Meta Nackedey and Kunigunde Rosenstiel, whose descriptions TM modeled on his real-life acquaintances Ida Herz (1894–1984) and Käte Hamburger (1896–1992). The presence of these devoted hangers-on strengthens both the Christological aspects of the work and its status as a "Nietzsche-novel." Back home from the War and recovering from a typhoid infection, Z. listens to L. describe the ideas that led him to compose Gesta Romanorum.

Time of composition: October 9–30, 1945. Time of narration: After April 1944. Narrated time: 1914–1915.

327/451	But we never got to Paris!	Note Z.'s unreflective use of the first-person plural throughout these pages.
327/451	*Je suis la dernière!* [...] *Méchants!*	French: "I am the last one! [...] You evil ones!"
328/452	an anxious, overcautious supreme commander	TM (or Z.) seems to be conflating the officer who gave the order to retreat, Lt. Col. Richard Hentsch (1869–1918), who was indeed regarded as anxious and overcautious, with German Chief of the General Staff Helmuth von Moltke the Younger (1848–1916), the nephew of the even more famous general Helmuth von Moltke the Elder (1800–1891).
329/454	*semper idem*	See 270/371.

331/456	elegiac habit of beginning every sentence	A first reference to elegy, a theme that will culminate with L.'s final composition, the *Lamentation of Doctor Faustus*. However, it is here treated in a comedic fashion. There is also a long tradition of anti-Semitic prejudice regarding the way Jews supposedly deform the German language. Z.'s description of Rosenstiel's speech patterns is a possible example of this, made all the more poignant by the fact that Rosenstiel's real-life model, the philosopher and literature professor Käte Hamburger, was a superb prose stylist.
332/459	Schildknapp had introduced Adrian to the book	On 322/445.
332/459	Rüdiger of the same-colored eyes	See 182/250.
334/462	*testo* in an oratorio	From Latin *testis*: witness. Traditional name for the narrator of an oratorio. Critics have pointed out that the orchestration of L.'s *Gesta Romanorum*, along with the use of a *testis*, moves the piece into close vicinity to Stravinsky's *L'Histoire du soldat* (1918).
334/461	*pièce de resistance*	French: "central/most important piece."
334/462	"Birth of Saint Gregory the Pope"	Like all the other stories summarized here, this is an actual tale from the *Gesta Romanorum*. TM would later use it as the subject for his novel *The Holy Sinner* (1951).
338/467	"Wolf's Glen" [...] "Bridal Wreath"	References to the Romantic devil's pact opera *Der Freischütz* by Carl Maria von Weber.
339/468	that person would be called art's redeemer	This passage adds the theme of "redemption" to the previously existing one of "breakthrough" and highlights L.'s endeavor to redeem art from the "intellectual coldness" and isolation into which it drifted during the nineteenth century. At the same time, L.'s dismissal of the "bliss of harmonic music's resolved cadences" indicates that he places himself in opposition to the redemptive efforts offered by the "harmonists," such as the last movement of Beethoven's Ninth Symphony as well as the "Leonore Overture" and the prisoner's chorus from *Fidelio*.

339/469	An art that is on a first-name basis with humanity	In his essay "What is German?" (1944, based on his 1943 lecture script "The War and the Future") TM differentiates between a base populism in which "little Mr. Smith or Jones slaps Beethoven on the back and shouts: 'How are you, old man!'" and the nobler attitude expressed by the line, "Be embraced, ye millions, this kiss to all the world" from the Ninth Symphony. While L.'s claim to an "art that is on a first-name basis with humanity" may thus seem innocuous, even desirable, TM clearly regarded it as full of dangers.

XXXII

In 1915, Inez Rodde weds Helmut Institoris. They settle down in a fancy apartment, where Z. soon becomes a frequent guest. He skeptically observes Inez's attempts to maintain a bourgeois household amidst the instability and uncertainty of the War period. One evening, Inez confesses her love of Rudi Schwerdtfeger to him.

Time of composition: November 9–29, 1945. Time of narration: After April 1944. Narrated time: 1915–1918.

341/471	"Pay heed before you wed for aye."	The German original, *Drum prüfe wer sich ewig bindet*, is a quotation from Friedrich Schiller's 1799 poem "Song of the Bell."
343/473	low building […] across from the Schweigestill's courtyard	This is based on an actual house in Polling (the real-world model for Pfeiffering), to which TM's mother Julia Mann moved in old age.
344/475	during the sparsest years	During the First World War, as well as perhaps the hyperinflationary period of 1922–1923.
345/476	*comme il faut*	French: "as was proper."
345/476	served as her abagail	A female servant who assists with matters of personal toilette.
346/478	for a world, so to speak, as it had been, not as it would become	Inez is trying against all odds to preserve a bourgeois form of life that the outbreak of the war has already rendered superannuated.
346/478	*une jeune fille accomplie*	French: "an accomplished young girl."

347/479	Käthe Kruse dolls		Käthe Kruse (1883–1968) was a world-famous dollmaker.
349/483	I had rented a room in Schwabing		Z.'s decision to rent a bachelor pad in Munich may well be driven by convenience, but his choice of address also places him close to the English Garden which, as the queer studies scholar Robert Tobin has pointed out, was and is a noted gay cruising area.
349/483	at the Allotria-Club		A Munich artist's association and social club, of which TM's father-in-law Alfred Pringsheim was a member.
350/484	"Vengeance is the Lord's"		Romans 12:19. The German actually quotes from Deuteronomy 32:35, with its very similar wording: "To me belongeth vengeance and recompense." Both quotations seem rather harsh given the context and reveal Z. at his most priggish.

XXXIII

The end of the First World War finds L. confined to his residence in Pfeiffering with near-constant gastro-intestinal attacks and migraines—a likely symptom of the outbreak of tertiary syphilis. He is visited by both Z. and Schwerdtfeger, who tries to commission a violin concerto. Meanwhile, the early stages of the German Revolution of 1918 unfold in Munich.

Time of composition: December 1–27, 1945. Time of narration: July 1944. Narrated time: 1918–1919.

354/488	a judgment that we did not [...] that first time	A highly ambiguous statement. On the one hand, Z. seems to be distancing himself from the nationalist rhetoric that framed the Treaty of Versailles as a catastrophe of Biblical proportions. On the other hand, he seems to also disavow German responsibility for the outbreak of the First World War.
355/489	our new retaliatory weapon	The V-1 rocket, first launched against London on June 13, 1944. The extent to which Z. is mixing sarcasm with genuine admiration throughout the following paragraph is an open question.

356/491	the Sarmatian flood	The Sarmatians were a group of tribes that harried the Eastern provinces of the Roman Empire. Z. is here using the term in a (perhaps unconsciously) derogatory fashion to refer to the Soviet army.
356/491	"It is a terrible thing to fall into the hands of strangers"	Possible allusion to Hebrews 10:31: "It is a fearful thing to fall into the hands of the living God."
357/493	those two saviors of European civilization [...] Uffizi in Florence	The joint visit of Hitler and Mussolini to the Uffizi Museum took place in May 1938.
357/493	Bolshevism has never destroyed works of art	Z. is being naïve, since the Russian Revolution was accompanied by widespread acts of iconoclasm.
358/494	rhetorical bourgeois who called himself a "son of revolution"	Not an actual person, but the compound figure already evoked in the previous paragraph. Also a possible allusions to TM's disputes with his brother Heinrich during the period of the First World War.
359/494	"Councils of Intellectual Workers"	A "Council of Intellectual Workers" was formed in Munich in December 1918; TM's brother Heinrich played a leading role, much to the disgust of his younger sibling.
359/495	a belletrist spoke [...] on the topic of "Revolution and Brotherly Love"	Thinly veiled reference to Bruno Frank (1887–1945), a friend of the Mann family and a participant in the Munich council movement.
360/497	the young lady from Bayreuth	See 223/304.
362/499	little mermaid in Andersen's fairy tale	See 246/337 and note that the mermaid's eye color matches L.'s.
366/506	technically perfect interpretation of Tartini	The Italian composer Giuseppe Tartini (1692–1770) is perhaps most famous for his "devil's trill" sonata for violin.
367/506	the marionette piece, "The Godless Cunning"	See the description of L.'s puppet opera on 333/460.

368/508	"Do you leave your garment in her hand and flee?"	An allusion to Genesis 39:12 and the attempted seduction of Joseph by Potiphar's wife. TM spent almost twenty years (from 1926–1943) adapting the story of Joseph into a literary tetralogy; this particular episode plays a prominent role in *Joseph in Egypt* (1936).
369/509	everything the word 'platonic' means to me	The term "Platonic love" can refer both to same-sex and to sexless relationships.

XXXIV

In the spring of 1919, L. begins composing his oratorio Apocalipsis cum figuris, *based on a cycle of Dürer woodcuts. Z. recognizes profound similarities between the themes of this work and contemporary events, Germany having been plunged into a state of chaos following the downfall of the Wilhelmine Empire.*

Time of composition: January 3–March 2, 1946, with a lengthy interruption. Time of narration: In or after July 1944. Narrated time: 1919.

371/512	almost breathless productivity	L.'s "breathless productivity" contrasts with Z.'s own "labored breathing" on 5/11.
373/514	John the Martyr in his cauldron of oil	The Apostle John is traditionally regarded as the author not only of the Gospel of John but also of several other books of the New Testament, including the Book of Revelation. Legend has it that either the Roman Emperor Domitian or the Emperor Nero (both of whom were noted for their persecution of Christians) ordered him boiled in oil, but could not harm him. Dürer included an image of John in the cauldron in his 1498 cycle of woodcuts illustrating the Apocalypse (Fig. 5). For his detailed descriptions of the woodcuts, TM relied on a biography of Dürer by Wilhelm Waetzoldt (1880–1945), which also provided him with inspiration for his description of the L. household in chapter III.
373/515	gables of Kaisersaschern	L.'s conflation of contemporary Kaisersaschern with medieval Nuremberg hearkens back to chapter VI.

375/517	as brothers, the two who have been down below		In the second canto of Dante's *Divine Comedy*.
375/517	*filia hospitalis*		Latin: "daughter of the house." A euphemism for prostitutes, giving a cruel edge to Z.'s joking remark.
376/519	"An end is come, the end is come [...]"		A word-for-word quotation of Ezekiel 7:6–7. Z. will again quote these words on 455/629, when he describes the downfall of Germany in 1945.
376/519	These words [...] a ghostly melody		For the detailed musical description of the *Apocalipsis cum figuris*, TM relied on the extensive help of his musical advisor Theodor W. Adorno, to whom he sent an outline of his intentions on December 30, 1945. Possible sources of inspiration also include Stravinsky's oratorio *Oedipus Rex* (1927) as well as Berlioz's *Symphonie Fantastique* (1830).
376/519	the eating of the book		See Fig. 6.
376/519	taken almost verbatim from Ezekiel		See Ezekiel 2:9–3:3.
377/521	a work so terrifying close to him		The *Apocalipsis* is close to Z. not only because he witnessed its creation, but also because it deals with a theme that has been close to his heart since the opening pages of *DF*: the end of the historical era of bourgeois humanism, and the anxiety over what will come next.
379/523	"The Bird's Cry of Woe"		See Revelation 8:13.
379/523	the words of Jeremiah		The following lines are taken from Lamentations 3:39–40, 42–43, and 45.
379/523	I call the piece a fugue		On the importance of fugues for L.'s musical formation, see Kretzschmar's second lecture in chapter VIII.

380/524	two luminol tablets	An error in the translation; L. is actually taking the barbiturate Luminal. (Luminol is a chemiluminescent agent used to detect blood in crime-scene investigations). TM himself regularly took Luminal during the stressful early years of his exile, when he was living in Switzerland and tried to continue working on the *Joseph* cycle despite all the bad news that were reaching him from Germany.
380/524	Awake, psaltery and harp!	Psalms 57:8.

XXXIV (continued)

The chapter that follows upon chapter XXXIV in Zeitblom's narrative is not labeled "XXXV," but rather "XXXIV (continued)." The unusual numbering highlights not only the centrality of this chapter to the themes developed in DF, but also draws attention to the number "thirty-four," which happens to be the sum of all verticals, horizontals, and main diagonals in a magic square like the one discussed in chapter XII.

While L. is working on the Apocalipsis *in his Pfeiffering study, Z. is a repeat visitor to the "intimate round-table sessions" (382/526) hosted by the art historian Sixtus Kridwiss in Munich. There, he gets to know a variety of arch-reactionary intellectuals who are all thinly-veiled portraits of real people of the time.*

Time of composition: As above. Time of narration: In or after July 1944. Narrated time: 1919.

381/525	hated by thousands	This is the first indication we get that any of L.'s works may have achieved renown beyond a very narrow circle of initiates. The statement needs to be taken with a grain of salt, since we learn on 396/547 that the *Apocalipsis* was publicly performed only once, although a printed edition is also available (410/564).
382/526	intimate round-table sessions	Emil Preetorius (1883–1973), the model for Kridwiss, hosted discussion evenings like the ones descried here in his Munich apartment.

383/528		"I entrust to you the plundering—of the world!"	An actual line from a poem by Ludwig Derleth (1870–1948), the model for Daniel Zur Höhe, who also wrote a volume of poems called *Proclamations*.
384/530		our democratic republic [...] a bad joke	TM's description of the Kridwiss Circle accurately reproduces the prevailing opinions in the conservative milieu in which TM himself moved during the years following the First World War. TM pledged his support to the Weimar democracy only in 1922, when he gave a public lecture "On the German Republic" that earned him the enmity of many of his former friends and associates.
385/530		freedom was a self-contradictory notion	Note the parallels to L.'s aesthetic theories, articulated most extensively in XXII.
385/531		a dialectical process that eventually turned freedom into [...] dictatorship	A dialectical approach to history in which "freedom" eventually turns into "order" (if not quite "dictatorship") also underlies Kretzschmar's lecture on Op. 111 in VIII.
385/531		*Réflexions sur la violence*	*Reflections on Violence* (1908) by the French syndicalist philosopher Georges Sorel (1847–1922), who was a major influence on reactionary intellectual circles in interwar Europe.
385/532		henceforth popular myths [...] would be the vehicle of political action	The realization that "fables, chimeras, phantasms that needed to have nothing whatever to do with truth, reason, or science" are oftentimes better motivators for political action than facts is central to the political thought not only of Sorel, but also of TM himself—who however sought to distance himself from the Frenchman by pointing out that whereas Sorel had pointed the way towards fascism, his own journey had ultimately been towards democracy.
386/533		they shared the fun of imagining a court of law	TM was a keen observer of Weimar jurisprudence and wrote several essays in which he decried the increasing sway that sloganeering and populist myths held over the court system during the final years of the republic.

387/534	It was far better for me to observe [...] instead of presenting [...] opposition	Whether this statement indeed holds true is one of the key questions in assessing Z.'s role in the novel.
389/537	My symbol of musical criticism, the "dead tooth"	See 161/220.

XXXIV (conclusion)

Z. offers a detailed description of the Apocalipsis cum figuris, *a work in which the earliest and most barbaric forms of sound production seem to recur in transmuted form as avant-garde musical expression.*

Time of composition: as above. Time of narration: In or after July 1944. Narrated time: 1919.

391/539	And now before my eyes the dramatic form was being superseded [...]	Z. here draws an explicit connection between L.'s musical modernism and the end of the bourgeois period in the years following the First World War.
391/540	"harmonic subjectivity" [...] "polyphonic detachment"	See 57/81.
391/541	"great multitude, which no man could number [...]"	Revelation 14:1. See also Fig. 7.
392/541	the antithesis that would replace bourgeois culture was not barbarism, but community	See 12/20 and 232/317.
393/542	We all know that the first concern [...] was to separate sound from nature	Z.'s reflections on the development of music in pre-modern times were heavily influenced by Paul Bekker's *The Story of Music*, which had already been a foundational text for chapters VIII and IX.
394/544	their distant classical model [...] the *St. Matthew Passion*	By Bach, written in 1727.
394/545	the whore of Babylon	See Fig. 8.

395/545	curvature of the world, which allows the earliest things		A reference to Kleist's "On the Marionette Theater," which had served as L.'s inspiration for *Gesta Romanorum*.
396/547	International Society for New Music		Possibly a reference to the "International Society for Contemporary Music," which held a festival in Frankfurt am Main in 1927 and is mentioned in Riemann's *Musical Encyclopedia*, a work that TM frequently consulted.
396/547	under Klemperer [...] Erbe		Otto Klemperer (1885–1973) was one of the most distinguished conductors of the twentieth century and especially renowned for his patronage of modern music during the 1920s. From 1933 to 1940 he was the chief conductor of the L.A. Philharmonic; TM repeatedly met him on social occasions. Karl Erb (1877–1958) was a tenor known especially for his performances as *testo* in Bach's Passion oratorios. The fact that his last name appears as "Erbe" in *DF* could be either an oversight or a sly joke: "Erbe" means "heritage" or "inheritance" in German.
396//547	jazz sounds for purely infernal purposes		Theodor W. Adorno was a notedly acerbic detractor of jazz.
397/548	pandemonium of laughter		See 18/29.
397/548	*Gaudium* of Gehenna		Latin: "delight." "Gehenna" is a valley west of Jerusalem, and is described in both Old and New Testament as a place of divine punishment.

XXXV

In 1922, Clarissa Rodde, who has tried to trade in her unsuccessful acting career for a bourgeois marriage to an Alsatian merchant, commits suicide when she is blackmailed by a former lover with a devilish appearance. At her funeral, Z. observes Inez who has been driven into morphine addiction by her own unhappy love life.

Time of composition: June 12–25, 1946. Time of narration: In or after July 1944. Narrated time: 1922.

399/500		resolutely took her life with [...] poison	The events of this chapter are closely modeled on the final weeks in the life of TM's sister Carla Mann (1881–1910), who poisoned herself in her mother's house in Polling in 1910.
400/551		*cidevant*	French: "former"
401/553		*Boche*	French: derogatory term for a German.
402/534		*Entrevue*	French: "interview."
404/557		a dose of cyanide	Carla Mann did indeed kill herself with cyanide, though in the context of 1946, it's hard not to also think of the high-ranking Nazis who killed themselves with cyanide pills.
404/557		*Je t'aime* [...] *mais je t'aime*	French: "I love you. Once, I cheated on you, but I love you." The actual wording of Clara Mann's suicide note.
404/557		*désolé*	French: "desolated." Z. is referring to the fact that the phrase *je suis désolé* is often used euphemistically to simply mean "I am sorry" and therefore does not necessarily imply the emotional devastation Henri is presumably trying to evoke here.
404/557		*Et maintenant— comme ça!*	French: "And now—just like that!"
406/559		a divorced Romanian authoress from Transylvania	Ms. Binder-Majoresku, whose name doesn't appear until 431/595

XXXVI

During the early 1920s, an increasing number of L.'s compositions find their first performances, though mostly with modest success. Z. learns that a mysterious Hungarian noblewoman named Frau von Tolna is behind some of these performances; a number of clues suggest that she may be identical with the prostitute Esmeralda. The year 1924 sees the world premiere in Vienna of a violin concerto that Rudi Schwerdtfeger commissioned from L. After the triumphant performance, Rudi and L. embark on a vacation to the Hungarian estates of Frau von Tolna. When they return, they are on familiar terms of address with one another, a fact that suggests sexual intimacy as well.

Time of composition: June 29–July 15, 1946. Time of narration: In or after July 1944. Narrated time: 1920–1924.

408/562	virulent sans-culottism	The term *sans-culottes* (French: "those without knee-breeches") referred to non-aristocratic people during the time of the French Revolution and quickly became synonymous with "revolutionary rabble."
409/563	a shift of cultural focus from France to Germany	It is not entirely clear what Z. has in mind, though it is true that the second half of the 1920s are generally regarded as the cultural glory days of the Weimar Republic, following upon the trauma of the 1918 Revolution and the inflationary period of 1922–1923.
409/563	first complete production [...] took place	See 396/547.
409/563	"cultural Bolshevism"	"Cultural Bolshevism" and "musical Bolshevism" were common derogatory epithets during the 1920s, applied by reactionary critics to avant-garde works.
409/564	Festival of Composers in Weimar [...] first music festival at Donaueschingen	Actual music festivals. The Donaueschingen festival in particular continues to enjoy renown as perhaps the most important venue for the premiere of contemporary classical music.
409/564	Bruno Walter	Important conductor (1876–1962) and a close friend and neighbor of TM's in both Munich and Pacific Palisades. In Germany he conducted both the Munich Royal Opera and the Salzburg Festival; in Los Angeles he was a frequent guest conductor of the L.A. Philharmonic.
410/564	Universal Edition	An actual music publishing house, though the name of its director is fictitious.
410/565	The *Anbruch*, a radically progressive Viennese music periodical	An actual publication, which published early essays by Adorno and was well-disposed towards Schoenberg. The name "Desiderius Féher" is fictive, however.
410/565	the eternal feminine	A reference to the closing lines of Goethe's *Faust, Part II*.
411/567	two needy female souls	See chapter XXXI

412/567	a palace in Pest	The eastern half of the city of Budapest, separated from Buda and Óbuda by the Danube. The fact that Frau von Tolna lives east of the Danube and maintains a country house in the Hungarian steppes marks her as exotic within the cultural geography of *DF*. It is notable that the only other major Hungarian character in the novel is Esmeralda. Frau von Tolna has often been interpreted as another manifestation of this succubus-like figure, now sent to advance L.'s fame throughout the world.
413/569	Frau Schweigestill [...] without having been seen	This passage emphasizes the similar roles as "mother figures" played by Signora Manardi and Frau Schweigestill in *DF*. The fact that Frau von Tolna did not reveal herself also implies an opposition between von Tolna's possibly demonic presence and Frau Schweigestill's position as a redeemer-figure.
413/569	the gem, a large-faceted emerald	A possible clue pointing towards Hetaera Esmeralda.
413/570	Apollo's sacred laurel tree	Another clue, since Apollo is associated (as the following paragraph reiterates) with both arrows and infection. TM's letters prove that he consciously played with these connotations when he wrote the passage.
413/570	Philoctetes of Chryse	The Greek hero Philoctetes suffered from a festering wound, the stench of which forced him to isolate himself on a desert island. L. also (albeit voluntarily) withdraws into solitude due to the effects of his syphilitic infection.
414/571	Old French rendition in verse of the *Vision of St. Paul*	See 374/517.
415/572	at Ehrbar Hall	Like almost all locations and institutions connected to the performance history of L.'s compositions, this is a real place.

XXXVII

In 1923, L. is visited by the French concert promoter Saul Fitelberg, who offers him a brilliant musical career in Paris. L. declines. Much of the chapter is taken up with Fitelberg's prattle in a mixture of French and German.

I've translated the French expressions, but the first-time reader can safely skip over them. They contain only platitudes and are there mostly for comical effect.

Time of composition: July 21–August 16, 1946. Time of narration: In or after July 1944. Narrated time: 1923.

418/576	*cher Madame* [...] *petite Maman*	French: "dear lady [...] little mother." In the original, TM intentionally misspells the French to emphasize Frau Schweigestill's Bavarian dialect—thus presumably Wood's decision to render *chère* as *cher*.
418/577	*Arrangements* [...] *artistes prominents*	French: "Musical arrangements. Representative of numerous prominent artists."
419/577	*Cher Maître* [...] *le professeur*	French: "My dear master, I am so happy, so touched to have found you! Even for a man who is as spoiled and hardened as I am, it's always a touching experience to meet a great man.—Pleased to meet you, professor."
419/577	*Vous maudirez* [...] *mille fois merci*	French: "You will be upset at my intrusion, Monsieur Leverkühn [...] But for me, since I happened to be in Munich, it would have been impossible to miss out [...] At any rate, I am convinced [...] For after all [...] Master [...] But yes, of course [...] Thank you, thank you a thousand times over!"
419/578	What I intend to record of his conversation	The joke, of course, is that there is no conversation. Neither Z. nor L. ever get a word in.
420/579	*Maître* [...] *le scandale*	French: "Master [...] and more, this house so full of dignity with its maternal and vigorous hostess. Madame Schweigestill! But that translates as: 'I will be silent.' Silence, silence! How charming! [...] Astounding [...] would you believe it? [...] ridiculously exaggerated. [...] That's the absolute truth, simply and irrefutably. [...] But to whom am I saying that. In the beginning there was scandal."
420/579	carry you off [...] on my cloak	This line established Fitelberg as another tempter figure and thus moves him into the vicinity of the devil.

CHAPTER SUMMARIES AND PAGE-BY-PAGE COMMENTARIES ♦ 209

420/579	of truly very simple Jewish parents	Fitelberg is perhaps the most prominent example in a long list of Jewish stereotypes that populate *DF* (Chaim Braisacher, Meta Nackedey, and Kunigunde Rosenstiel are other examples). During the composition of *DF*, TM's oldest son Klaus pointed out to this father that these stereotypical descriptions might open him up to charges of anti-Semitism, but TM rejected this.
420/580	*Au commencement était le scandale*	French: "In the beginning there was scandal." A parody of John 1:1, which in French reads *Au commencement était la parole* (*la parole*: the word). In Goethe's *Faust*, the protagonist also tries his hand at translating this Bible verse, eventually settling on the equally unusual *In the beginning was the deed*.
420/580	*à la longue* [...] *Fourberies gracieuses*	French: "In the long run [...] interlocutor [...] a hole in the wall, a little cave [...] called "Theater of the Gracious Deceits" [...] I can assure you [...] In a word [...] Gracious Deceits."
421/580	James Joyce [...] Duchess de Clermont-Tonnière	James Joyce, Pablo Picasso (1881–1973), Ezra Pound (1885–1972), and the Duchess de Clermont-Tonnère (1875–1954) are here largely invoked as short-hand for the Parisian avant-garde of the early 1920s, although it's also significant that only the Duchess was French, a fact that emphasizes the cosmopolitan nature of the world to which Fitelberg would like to introduce L. TM's references to interwar Paris are heavily indebted to Igor Stravinsky's memoirs; while TM himself visited the city several times during this time period, he did not associate with avant-garde circles, preferring the company of an older generation of artists.
421/581	*crème de la crème* [...] *fanatique de musique*	French: "the elite [...] Ah madame, oh, madame, what do you think, one tells me, madame, that you are absolutely crazy about music?"

421/581	*Enfin* [...] *C'est suprême*		French: "Finally [...] that's where I find satisfaction and pleasure [...] and we discover ourselves in this longing [...] which furnishes the subject [...] "Insult! Impudence! Execrable foolishness!" [...]"What precision! What spirit! It's divine! It's superb!"
421/582	Erik Satie, a few surrealists, Virgil Thomson		Erik Satie (1866–1925) and Virgil Thomson (1896–1989) were both modernist composers who celebrated their chief successes in Paris during the early 1920s. TM's musical advisor Theodor W. Adorno held a generally dim view of them.
422/582	*un boche* [...] *énormement caractéristique*		French: "A boche who on account of his genius belongs to the world and who marches at the head of musical progress [...] Ah, that's truly German, for example! [...] dear master, why not say it? [...] that *Phosphorescence of the Sea* [...] and that you enchain your art in a system of inexorable and neoclassical rules [...] German quality [...] roughness [...] indeed, just between us [...] No, I am certain of it! [...] That's "boche" to a fascinating degree! [...] enormously characteristic."
423/584	*ce cosmopolitisme généreux et versatile*		French: "that generous and versatile cosmopolitanism."
423/584	Maja de Strozzi-Pečič		Croatian soprano (1882–1962).
423/584	Flonzaley Quartet [...] Pro Arte Quartet		Actual string quartets of the era.
423/584	*Cher Maître* [...] *c'est dommage, pourtant*		French: "Dear master, I understand your meaning. But still, that's too bad."
423/584	*particulièrement à Paris* [...] *barrière*		French: "Especially in Paris [...] Everybody knows, madame, that your musical judgment is infallible! [...] barrier."
423/585	Diaghilev's Ballets Russes		The Ballets Russes are another example of the avant-garde culture of the time and were closely associated with Igor Stravinsky.
424/585	*Entre nous* [...] *un peu gauche*		French: "Between us [...] Master [...] Tell me then [...] severity [...] a solemn state of mind and a little bit awkward."

424/586	Jean Cocteau [...] Les Six	Jean Cocteau (1889–1963), Léonide Massine (1896–1979), Manuel de Falla (1876–1946), and the musical collective Les Six are further illustrations of the international modernism that characterized Paris during the interwar years.
424/586	*Embarrass* [...] *une espèce d'infirmier, voilà!*	French: "Embarrassment [...] this strange and hermit-like refuge [...] well [...] excentric semi-fools [...] a kind of nurse, that's all!"
424/586	*dans quelle manière* [...] *une confusion tragique*	French: "In what maladroit fashion [...] destiny [...] destinies [...] a nuisance [...] annihilation [...] the last enemy [...] with some justification [...] which are absolutely stupefying [...] All that is a little embarrassing, isn't that right? A tragic mistake."
426/588	*A la bonne heure* [...] *c'est mélancolique, tout ça!*	French: "Splendid! [...] Oh, how gloomy all that is!"
426//588	*Sincèrement* [...] *un grand homme*	French: "Sincerely [...] to pay tribute to a great man."
426/589	*en psychologue* [...] *qui est essentiellement anti-sémitique*	French/German: "as a psychologist [...] folkish [...] which is essentially anti-Semitic."
427/590	Gounod's and Goethe's *Faust*	Charles Gounod (1818–1893) composed an operatic adaptation (1859) of Goethe's *Faust II* that TM loved.
427/590	*pour prendre congé* [...] *Tiens*	French: "To take my leave [...] a beautiful treasure [the French *marguerite* is also an allusion to the name of the main female character in Goethe/Gounod's *Faust*] [...] Let me, let me think about it [...] he too [...] well!"
427/590	Even Massenet is bewitching	Jules Massenet (1842–1912) is another nineteenth-century French composer known primarily for his operas. Among his many works is the unfinished opera *Esméralda*, after Victor Hugo's *The Hunchback of Notre Dame*.
427/590	Should we Jews [...] not feel ourselves drawn to Germanness	The thesis of a fundamental correspondence between Jewish and German identity is a constant of Thomas Mann's thought, especially in the 1930s and 1940s.

427/591	*Comme c'est respectable* [...] *nom de guerre*	French: "How respectable it is! Not exactly humane, but extremely respectable [...] A striking analogy! [...] code name."
428/591	*je vous le jure* [...] *Adieu, adieu*	French: "I swear it [...] Mediator [...] But it is in vain. And that is truly too bad [...] Dear master, it was a pleasure. I failed at my mission [...] My respect, Monsieur le Professeur. You helped me far too little, but I will not hold it against you. Thousand regards to Mme. Schwei-ge-still. Good-bye, good-bye!"

XXXVIII

Z. provides a more detailed description of L.'s violin concerto and recalls some of the circumstances that led to its composition, including a conversation about popular music in the salon of the paper manufacturer Bullinger. The episode strengthens the impression that L.'s ambitions in writing this piece were fundamentally parodic in nature.

Time of composition: August 23–September 5, 1946, with later revisions. Time of narration: In or after July 1944. Narrated time: 1924.

429/593	B minor, C minor, and D minor	A significant error on Woods's part, for the original has "B-flat major, C major, and D major." The ensuing technical discussion doesn't make sense when applied to minor scales.
429/593	Dominant of the second degree [...] exactly in between	The dominant is the fifth scale degree of the diatonic scale. D is thus the dominant of the scale built on G, which in turn is the dominant of the scale built on C. The subdominant is the fourth scale degree of the diatonic scale, which is harmonically equivalent to moving five degrees downwards rather than upwards. Performing such a downwards movement twice from C yields first F, then B♭. B♭ is thus the subdominant of the second degree to C, while D is the dominant of the second degree. TM accidentally omitted the words "of the second degree" when describing the subdominant, the result of a transcription error from Adorno's notes, which heavily influenced these paragraphs.

430/593	the tonic triad of each of the three main keys	The tonic triad of C major is C–E–G, while the tonic triad of B-flat major is B♭–D–F, and the tonic triad of D major is D–F♯–A.	
430/594	In its physical effect, in the way it grabs one by the head and shoulders [...]	The original is even stronger, having *körperlich* (= "corporeal") rather than "physical." The musical structure of the piece that L. wrote for Schwerdtfeger thus anticipates the physical union that took place during their trip to Hungary in XXXVII.	
430/594	Tartini's "Devil's Trill" Sonata	See 366/506.	
431/594	"apotheosis of drawing-room music"	The original *Salonmusik* does indeed mean "drawing-room music," but could also be translated more literally as "salon music." Since Z. has repeatedly used the term "salon" to refer to the various social circles in which he and L. move in Munich, the violin concerto might also be understood as a commentary on its own time.	
431/596	from some land where no one else dwells.	A phrase drawn from a description of Friedrich Nietzsche in a letter by Erwin Rohde dated January 24, 1889. TM copied the passage into his notebooks and wrote "dementia" next to it.	
432/597	Berlioz's *Symphonie fantastique*	Berlioz's programmatic *Symphonie fantastique* features both hallucinatory visions and a witches' sabbath—themes of some relevance to *DF*.	
433/598	Saint-Saëns' *Samson*	The opera *Samson and Delilah* (1877) by Camille Saint-Saëns is about a man who is robbed of his supernatural powers by a woman in a moment of intimacy—the exact inverse of the plot of *DF*.	
433/599	*Mon coeur s'ouvre à ta voix*	French "My heart opens at the sound of your voice." Title of a popular duet [here mistakenly called an aria] from *Samson and Delilah*.	
434/600	Philine [...] Wilhelm Meister	Characters in Goethe's novel *Wilhelm Meister* (1795/96).	
435/600	A knight who defends fear and reproach	The original here is *Ein Ritter der Furcht und des Tadels*—an ironic inversion of the idiomatic *Ritter ohne Furcht und Tadel* ("Knight without Fear and Reproach").	

214 ♦ CHAPTER SUMMARIES AND PAGE-BY-PAGE COMMENTARIES

XXXIX

During a visit to Zurich, L. makes the acquaintance of the French Swiss stage designer Marie Godeau. Soon after, he announces to a surprised Z. that he intends to marry her. (Z. does not yet know that by doing so L. would transgress against the pact discussed in chapter XXV). We also get an overview of Munich social life during the mid-1920s, which has changed quite a bit from what we saw in chapter XXXIV.

Time of composition: September 7–22, 1946. Time of narration: In or after July 1944. Narrated time: 1924–1925.

437/604	Luckless "you"!		Z. is referring specifically to the informal pronoun of address *du*, which Rudi has been using with L. ever since their stay in Hungary.
437/604	In the final days of 1923		An error on Woods's part. The original has "1924," which is consistent with the chronology established in chapters XXXVI and XXXVIII.
437/604	the Swiss Chamber Orchestra [...] Herr Paul Sacher		Another real-life ensemble, though not founded until 1926 as the "Basel Chamber Orchestra."
439/606	Dr. Andreae		See 196/269.
439/606	Dr. Schuh, the excellent music critic		Willi Schuh (1900–1968), music critic of the *Neue Zürcher Zeitung*, publicly defended TM against his ultra-nationalist critics following the publication of TM's controversial *Sorrows and Greatness of Richard Wagner* (1933).
439/606	the most beautiful black eyes		Godeau's black eyes and dark brown hair move her into the vicinity of Rosaline in *Love's Labour's Lost*, and through Rosaline also to the "Dark Lady" from Shakespeare's sonnets. See 231/315.
441/609	resemble Elsbeth Leverkühn's voice		A resemblance that possibly elevates Godeau into the company of the various protective mother figures that populate *DF*.
441/610	the Pension Gisella		See 267/366.
442/611	You once tendered me kindred disclosures		In chapter XXII, when Z. announced his impending marriage to L.

CHAPTER SUMMARIES AND PAGE-BY-PAGE COMMENTARIES ♦ 215

| 443/613 | the affair was almost beyond belief | But only "almost," since this episode actually took place and received extensive news coverage. On Gleichen-Russwurm, see 215/294. |

XL

In an attempt to court Marie Godeau, L. arranges for all of his closest friends to go on a communal outing to Linderhof Castle, one of the fairy-tale castles built by King Ludwig II in the Bavarian Alps. During the trip, Z. finds himself defending the mad king against a skeptical Schwerdtfeger. Their discussion touches upon the relationship between art and politics: should art put itself at the service of political madness, as Hans von Bülow and Wagner did with Ludwig II, or should it aid in its overthrow?

Time of composition: ca. September 22–October 4, 1946. Time of narration: In or after July 1944. Narrated time: 1925.

445/615	Oberammergau	Municipality in the Bavarian Alps, roughly thirty miles southwest of Munich. Famous for the passion play that is performed there once every decade. L. has visited the town, and the other attractions that follow, before, with Rüdiger Schildknapp (see 218/298).
445/615	Monastery at Ettal […] Linderhof Castle	Kloster Ettal is a Benedictine Abbey a couple of miles southeast of Oberammergau. Like Castle Neuschwanstein, which L. considers but rejects as a destination, Linderhof was constructed by King Ludwig II of Bavaria (1845–1886), colloquially known as "Mad King Ludwig." Ludwig II was known as a patron of the arts (and especially of Richard Wagner), but also shrouded in scandal because of his homosexuality. He committed suicide by drowning himself in Lake Starnberg, a fate that foreshadows L.'s own actions following the onset of his madness. At the time of his death, he was almost exactly the same age as L. is in this chapter.
446/617	elfin Platonist	See 369/509.

446/617	a kind of rehearsal for something yet to come	See chapter XLI. At the same time, Z.'s mission recalls the plot of *Love's Labour's Lost*.
447/619	the black, the blue, and the same-coloured eyes […] under Adrian's eye	The black eyes belong to Marie Godeau (439/606), the blue ones to Schwerdtfeger (213/293), and the "same-coloured" (blue-grey-green) ones to Schildknapp (182/250).
448/620	"Let us not speak […] of these pious sins!"	A possible sign that Marie Godeau's presence is causing L. to have second thoughts about the work that is the most obvious product of his syphilitic infection so far.
450/623	letting von Bülow play the piano	Hans Guido Count Bülow (1830–1894), pianist, conductor, and first husband of Cosima Wagner. Von Bülow tolerated his wife's love affair with Wagner and even recognized a daughter that resulted from this affair as his own. The menage-à-trois possibly foreshadows events in the next few chapters, but Bülow is also significant because his piano playing for Ludwig II alludes to the relationship between music and melancholia.
450/623	Kainz's enchanting voice	Joseph Kainz (1858–1910), famous nineteenth-century actor.
451/624	Ludwig's so-called madness, which […] I declared an unjustified and brutal act	Throughout the following discussion, Z., not for the first time, reveals his essentially conservative nature as well as a secret fondness for mythmaking against which he on other occasions publicly protests. The "shallow" Schwerdtfeger, on the other hand, seems more closely aligned with the tenets of liberal democracy. Z.'s compassion for King Ludwig also foreshadows his later care for the paralytic L.

XLI

Shortly after the outing to Linderhof, L. summons Schwerdtfeger and asks him to woo Marie Godeau on his behalf. In doing so, he enacts a Shakespearean thematic—his interest in the Bard having remained unbroken since he set Love's Labour's Lost *to music. L. insists Schwerdtfeger go through with his commission even after he learns that the violinist harbors feelings of his own for Godeau.*

Time of composition: October 6–12, 1946. Time of narration: Late March 1945. Narrated time: 1925.

455/629	An end is come, the end is come	See 376/519. Z. is ironically conflating the First World War, which inspired L.'s *Apocalipsis*, with the Second.
456/630	That "Tenth" Symphony again?	Because of its stylistic similarities to Beethoven, Brahms' First Symphony is sometimes jokingly called "The Tenth Symphony." The epithet also strengthens the general argument of *DF*, which casts nineteenth-century music history as a singular tradition emanating from Beethoven.
458/633	whose stout-hearted perseverance overcame death	L. is ascribing Christ-like traits to Schwerdtfeger whom he, after all, is about to send on a mission to nullify the devil's pact, which demands that its subject may never love (264/363).
459/635	nuncio	Official title of a papal ambassador. The original simply has *Werber* ("courter").
460/635	the most secret pages in the book of my heart have been opened	A quotation from I.4 of Shakespeare's *As You Like It* (1599), one of several plays that deal with a courtship triangle very much like the one described here (*Much Ado about Nothing* [1598] and *The Two Gentlemen of Verona* [1599] are the others). All three were found on L.'s desk on 322/445.
460/636	the lass—but you don't like that word	The word that L. tries to avoid is *Mädel*, which also occurs in the title of *O lieb Mädel, wie schlecht bist du*, the poem by Clemens Brentano that L. set to music around 1906, and in which he first employed the H-E-A-E-Es logogram (see 194/266). In the earlier passage, Woods translated the term as "maiden" rather than "lass."

XLII

Schwerdtfeger delivers L.'s marriage proposal and is rejected. Shortly after, feeling encouraged by the way Godeau reacted during their meeting, he proposes on his own behalf and is accepted. The news spreads and soon after, Z. and many of L.'s friends assemble to hear Schwerdtfeger give one last concert with the Zapfenstösser orchestra before he and Godeau will move to Paris. At the concert, Z. witnesses the oppressive atmosphere that has fallen upon

Munich cultural life. In the aftermath of the performance, a distraught Inez Institoris shoots Schwerdtfeger on a public tram. He dies in Z.'s arms, and Z. is left to deliver the news to her husband.

Time of composition: October 13–23, 1946. Time of narration: Late March 1945. Narrated time: 1925.

463/639	to walk with his head and upper body tilted to one side	Impediments that also characterized Nietzsche in the years immediately preceding his syphilitic collapse in 1889.
463/639	when one's own right hand is perjured to the bosom […] such a friend is now.	Quotations from V.3 of *The Two Gentlemen of Verona*. See 460/635.
463/639	so foolish that it reminds me […] It is no sin or shame to be trusting	A quotation from *Much Ado about Nothing* II.1. Remarkably, Z. answers L. with the correct line, even though he does not seem cognizant of the allusive game.
467/645	faithfully restrained emotions might burst forth	The original is *Durchbruch*: the same term that has been used for several other kinds of "breakthroughs" over the course of the book. (See 258/354).
468/646	Orchestre Symphonique	Name of an actual musical ensemble in Paris, which was, however, not founded until 1933.
469/648	*Art and Artist*	An actual journal that was published from 1902–1933.
470/649	Sparks of electricity constantly flashed […] cold flames scattered	The association of electrical sparks with fire is even stronger in the original, which speaks of *elektrisches Feuer* rather than "sparks of electricity." The notion of a "cold" electrical fire links this scene to a thematic cluster first introduced on 8/15.
471/651	never had he more regretted […] but a mere numismatist	Kranich will voice the same sentiment again on 527/728.
471/652	doctors tend to be musical […] so many who are Jewish	Another example of Z.'s unconscious anti-Semitism, first noted on 10/17.

XLIII

Following Schwerdtfeger's death, L. suffers through a period of poor health and stagnating creative powers. By 1927, however, he has fully recovered and not only composes a number of new pieces, but also conceives the first ideas for what will become his final work, The Lamentation of Doctor Faustus.

Time of composition: October 30–November 7, 1946. Time of narration: March 1945. Narrated time: 1926–1927.

474/655	whose thousand-year history [...] proven by its outcome to have gone fatally amiss		The question whether something essential had gone amiss with German culture was vigorously debated during the postwar years, as was the question whether Germans as a whole were to be blamed for the crimes committed during the Nazi period. Mann commented on these questions not only in fiction, but also in important essays and lectures, such as "The End," "The Camps," and "Germany and the Germans" (all 1945).
474/655	as the German proverb has it		Not exactly a proverb, but the summary of a couplet from Goethe's *Tame Xenias*.
475/657	his neglected and decaying teeth		TM had already used decaying teeth as a symbol of larger cultural decline in his early novel *Buddenbrooks*.
476/658	"emptiness, virtual idiocy" [...] "pray for my poor soul"		The quotations in this paragraph all first occur in the conversation with the devil on 251/344, though Woods varies the translation somewhat.
478/661	tendency towards musical "prose"		The term "musical prose" was commonly used by Schoenberg and his disciples.
479/663	Trio for violin, viola, and cello		Schoenberg completed just such a trio shortly before TM wrote this chapter in November 1946.
480/664	"his spirit and capercaillie"		See 282/388.
480/664	University of Cracow		Some early modern sources used by TM also report that Doctor Faustus studied in Cracow.
481/664	"Sorowe did move Dr. Faustum that he made writ of his lamentation"		A quote from chapter 63 of the Chapbook.

XLIV

In 1928, Leverkühn's sister Ursula Schneidewein, whose wedding in chapter XXII precipitated L.'s and Z.'s conversation about the "strict style," entrusts her five-year-old son Nepomuk, who is recovering from a case of the measles, to the care of her brother in Pfeiffering. Nepomuk is one of the most complex and also most contentious characters in Doctor Faustus. *He is modeled on TM's own beloved grandson Frido, who was six years old when his grandfather wrote these lines. Nepomuk is depicted as an elfin, even angelic, child, and also repeatedly compared to the wind spirit Ariel from Shakespeare's* The Tempest *(1611), songs from which L. is at that time setting to music. L., Z., and all the other residents of the Schweigestill farm are exceedingly taken by the boy. L. even seems to experience something resembling paternal love.*

Time of composition: November 7–December 11, 1946. Time of narration: Late March 1945. Narrated time: 1928.

483/667	"Echo," as [...] he called himself	"Echo" is a figure from Ovid's *Metamorphoses*. Critics have also compared Nepomuk to Ariel, the wind spirit from Shakespeare's *Tempest*, whose songs L. is setting to music, and to Mignon, a child with a tragic fate in Goethe's *Wilhelm Meister's Apprenticeship* (1795/96).
484/668	solemn and imposing Swiss drawl	Frido Mann (1940–), TM's grandson on whom the figure of Nepomuk is based, had a Swiss mother who influenced his childhood speech patterns. Swiss German also maintains many elements that sound antiquated in contemporary High German, linking Echo to the early modern past with which L. is so studiously engaged. TM doubles down on this by having the child occasionally quote from early modern literary sources in the following pages.
485/669	sweet light of the azure smile	Nepomuk's "azure" eyes offer yet another variation on the theme of blue eyes that runs throughout *DF*. "Azure" is also a synonym for "sky-blue," emphasizing the child's possible relationship to the wind-spirit Ariel.

CHAPTER SUMMARIES AND PAGE-BY-PAGE COMMENTARIES ♦ 221

486/671	"Shock-headed Peter"	*Der Struwwelpeter* (1845) is an instructional children's book by Heinrich Hoffmann (1809–1894), highly influential in the German-speaking world until the late twentieth century. Significantly, all the children in the book meet with cruel and untimely fates.	
488/674	A puppy dog and no one else	The children's rhymes on this page appear to be TM's own invention.	
489/676	A conceptual sphere that is mythic and timeless	This has been a recurring theme throughout the novel. See, e.g., 39/57.	
491/678	he was not allowed into the abbot's study	TM's own children similarly remembered how they were not allowed into their father's study for hours on end when he was writing.	
492/680	A letter opener [...] the chiming table clock	These are all objects from the Mann household that were favorite toys of Frido's when he came to visit his grandparents.	
492/681	"Come unto these yellow sands" [...] "Where the bee sucks, there suck I"	These songs can be found in I.2 and V.1 of *The Tempest*, respectively.	
493/681	"Where should this music be? I' th' air or th' earth?"	*The Tempest* I.2.	
493/681	Sycorax and her little servant	The servant is, of course, Ariel.	
493/682	Rumpelstiltskin [...] Leaping Lark	All characters from *Grimm's Fairy Tales*.	
494/682	For whoso heedeth Goad's command	TM adapted Echo's evening prayers from a book of thirteenth-century verses. He overshot the mark a little, however. "Goad" (*Got* in the original) may sound like a Middle High German pronunciation of "God" but is not authentic.	

XLV

Two months after his arrival in Pfeiffering, Nepomuk Schneidewein comes down with cerebrospinal meningitis, an affliction closely related to the symptoms suffered by patients with tertiary neurosyphilis. He dies soon after amidst horrible pains. In a conversation with Z., L. takes responsibility for these events, identifying them as the means by which the devil is punishing him for transgressing against his obligation not to love. He darkly vows to compose a work that will "take back" the Ninth Symphony. At the same time, however, he expresses his conviction that Nepomuk will enter into heaven and be forever beyond reach of dark forces.

Time of composition: December 2–11, 1946 (the chapter was originally part of XLIV). Time of narration: Late March 1945. Narrated time: 1928.

496/685	Sniffles now dulled the sweet clarity of his eyes	As was his custom, TM consulted with a doctor to create the following detailed and medically accurate account of the progression of cerebrospinal meningitis.
497/687	"There's something about it that's not quite right"	The original German for "not quite right" is *nicht ganz geheuer*, an adjectival phrase that is commonly used to refer to supernatural phenomena. L.'s reaction shows that he is catching on to the fact that Echo's illness may be a consequence of the devil's pact, which prohibits L. from loving anyone.
500/691	"I had thought [...] that He would permit it"	A reference to the interdiction to love, as discussed in chapter XXV.
501/692	"I shall take it back [...] The Ninth Symphony"	Throughout the course of *DF* (and especially in chapter XXII), L. has described his intentions to somehow "correct" the course of musical history that was set into motion by Beethoven's late work. Here now, he links musical history explicitly to social progress, choosing as his central symbol the Ninth Symphony, whose jubilant final choral movement not only revolutionized classical music, but also clearly vocalizes Enlightenment ideology.
502/693	it was good still to see some reflective blackness	Nepomuk's azure eyes have turned black, bringing to an end the color game started on 26/39. Schwerdtfeger's blue eyes, of course, were already extinguished in chapter XLII.
503/694	"Then to the elements [...] fare thou well."	The lines with which Prospero sets Ariel free in V.1 of *The Tempest*. The lines are in English in the original as well.

XLVI

In May 1945, Germany unconditionally surrenders to the Allies, and Z. reflects on what the horrors that were brought to light by the liberation of the concentration camps say about Germany and its future. Back in 1929, L., now in the final throes of his syphilitic infection, begins the composition of The Lamentation of Doctor Faustus, *which is at once his attempt to take back the progressive optimism of the Ninth Symphony and a heartfelt cry of despair.*

Time of composition: December 17, 1946–January 1, 1947. Time of narration: April 25, 1945. Narrated time: 1929–1930.

504/695	For almost four weeks […] added nothing	TM's chronology is hardly plausible, for it would imply that Z. wrote chapters XLI–XLV in the span of about a week.
505/695	"Werwolf," a unit of berserk boys	TM first commented on the "Werwolf" resistance movement, which never constituted a serious threat to the victorious Allies, in a diary entry for April 2, 1945.
505/695	a transatlantic general	The American general George S. Patton (1885–1945). TM was one of the first Germans to comment on the liberation of the concentration camps in writing, in his essay "The Camps" (May 1945), to which the following two paragraphs are heavily indebted. The "local concentration camp" Z. mentions is Buchenwald.
506/697	it was in fact tens of thousands […] who committed the acts	Statements like this one, uncontroversial as they may seem to the contemporary American reader, were highly provocative during Mann's lifetime and earned him the instant enmity of many of his compatriots.
506/697	like the Jews of the ghetto	A very strange comparison, but indicative of TM's thoughts about Judaism. See 427/590.
506/697	Damn, damn those corruptors	The question whether Germans were willing participants in the crimes of the Nazis or had to be "corrupted" first remained controversial for many decades to come, as is shown by the controversy surrounding Daniel Goldhagen's 1996 study *Hitler's Willing Executioners*.

506/698	A patriotism [...] be more high-minded than conscientious	This attitude that Nazism was "without roots" in German history was characteristic of many left-leaning émigrés, such as Bertolt Brecht, Ludwig Marcuse (1894–1971), and TM's older brother Heinrich. In 1943, these men urged TM to publicly declare himself along similar lines. The author at first assented, but to the chagrin of his compatriots retracted his signature after further deliberation. TM's Library of Congress lecture "Germany and the Germans" can in part be understood as a response to this controversy.
507/698	Because the last years [...] belong in fact to the ascent and spread of that usurping power	In the German federal elections of September 1930, the Nazis' share of the popular vote jumped from roughly 2.6% to 18.3%.
507/699	a kind of imperial	See 26/39.
508/700	pupils [...] as if they were not subject to the influence of any change in light	A characteristic symptom of tertiary syphilis, but perhaps also a symbolic indicator of the fact that L. is now beyond the reach of saving grace. Compare Echo's similar development on 502/693.
509/702	a chaconne by Jacopo Melani	Jacopo Melani (1623–1676) was an Italian composer whose potential usefulness for *DF* was pointed out to TM by his musical advisor Theodor W. Adorno. As with most of the other of L.'s musical works, the description of the *Lamentation* in the following pages owes a great deal to written suggestions provided by Adorno.
509/702	Germany's liberation, its liberation of itself	The German employs the reflexive noun *Selbstbefreiung*, which makes it even clearer that Z. is dreaming of a liberation of Germany not only "of itself" but also "by itself." Over the course of the 1940s, TM became increasingly convinced that such a self-liberation was impossible and would have to come by a conquering force, as it indeed did in 1945.
509/703	*de profundis*	Latin: "out of the depths." See Psalms 130:1.

509/703–4	In order for such an event [...] to occur	The German carries a clear allusion to a couplet from the concluding chorus of Goethe's *Faust II*: "Das Unzulängliche, / Hier wird's Ereignis."
510/703	*Ecce homo* gestures	Latin: "behold the man!" The words and gesture used by Pilate in John 19:5 when he presents Jesus to the Jewish people. *Ecce Homo* is also the title of a book by Friedrich Nietzsche, who served as one of the models for L. throughout *DF*.
510/703	all expression is in fact lament [...] music becomes a lament	The two earliest known operas, *L'Orfeo* (1607) and *L'Arianna* (1608) by Claudio Monteverdi (1567–1643), both revolve around musical lamentations.
510/703	*Lasciatemi morire*	Latin: "Let me die." Title of an aria from the (otherwise lost) opera *L'Arianna* by Claudio Monteverdi.
510/704	a conversation I had with Adrian	See XXII.
511/705	lasting approximately an hour and a quarter.	*The Lamentation of Doctor Faustus* has almost exactly the same performance length as Beethoven's Ninth Symphony, the work that it is meant to "take back."
511/705	It will be recalled that in the old chapbook	Specifically, in chapters 67 and 68 of the Chapbook.
511/705	"St. John's Farewell"	This phrase refers to the custom, popular in the Catholic world until the eighteenth century, to dedicate the last glass of wine at a communal meal to St. John the Apostle. The custom recalls the Last Supper, of which Faust's final meal with his students is a parody.
511/706	*oratio Fausti ad studiosus*	Latin: "Faust's speech to the students."
511/705	"For I die as both a wicked and good Christian"	In the original: *Denn ich sterbe als ein böser und guter Christ*. See 5/11.

512//707	Working uninhibitedly within preorganized material [...] can abandon himself to subjectivity.	These lines distill the ultimate essence of the political allegory at the heart of *DF*: the idea that the inhabitants of the "new Germany" dreamt up by Nazism, just like the composers who embrace the twelve-tone technique, are free to express their subjectivity in whichever way they choose, as long as they do not in any way challenge the "preorganized material" of the state itself.
512/707	The episode where Faust calls up Helen	In chapters 49 and 59 of the Chapbook.
513/707	a kind of process of alchemistic distillation	Music has been linked to alchemy throughout *DF*, starting on 44/63.
514/710	the "Watch with me!" of Gethsemane	See Matthew 26:38.
514/710	the good old "physician and gossip"	See chapter 52 of the Chapbook. There, however, the pious neighbor is depicted not as a tempter-figure, but rather as a genuine Christian who makes a last-ditch effort to save the soul of Faustus.
515/710	*Apage!*	See 107/146.
515/711	But yet another final [...] a light in the night.	The description of the *Lamentation* ends on a hopeful note, however uncertain. TM's original draft of the passage was even more explicit in this regard; he changed it at the insistence of Adorno.
515/711	One instrumental group after the other steps back	Likely real-world models for this technique include the "Farewell Symphony" (1772) by Joseph Haydn (1732–1809), and the "Lyric Suite" (1926) by Alban Berg.

XLVII

In May of 1930, L. invites all of his friends and associates to Pfeiffering to play them piano extracts from his recently completed The Lamentation of Doctor Faustus. *The resulting assembly serves as a kind of group portrait of many of the secondary characters from the last twenty-five chapters. Once everybody has arrived, L. delivers a monologue in antiquated German that recalls a similar speech in the closing chapters of the Chapbook. He claims responsibility for the deaths of Rudi Schwerdtfeger and Nepomuk Schneidewein and claims to have had sexual intercourse with several succubae. Most of his scandalized guests flee the room. When only a small circle of his closest friends is left, L. attempts to perform his work, but suffers a paralytic stroke and falls to the floor.*

Time of composition: January 2–19, 1947. Time of narration: Late April 1945. Narrated time: 1930.

516/711	"Watch with me! [...] in my hour!"		Matthew 26:40. Compare Kretzschmar's Beethoven lecture on 62/89 as well as Z.'s explanation on 514/710.
519/717	He sat with his hands folded, his head tilted to one side		A Christological posture, though also one frequently affected by Nietzsche during his final years.
519/717	in that slightly monotone [...] fashion		Monotone and halting speech is another common symptom of tertiary syphilis, also attested in Nietzsche.
520/719	he used a kind of antiquated German		L.'s antiquated figures of speech are largely derived from the Chapbook, and in fact, parts of his address faithfully summarize similar passages in the original source.
520/718	famulus		See 56/79.
520/718	our hound Praestigiar		This name is derived from the Latin *praestigiator* (swindler, con man) and occurs in a later adaptation of the Chapbook that TM consulted during his research.
521/719	Goad		See 494/682.
521/720	The Angel of Poison		See Echo's chatter on 244/333.
521/720	you must set pins if you would bowl		A phrase that L. derives from the theology professor Kumpf. See 104/142.
522/721	for indeed St. Thomas already teaches		TM found these teachings in the *Malleus Maleficarum*.
523/722	my *datum* was fixed		Latin: "that which is given," though in German, *Datum* simply means "date."
523/723	the great *religiosus*		This reference to the devil as "the great religiosus" is unusual, but must be understood in light of the teachings of Eduard Schleppfuss in XIII.
523/723	*figuris* [...] *characteribus*		See 263/362.

524/724	should a man make the Devil [...] and break through	The summation of the "breakthrough" theme in *DF*, which is here applied not only to L.'s personal musical development, but also quite clearly to the German nation.
524/724	*Nigromantia, carmina, incantatio, veneficium*	Latin: "black arts, [magical] songs, incantation, preparation of poisons and potions." All terms that can be found in the Chapbook.
524/724	Hyphialta by name	Another term for "succubus" that TM found in early modern sources.
524/724	as my concubine	The original here has the antiquated term *Schlafweib*, which the Chapbook uses to describe Helen after Faustus employs her as his concubine.
525/725	Therefore I must needs kill him	The reference is, of course, to Schwerdtfeger. L.'s confession here suggests he knew exactly what would happen to his friend when he sent him to Marie Godeau's house.
525/725	*magisterulus*	Latin: "little master."
525/726	"He who seeketh hard things shall have it hard."	See 232/987. TM removed the earlier reference from the novel following the publication of the first edition, thus interfering with the tightly woven net of self-quotations that characterize L.'s final monologue.
527/728	"I, as a numismatist, consider myself completely incompetent here."	See 471/651.
527/728	We saw tears trickle [...] and fall on the keys	A similar occurrence is attested in the life of Hugo Wolf, another victim of syphilis that served as a model for L.
527/728	held his upper body in her motherly arms	Another instance of the pietà motif that we already saw on 137/188.

Epilogue

After his paralytic stroke, L. at first spends several months in an asylum, then returns home to the Schweigestill farm. There, he tries to wade into the Klammer Pool—possibly in an attempt to commit suicide, possibly in a gesture of baptism—but is saved from drowning by the farm hand. Soon after, his mother takes him home to Buchel Farm, where he will live for ten more years before succumbing to his illness. A distraught Z. remains to offer a prayer for his fatherland.

Time of composition: January 21–29, 1947. Time of narration: May 1945. Narrated time: 1930–1940.

528/729	"It is done."		Variation on John 20:15: "It is finished."
528/729	the large pile of enlivened paper		Z. may here be playing with the traditional humanist trope of "living letters," but may also be referring to the possibly demonic force that has been showing itself to work throughout *DF*.
528/730	poisoned by their doctors, then drenched in gasoline		Reference to the deaths of Adolf Hitler and Joseph Goebbels (1897–1945) on May 1, 1945.
529/730	means for having these pages reach America		See the "Contexts" section of this book for a summary of the transatlantic publication history of *DF*.
529/730	I fear that over this savage decade		This fear was TM's as well.
530/732	old woman appeared […] in order to take her back with her		As did Nietzsche's mother, who accompanied her son back to his native Naumburg in 1889.
530/733	"Woman, what have I to do with thee?"		See John 2:4.
532/735	he who invokes the Devil […] only by "consigning the body"		This idea is mentioned several times in the Chapbook. There are several other ways to interpret L.'s suicide attempt, most importantly as an attempted baptism or as an allusion to *The Little Mermaid*.
532/735	the son erupted into anger against his mother		Another episode from the life of Nietzsche, who erupted into a similar fit of rage during the train journey from Frankfurt to Naumburg.
533/736	An *Ecce homo* countenance		See 153/211.
533/737	nobleman by El Greco		Presumably a reference to "Nobleman with a Hand on His Chest" (~1580) by El Greco (1541–1614). The subject of this painting does indeed closely match the description of L. that Z. offered in the last two chapters.

534/738	"May God have mercy on your poor soul"	TM found similar phrases both in a biographical volume on Nietzsche and in the letters of Hugo Wolf, tying L.'s final fate closely to that of two of his real-life models.

Author's Note

The "Author's Note," which TM added to appease Arnold Schoenberg, first appeared in 1948 in an edition licensed to the Suhrkamp Verlag in Germany.

13: Cast of Characters

Roughly 150 named characters populate the pages of *Doctor Faustus*. The following list includes only fictional characters and only those who are mentioned in more than one place in the novel. Historical figures who make cameo appearances are glossed in the main commentary.

Arzt, Matthäus	Member of the Winfried fraternity in Halle. Mann found the last name in a biography of the German sculptor and woodcarver Tilmann Riemenschneider (ca. 1460–1531), although "Arzt" also means "medical doctor" in German. His first name is that of the Apostle Matthew in German.
Baworinski	Presiding officer of the Winfried fraternity in Halle. Mann found the name in the letters of Martin Luther.
Binder-Majoresku, Frau	Divorced Romanian authoress of light comedies; maintains a Bohemian salon in Munich. Possibly supplies Inez Rodde with morphine.
Breisacher, Dr. Chaim	Independent scholar in Munich, first a guest of the Schlaginhaufen salon, later of the Kridwiss Circle. Advocates *völkisch* and proto-fascist ideas. Modeled on the historian and philosopher Oskar Goldberg (1885–1953).
Bullinger	Acquaintance of Rüdiger Schildknapp's. A paper manufacturer in Munich. Mann found the name in the letters of Martin Luther.

Cimabue, Luca	Apprentice violin-maker in the household of Nikolaus Leverkühn Family name derives from the Italian painter Cenni di Pepo (ca. 1240–1302), popularly known as Cimabue.
Deutschlin, Konrad	Member of the Winfried fraternity in Halle. Mann found the name in a biography of Tilmann Riemenschneider, but it also alludes to "deutsch," meaning "German."
Dungersheim	Member of the Winfried fraternity in Halle. Mann found the name in the letters of Martin Luther.
Edelmann, Dr.	Director of the music publishing house that publishes *Apocalipsis cum figuris*.
Edschmidt, Dr.	Conductor of the Zapfenstösser Orchestra. Name probably derives from the writer Kasimir Edschmid (1890–1960).
Erasmi, Dr.	Leipzig medical doctor. Specialist in venereal diseases who briefly treats Leverkühn before suddenly dying. Name presumably derives from Erasmus of Rotterdam (1466–1536).
Esmeralda, or "Hetaera Esmeralda"	Prostitute who offers her services to Leverkühn in a brothel in Leipzig, then is subsequently visited by him in Pressburg. Source of Leverkühn's syphilitic infection. Strongly hinted by Zeitblom to be a succubus. Possibly reappears later as Frau von Tolna, Leverkühn's mysterious benefactress.

Fitelberg, Saul	International music agent and concert producer. First name derives from the film agent Saul C. Colin (1909–1967), who tried to facilitate a cinematic adaptation of Mann's *Joseph* tetralogy. Mann found the last name in the memoirs of Igor Stravinsky. Fitelberg's behavior was partly modeled on that of Riccault de la Marlinière, a character in the play *Minna von Barnhelm* (1767) by Gotthold Ephraim Lessing (1729–1781).
Godeau, Isabeau	Aunt of Marie Godeau.
Godeau, Marie	French-Swiss artist; stage designer in Paris. Love interest of both Leverkühn and Rudi Schwerdtfeger, the latter of whom proposes marriage to her in his own name, rather than in that of Leverkühn, who had commissioned him to woo Godeau. External appearance is modeled on Mann's wife Katia; name is a composite of various people from the memoirs of Igor Stravinsky.
Hanne	Floppy-bosomed milkmaid at Buchel. Introduces Leverkühn to musical rounds.
Hinterpförtner, Monsignore	Head of the Theological Seminary in Freising. Friend of Zeitblom. Name translates as "warden of the back door."
Holzschuher, Prof. Gilgen	Art historian and Dürer scholar; member of the Kridwiss Circle. Name is a compound derived from biographies of Riemenschneider and Dürer. The possible model is Wilhelm Waetzoldt, whose Dürer biography forms one of the main sources for *Doctor Faustus*.
Hubmeyer	Member of the Winfried fraternity in Halle. Mann found the name in a biography of Tilmann Riemenschneider.

Institoris, Dr. Helmut	Aesthetician and art historian, instructor at the Munich Technical Institute. Marries Inez Rodde. Name derives from Henricus Institoris, the author of the fifteenth-century inquisitor's manual *Malleus Maleficarum*.
Kaschperl	Farm dog at Pfeiffering. Name is a dialectal diminutive of *Kaspar*, a common designation for the devil and also the name of a character in the Faust opera *Der Freischütz* (1821) by Carl Maria von Weber (1786–1826).
Kjoejelund, Harald	Heldentenor at the Munich opera. Model unknown.
Knöterich, Konrad	Amateur painter and musician, member of Frau Rodde's Munich salon. Possibly modeled on a certain Herr Knötzinger, an acquaintance of Mann's mother.
Knöterich, Natalia	Amateur painter, wife of Konrad K, rumored to be addicted to morphine.
Kranich, Dr.	Numismatist and curator of a coin museum in Munich. Last name means "crane" in German. Likely modeled on Professor Georg Habich, the director of Munich's Numismatic Collection, whose last name means "hawk" in German.
Kretzschmar, Wendell	Leverkühn's music teacher in Kaisersaschern and Leipzig. Name most likely derives from the musicologist Hermann Kretzschmar (1848–1924). Born in Pennsylvania into a German-American family. Pursues career as conductor and organist in Germany and Switzerland. Composer of several musical works, including the opera *The Marble Statue*. Organist in Kaisersaschern during Leverkühn's youth, later instructor of organ and piano classes at Hase's Private Conservatory in Leipzig. Arranges first public performance of a Leverkühn work and has others published.

Kridwiss, Sixtus	Graphic artist and collector of East Asian art. Leader of the proto-fascist "Kridwiss Circle" in Munich during the years following the First World War. Mann found both first and last name in the letters of Martin Luther, although the figure as a whole is modeled on Mann's friend, the graphic artist and stage designer Emil Preetorius, who was President of the Bavarian Academy of Fine Arts in the 1920s. Preetorius stayed in Germany after 1933 and rose to a prominent position at the Bayreuth Festival during the Nazi period, which led to a cooling-off of his relationship with Thomas Mann. However, they resumed their old relations in 1947, and Preetorius appears not to have been bitter about what Mann characterized as one of his "literary murders."
Kumpf, Ehrenfried	Professor of systematic theology at Halle, teacher to both Leverkühn and to a reluctant Zeitblom. Mann found the name in a biography of Tilmann Riemenschneider. Kumpf's archaic language and his behavior strongly allude to Martin Luther, although the character also resembles the German theologian Martin Kähler (1835–1912), one of the teachers of Mann's friend Paul Tillich.
Kürbis, Dr.	Quack doctor who treats Leverkühn for syphilitic symptoms in 1918/1919 and attempts to treat Nepomuk Schneidewein ten years later. Name means "pumpkin" in German.
Leverkühn, Adrian	German composer. A Dr. August Leverkühn served as a court-appointed guardian for the Mann children after the death of Thomas Mann's father, but the more pertinent etymology is from *Leben* = life + *kühn* = audacious. The exhortation to "live audaciously" alludes to an aphorism from Friedrich Nietzsche's *The Gay Science* (Bk. 4 §283), as well as possibly to the ethos of fascism.

Leverkühn, Elsbeth	Leverkühn's mother. Mistress of Buchel. Physical description is modeled on the *Portrait of a Venetian Woman* by Dürer. See Fig. 2.
Leverkühn, Georg	Leverkühn's older brother; his senior by five years. Heir to the family farm at Buchel.
Leverkühn, Jonathan	Leverkühn's father. Farmer at Buchel and amateur naturalist. Physical description is modeled on a copper etching by Dürer of Luther's friend and collaborator Philip Melanchthon (1497–1560), a leading intellectual voice of the Reformation. See Fig. 1.
Leverkühn, Nikolaus	Leverkühn's paternal uncle. Owner of a musical instrument shop in Kaisersaschern and a violin-maker. Physical description is modeled on the sketch *The Master-Builder Jerome of Augsburg* by Dürer. See Fig. 3.
Leverkühn, Ursula	Leverkühn's younger sister. Marries Johannes Schneidewein, with whom she has four children, among them Nepomuk Schneidewein.
Luder, Frau	Manager of the dairy at Buchel Farm. Name means "hussy" in German.
Manardi, Peronella	Mistress of the Manardi household in Palestrina. Name derives from Giovanni Manardi (1462–1532), Italian humanist and pioneering syphilis researcher.
Michelsen	Schoolmaster at Weissenfels. Private tutor of the young Leverkühn.
Nackedey, Meta	Admirer of Leverkühn. Last name translates as "naked child." Modeled on Ida Herz, a fervent admirer of Mann who served as his sometime archivist and librarian.

Nonnenmacher, Kolonat	Professor of ancient philosophy at the University of Halle, teacher of both Zeitblom and Leverkühn. Mann found both the first and the last name in a biography of Tilmann Riemenschneider, but the last name also translates as "creator of nuns," alluding to the early modern custom of locking away in nunneries women who had become pregnant out of wedlock.
Nottebohm	Painter and friend of the Institoris household. Name derives from the Beethoven scholar Martin Gustav Nottebohm (1817–1882), although in all other regards he is modeled on the painter Walter Geffcken (1872–1950), a friend of the Mann family.
Orlanda, Tanya	Wagnerian heroine in Munich. Likely modeled on the soprano Milka Ternina (1863–1941), the mistress of Mann's father-in-law Alfred Pringsheim.
Platner, Hans	Owner of the marionette theater that first performs *Gesta Romanorum* at Donaueschingen in 1921.
Probst	Member of the Winfried fraternity in Halle. Mann found the name in the letters of Martin Luther.
Radbruch	Publisher of Rüdiger Schildknapp and member of the prewar salons frequented by Leverkühn and Zeitblom in Munich.
Reiff, Herr and Frau	Wealthy Swiss industrialists who introduce L. to Marie Godeau. Modeled on Swiss friends of the Mann family who frequently hosted TM during the 1930s.
Riedesel, Baron von	Guest at the Munich salon of the Schlaginhaufens. General intendant of the Royal Bavarian Court Theater. Mann found the name in the letters of Martin Luther. The figure is a composite of two actual general intendants, Ernst Ritter von Possart and Albert Freiherr von Speidel.

Rodde, Frau	Widow of a senator from the Hanseatic town of Bremen. Society host in Munich. The character is modeled on Mann's mother, Julia Mann née Silva-Bruhns, who hosted a modest salon in Munich after the death of Mann's father, Senator Thomas Johann Heinrich Mann (1840–1891). Her last name is presumably modeled on Senator Matthias Rodde (1754–1825), whose biography provided Mann with fertile material for his novel *Buddenbrooks*.
Rodde, Clarissa	Younger daughter of Frau Rodde. Modeled on Mann's sister Carla Mann.
Rodde, Inez	Older daughter of Frau Rodde. Modeled on Mann's sister Julia Elisabeth Mann (1877–1927). "Ines" in German original.
Rosenstiel, Kunigunde	Admirer of Leverkühn. Provides him with the *Visions of St. Paul* that become a source of the *Apocalipsis cum figuris*. Last name translates as "rose stem." Modeled on Mann's fervent admirer and part-time secretary Ida Herz (see also "Nackedey, Meta"), as well as on German-Jewish literary critic Käte Hamburger, who wrote pioneering studies of Mann.
Schappeler	Member of the Winfried fraternity in Halle. Mann found the name in a biography of Tilmann Riemenschneider.
Scheurl, Jeanette	Novelist and acquaintance of Leverkühn in Munich. Mann found the name in the letters of Martin Luther, but the character is otherwise modeled on Annette Kolb (1870–1967), a friend of Mann's and a famous novelist in her own right. She never forgave her friend for this portrait.

Schildknapp, Rüdiger	Writer and translator. Close friend of Leverkühn, whom he meets during their mutual time in Leipzig. Last name means "shield bearer" in German. Physical description and behavior are patterned on Mann's friend Hans Reisiger, a translator most famous for his translations into German of *Leaves of Grass* (1855) by Walt Whitman.
Schlaginhaufen, Dr. and Frau	Hosts of a Munich salon. The name derives from the letters of Martin Luther and could be translated as "heap of punches" or "punch the rabble." Frau Schlaginhaufen's maiden name is von Plausig, marking her as a member of the aristocracy.
Schleppfuss, Eberhard	Private lecturer teaching psychology of religion at Halle. Teacher to both Leverkühn and Zeitblom. Last name means "dragfoot" in German, an obvious reference to the traditional depiction of Satan with a cloven hoof.
Schneidewein, Johannes	Leverkühn's brother-in-law. Husband of Ursula Leverkühn, father of Nepomuk Schneidewein. Optician in Langenselza. Mann fond the last name in the letters of Martin Luther.
Schneidewein, Nepomuk	Nephew of Leverkühn. Known to his family as "Echo." Modeled on Frido Mann, Mann's grandson by way of his youngest son Michael.
Schweigestill, Clementina	Daughter of Max and Else Schweigestill. Reads to Leverkühn during his long period of illness in 1918/19. "Clementine" in German.
Schweigestill, Else	Mistress of the Schweigestill farm in Pfeiffering. Name translates as "be silent" or "I will be silent."
Schweigestill, Gereon	Son of Max and Else Schweigestill. Heir to the family farm in Pfeiffering.

Schweigestill, Max	Master of the Schweigestill farm in Pfeiffering.
Schwerdtfeger, Rudolf	Violinist, later concertmaster, of the Zapfenstösser Orchestra in Munich. Modeled on Mann's childhood friend and love interest Paul Ehrenberg (1876–1949). The name derives from an old-fashioned word for "sword maker," but literally means "sword polisher."
Spengler, Baptist	Painter, member of the Rodde salon in Munich. Suffers from syphilis, though not with the same creative effects the disease precipitates in Leverkühn. Passes away in 1930, six weeks before Leverkühn's descent into madness. Modeled on a friend of Mann's mother, the painter Baptist Scherer (1869–1910), though the last name likely alludes to the reactionary cultural philosopher Oswald Spengler (1880–1936).
Stoientin, Dr.	Director of the School of the Brethren in Kaisersaschern. Leverkühn's teacher in Greek, Middle High German, and Hebrew. Later Zeitblom's superior. Name derives from David Friedrich Strauß's biography of the German humanist Ulrich von Hutten.
Suso	Farm dog at Buchel. Name derives from the medieval mystic Henricus Suso (1295?–1366).
Teutleben, Carl von	Member of the Winfried fraternity in Halle. Mann found the name in the letters of Martin Luther, but might also be read as an allusion to *deutsches Leben* = German life.

Tolna, Madame de	Mysterious Hungarian noblewoman, benefactress of Leverkühn. Arranges for the publication of *Apocalipsis cum figuris* by seducing a music critic and convincing him to write a positive review. Follows Leverkühn around at a distance. Owns a large estate in Hungary where Leverkühn and Schwerdtfeger embark on a holiday after first performance of Leverkühn's violin concerto and become intimate. Likely identical with the prostitute Esmeralda. Most obvious model is Tchaikovsky's benefactress Nadezhda von Meck (1831–94), although several other possible sources have been identified.
Unruhe, Dr. Egon	"Philosophical paleozoologist" and member of the Kridwiss Circle. Mann found the name in the letters of Martin Luther, although the character is otherwise modeled on the philosopher and paleozoologist Edgar Dacqué (1878–1945).
Vogler, Professor Georg	Literary historian of a nationalist bent; member of the Kridwiss Circle. Mann found the name in the letters of Martin Luther, although the character is modeled on the philologist Josef Nadler (1884–1963), the author of a *Literary History of the German Tribes and Landscapes* (1912–1928).
Waltpurgis	Milkmaid at Pfeiffering. Early modern sources commonly refer to presumptive witches by this name, which also recalls the Walpurgis Night of April 30–May 1, on which evil spirits were thought to assemble.
Zeitblom, Helene (née Ölhafen)	Wife of Zeitblom. Mann found the name in the letters of Martin Luther; it translates as "oil harbor."
Zeitblom, Helene	Daughter of Zeitblom and Helene Zeitblom, née Ölhafen. Married to the manager of the Regensburg branch of the Bavarian Security and Exchange.

Zeitblom, Serenus	Biographer of Leverkühn and narrator of *Doctor Faustus*. Mann found a model for the given name in the *Malleus Maleficarum*, a model for the surname in Wilhelm Waetzoldt's *Dürer and his Times*. Taken together, the name translates as "serene blossom of time." In ancient thought, "serenity" is sometimes also characterized as a "Jovial" (i.e. Jupiter-affiliated) quality that stands in opposition to the "Saturnine" melancholia afflicting Leverkühn.
Zimbalist, Dr.	Leipzig medical doctor. Specialist in venereal diseases who briefly treats Leverkühn before being arrested. Name alludes to the violin virtuoso Efrem Zimbalist (1889–1985), director of the Curtis Institute of Music at the time that *Doctor Faustus* was written.
Zink, Leo	Austrian painter, member of the Rodde salon in Munich. Modeled on a friend of Mann's mother, Leo Putz (1869–1940).
Zur Höhe, Daniel	Poet and member of the Kridwiss Circle. Modeled on the poet Ludwig Derleth (1870–1948), whom Mann had already parodied forty years earlier in his short story "At the Prophet's" (1904).
Zwitscher, Rosa	Actress at the Munich Hoftheater and member of the Rodde circle. Last name means "twitter" in German.

14: Timeline of Events in the Novel

(Note: Mann's chronology for the years 1900–1910 is not entirely consistent. This timeline represents the most plausible dating of events.)

1883	Zeitblom born in Kaisersaschern on the Saale (II).
1885	Leverkühn born in Oberweiler near Weissenfels (III).
1893	Schoolmaster Michelsen becomes private tutor of Leverkühn (V).
1895	Leverkühn enters Boniface Gymnasium in Kaisersaschern (V).
1899 or 1900	Leverkühn starts taking private music lessons from Wendell Kretzschmar (VII).
1900–1901	Leverkühn attends Kretzschmar's public lectures on music (VIII).
1901	Zeitblom begins studies at Jena (XI).
1902	Zeitblom moves to the University of Giessen (IX).
1903–05	Zeitblom and Leverkühn reunited in Halle, where Zeitblom studies classical philology and Leverkühn theology (II).
1905	Leverkühn moves to Leipzig to begin formal studies of music with Kretzschmar. Zeitblom begins military service in Naumburg (XV). Leverkühn's first encounter with the prostitute Esmeralda (XVI).
1906	Leverkühn travels to Pressburg in search of Esmeralda and sleeps with her, contracting syphilis and initiating devil's pact (XIX). Zeitblom moves to Leipzig to resume his studies (XVIII).
1906–1910	Leverkühn composes song cycles on Mediterranean themes as well as on poems by Brentano. Further compositions include several piano pieces, a concerto for string orchestra, and a quartet for flute, clarinet, *corno di bassetto*, and bassoon (XX–XXI).

1908–1909	Zeitblom travels to Greece (XVIII). First public performance of a composition by Leverkühn, the *Phosphorescence of the Sea* in Basel (XXI).
1909	Zeitblom starts teaching classical languages and history at Kaisersaschern (II).
1910	Zeitblom marries Helene Ölhafen. Leverkühn moves to Munich and formulates first ideas for a "strict style" (XXII).
1911	Leverkühn leaves Munich in June to spend a year in Italy with Rüdiger Schildknapp. They pass the summer in Palestrina, the winter in Rome (XXIV).
1912	Leverkühn moves from Rome to Palestrina in May before returning to Germany at the end of the summer. Conversation with the devil (XXV). Leverkühn finishes *Love's Labour's Lost* (XXVI). Zeitblom visits Leverkühn in Palestrina. Leverkühn takes up residence on the Schweigestill Farm in Pfeiffering. (XXVI).
1913	Zeitblom starts teaching classical languages and history at both the high school and the theological seminary in Freising (II). Leverkühn composes songs to poems by Blake and Keats, as well as "The Festival of Spring," on a poem by Klopstock, in a setting for baritone, organ, and string orchestra (XXVII).
1914	First public performance of *Love's Labour's Lost* in Lübeck. Leverkühn composes orchestral fantasy *Marvels of the Universe* (XXVII). Zeitblom is called up for active duty and participates in invasion of France (XXI).
1915	Zeitblom contracts typhoid fever and is discharged from military, returning to his teaching post in Freising. Leverkühn composes *Gesta Romanorum*, an opera for puppets (XXX). Inez Rodde marries Dr. Helmut Institoris, despite being secretly in love with Rudi Schwerdtfeger (XXXII).
1918	Leverkühn and Zeitblom witness the end of the First World War, the November Revolution, and the birth of the Soviet council movement in Munich. Leverkühn suffers from intense migraines as a result of his syphilitic infection (XXXIV).

1919	Leverkühn recovers from his illness, writes the oratorio *Apocalipsis cum figuris*. First appearance of Frau von Tolna. Zeitblom and Leverkühn attend meetings of the "Kridwiss Circle" (XXXIV).
1920	First public performance of *Marvels of the Universe* in Weimar (XXXVI).
1921	First public performance of *Gesta Romanorum* in Donaueschingen (XXXVI).
1922	Suicide of Clarissa Rodde. First performance of the Brentano Songs in Zurich (XXXV).
1923	Saul Fitelberg visits Pfeiffering. (XXXVII). Birth of Nepomuk Schneidewein (Echo) (XLIV).
1924	Fragments of the *Apocalipsis cum figuris* first performed at a festival of the International Society for New Music in Prague. Leverkühn finishes his Violin Concerto (XXXVIII), which receives its first performance in Vienna, with Schwerdtfeger playing the solo part. Leverkühn and Schwerdtfeger visit Schloss Tolna in Hungary, where they commence an intimate relationship (XXXVI). In the closing days of the year, Leverkühn attends a performance of the concerto in Zurich, where he first meets Marie Godeau (XXXIX).
1925	The excursion to the Bavarian Alps (XL). Schwerdtfeger courts Marie Godeau on Leverkühn's behalf, then becomes engaged to her himself (XLI). A vengeful Inez Rodde shoots Schwerdtfeger (XLII).
1926	Only complete public performance of *Apocalipsis cum figuris* at the festival of the International Society for New Music in Frankfurt am Main (XXXIV). Max Schweigestill and Jonathan Leverkühn both pass away in the week between Christmas and the New Year.
1927	Leverkühn's "annus mirabilis." Composes music for an ensemble of strings, woodwinds, and piano; a string quartet; and a trio for violin, viola, and cello. First plans for *The Lamentation of Dr. Faustus* (XLIII).
1928	Leverkühn's nephew Nepomuk Schneidewein ("Echo") comes to Pfeiffering to recuperate from a case of the measles (XLIV). Leverkühn works on a musical setting of Ariel's songs from *The Tempest*. Death of Nepomuk Schneidewein from cerebrospinal meningitis (XLV).

1929	Leverkühn begins composition of symphonic cantata *The Lamentation of Dr. Faustus* (XLVI).
1930	Leverkühn concludes composition of *The Lamentation of Dr. Faustus* and suffers paralytic stroke (XLVII). After three months in a sanatorium in Nymphenburg he returns to Pfeiffering, where he tries to drown himself in the Klammerweiher. Brought home to Buchel by his mother towards the end of the year (epilogue).
1934	Zeitblom retires from his teaching position in Freising following the ascent of the Nazis (I).
1939	Final meeting between Leverkühn and Zeitblom (epilogue).
1940	Death of Leverkühn (I).
1943	Zeitblom begins composition of *Doctor Faustus* (I).
1945	Zeitblom concludes composition of *Doctor Faustus* (epilogue).

15: List of Adrian Leverkühn's Major Compositions

(Note: The division of Leverkühn's oeuvre into "early," "middle," and "late" periods is my own and not attested in the novel. My justification for this schema is given in chapter 10, "Music Theory and Political Allegory")

Early period. Compositions completed prior to the devil's pact (1905–1906)

Characterized by high degree of fidelity to late-nineteenth-century musical conventions.

> "His whole life long [Leverkühn] would no more count this demonstration of talent for coloristic orchestration among his actual compositions than he did the calligraphic, wrist-loosening exercises over which he had previously labored for Kretschmar" (161/221).

Choruses for six to eight voices (XVIII)	1905–1906
Fugue with three themes for string quintet with piano accompaniment (XVIII)	1905–1906
Symphony (XVIII)	1905–1906
Cello sonata in A major (XVIII)	1905–1906
Phosphorescence of the Sea (symphonic fantasy) (XVIII)	1905–1906

Middle period. From the devil's pact to the outbreak of tertiary syphilis (1906–1918)

Characterized by a predilection for vocal music and the embrace of early modern musical forms.

> "I discovered that he was increasingly preoccupied with an interest in music wedded to word, with its vocal articulation" (172/235).

> "And now before my eyes the dramatic form was being superseded by the epic, music drama being transformed into oratorio, opera

drama into opera cantata [...]—out of an attitude, I mean, which, being no longer interested in things psychological, insisted on being objective, on a language that expressed something absolute, binding, and obligatory, and that therefore preferred to put on the gentle chains of pre-classical strict forms" (391/539–40).

Songs on Mediterranean themes (XX)	1906–1910
Songs on poems by Verlaine and Blake (XX)	1906–1910
Piano pieces (XXI)	1906–1910
"Concerto" for string orchestra (XXI)	1906–1910
Quartet for flute, clarinet, *corno di bassetto*, and bassoon (XXI)	1906–1910
13 Brentano Songs (XXI)	1906–1910
Love's Labour's Lost (opera) (XXIV)	1912
Songs on poems by Keats and Klopstock (XXVII)	1913
Marvels of the Universe (orchestral fantasy; also referred to by Zeitblom as *Cosmic Symphony*) (XXVII)	1914
Gesta Romanorum (puppet opera) (XXX)	1915
Apocalipsis cum figuris (oratorio, also referred to by Zeitblom as *The Revelation of St. John*) (XXXIV)	1919

Late Period. From the outbreak of tertiary syphilis to the paralytic stroke (1919–1930)

Continued emphasis on vocal music and early modern forms, but with added degree of parody. Full embrace of the "strict style" first discussed in 1912. Lamentation as an artistic genre.

"The tendency to hybridize forms, to mix and switch them [...] was now indeed growing. 'In studying philosophy,' he in fact said, 'I learned that to set limits is to go beyond them. I've always held to that notion.' What he meant was Hegel's critique of Kant" (479/662–63).

Violin concerto (XXXVIII)	1924
Chamber piece for three strings, three woodwinds, and piano (XLIII)	1927
String quartet (XLIII)	1927
Trio for violin, viola, and cello (XLIII)	1927
Songs from *The Tempest* (XLIV)	1928
The Lamentation of Doctor Faustus (symphonic cantata; also referred to by Zeitblom as an oratorio) (XLVII)	1930

16: Suggestions for Further Reading and Research

*D*OCTOR *F*AUSTUS is one of the most influential and most talked-about literary works of the twentieth century. The period from 1947 to 1950 alone saw the publication of over three hundred popular reviews; academic journals began printing studies of *Doctor Faustus* in 1948, within a year of the novel's original publication date. Naturally, these first academic articles appeared in American journals, because the German university establishment still lay in ruins so shortly after the war.

In the seventy-five years that have passed since then, interest in the novel has continued unabated. It would be impossible to summarize all the pertinent critical developments in a short essay, and also unnecessary for a first-time reader. My aim in this chapter is instead to equip readers with the best possible tools to help them delve deeper into the novel, and into the life and thought of Thomas Mann more generally. To this end, I first provide an annotated list of what I consider standard reference works on *Doctor Faustus*. Then, I present a curated selection of article-length scholarship that has been published in English over the past fifty years. Readers with an advanced knowledge of German will, of course, have access to a much wider range of research. A comprehensive bibliography that is current up to 2007 can be found in the commentary volume to the *Große kommentierte Frankfurter Ausgabe* of *Doctor Faustus* (see further information in chapter 2 of this guide). For scholarship since then, the yearbook of the German Thomas Mann Society, the *Thomas Mann Jahrbuch* currently edited by Katrin Bedenig, Marc von Moos, and Hans Wißkirchen, is an invaluable starting point.

Standard Reference Works

Guides and Introductions

Beddow, Michael. *Thomas Mann: "Doctor Faustus."* Cambridge: Cambridge University Press, 1994.

> A useful and compact introductory guide, even though one occasionally gets the impression that Beddow does not actually like *Doctor Faustus*.

Bergsten, Gunilla. *Thomas Mann's "Doctor Faustus": The Sources and Structure of the Novel*. Translated by Krishna Winston. Chicago: University of Chicago Press, 1963.

> Pathbreaking analysis on the sources and inner structure of *Doctor Faustus*, frequently quoted even today. Possibly the single most important monograph ever published on the novel.

Kontje, Todd. *The Cambridge Introduction to Thomas Mann*. Cambridge: Cambridge University Press, 2010.

> Concise and well-written introductory guide to Thomas Mann. Includes a short chapter on *Doctor Faustus*.

Reed, Terence J. *Thomas Mann: The Uses of Tradition*. Oxford: Clarendon University Press, 1974.

> If Bergsten's study is the most important monograph to ever be published on *Doctor Faustus*, then Reed's book can arguably make the same claim about Mann's oeuvre as a whole, at least in English. Focuses on Mann's debts to the German cultural and intellectual tradition, but touches upon almost all major aspects of his work as well. For students who want to delve deeper than the Kontje volume allows.

Vaget, Hans Rudolf. "'German' Music and German Catastrophe: A Re-Reading of *Doctor Faustus*." In *A Companion to the Works of Thomas Mann*, edited by Herbert Lehnert and Eva Wessell, 221–44. Rochester, NY: Camden House, 2004.

> Thorough introductory article on *Doctor Faustus*, divided into similar sub-divisions as this *Guide*. Makes a strong argument for the novel as a commentary specifically on the "German Catastrophe" of Nazism and the Holocaust.

Letters, Essays, and Autobiographical Documents with Special Relevance to *Doctor Faustus*

Mann, Thomas. *The Letters of Thomas Mann 1889–1955. Volume 2: 1943–1955*. Edited and Translated by Richard and Clara Winston. London: Martin Secker & Warburg, 1970.

> Unfortunately, Mann's diaries from the 1940s have not been translated into English, and only a small fraction of his many letters are included in this volume. Nevertheless, the 150 or so pages of this volume that deal directly with the 1940s provide unparalleled insight into Mann's life and mindset during the years in which he wrote *Doctor Faustus*.

Mann, Thomas. *Thomas Mann's Antifascist Radio Addresses, 1940–1945: German Listeners!* Edited and translated by Elaine Chen, Jeffrey L. High, and Hans Rudolf Vaget. Rochester, NY: Camden House, 2025.

> While working on the first half of *Doctor Faustus*, Mann recorded a series of anti-fascist radio broadcasts for the BBC. These provide valuable insight into his political thinking at the time and make for especially interesting reading when compared to Zeitblom's parenthetical reflections in the novel.

Mann, Thomas. *The Story of a Novel: The Genesis of "Doctor Faustus."* New York: Alfred A. Knopf, 1961.

> Mann's book-length account of the composition of *Doctor Faustus* is a fascinating and highly informative document, even though it needs to be treated with a certain amount of circumspection. (The original German title translates as *The Genesis of "Doctor Faustus": Novel of a Novel*).

Mann, Thomas. *Thomas Mann's Addresses. Delivered at the Library of Congress, 1942–1949.* Washington, DC: The Library of Congress, 1963.

> Contains two important lectures that deal directly with themes presented in the novel, "Germany and the Germans" (1945) and "Nietzsche's Philosophy in the Light of Contemporary Events" (1947).

Schoenberg, E. Randol, ed. *The Doctor Faustus Dossier: Arnold Schoenberg, Thomas Mann, and Their Contemporaries, 1930–1951.* Berkeley: University of California Press, 2018.

> Comprehensive dossier of the Schoenberg-Mann controversy precipitated by Mann's supposed act of plagiarism in chapter XXII. Contains not only many letters by both figures but also a number of interesting early critical studies.

Biographies

Boes, Tobias. *Thomas Mann's War: Literature, Politics, and the World Republic of Letters.* Ithaca, NY: Cornell University Press, 2019.

> Explores Mann's political activism and his self-stylization as a public intellectual during the period of his American exile.

Heilbut, Anthony. *Thomas Mann: Eros and Literature.* Berkeley, CA: University of California Press, 1996.

> Probably the most readable biography of Mann available in English. Focuses on Mann's suppressed homoeroticism and deals mainly with the first half of his life, not his American exile.

Kurzke, Hermann. *Thomas Mann: Life as a Work of Art.* Translated by Leslie Wilson. Princeton, NJ: Princeton University Press, 2002.
> Generally recognized as the most critically astute biography of Mann, by a major German Mann scholar. Unfortunately, the English translation is not always fortuitous.

Bibliographies

Fetzer, John F. *Changing Perceptions of Thomas Mann's "Doctor Faustus": Criticism 1947–1992.* Columbia, SC: Camden House, 1996.
> Contains a detailed overview of the first fifty years of *Doctor Faustus* criticism and includes a bibliography with over 750 entries.

Selected Criticism, 1980–2025 (in chronological order)

Palencia-Roth, Michael, "Albrecht Dürer's *Melencolia I* and Thomas Mann's *Doktor Faustus.*" *German Studies Review* 3, no. 4 (1980): 361–75.
> Detailed analysis of Dürer's *Melencolia I* and the theme of melancholia more generally in *Doctor Faustus.* Argues that Mann deeply identified with Leverkühn, at least in the sense that he believed great art could only be created from a spirit of profound melancholy.

Cerf, Steven. "Love in Thomas Mann's *Doktor Faustus* as an Imitatio Shaekespeari." *Comparative Literature Studies* 18 (1981): 475–86.
> Examines the numerous references to Shakespeare in *Doctor Faustus* and argues that each successive encounter with the Bard reflects a stage in the evolution of Leverkühn's attitudes towards love.

Durrani, Osman. "Echo's Reverberations: Notes on a Painful Incident in Thomas Mann's *Doktor Faustus.*" *German Life & Letters* 37, no. 2 (1983): 125–34.
> Provides a run-down of various literary and historical models that may have influenced the creation of Nepomuk Schneidewein and examines the ambiguous role he plays in the novel.

Ryan, Judith. "The Flowers of Evil: Thomas Mann's *Doctor Faustus.*" In The *Uncompleted Past: Postwar German Novels and the Third Reich,* 42–55. Detroit: Wayne State University Press, 1983.
> Analyzes Thomas Mann's analysis of Nazism, positioning *Doctor Faustus* as a paradigmatic novel of exile. Connects it to a larger "turn towards myth" amongst novels of the early postwar period.

Lehnert, Herbert. "The Luther-Erasmus Constellation in Thomas Mann's *Doktor Faustus.*" *Michigan Germanic Studies* 10 (1984): 142–58.

> Maps the Luther-Erasmus dichotomy in *Doctor Faustus* onto various other facets of Mann's cultural and intellectual formation. In the process, presents a highly readable synthesis of Mann's intellectual origins. Defends Luther against his portrayal in the novel.

Durrani, Osman. "The Tearful Teacher: The Role of Serenus Zeitblom in Thomas Mann's *Doktor Faustus.*" *Modern Language Review* 80, no. 3 (1985): 652–58.

> Analyzes Zeitblom's role as a narrator in *Doctor Faustus*. Ultimately takes a positive view of him, arguing that Zeitblom's prose style is ideally attuned to its subject and that his ambivalences are no less indicative of the age in which he lives than is the fate of Leverkühn.

Roche, Mark W. "Laughter and Truth in *Doktor Faustus*: Nietzschean Structures in Mann's Novel of Self-Cancellation." *Deutsche Vierteljahrsschrift für Literatur und Geistesgeschichte* 60 (1986): 309–32.

> Examines *Doctor Faustus* as a Nietzsche novel, paying special attention to Leverkühn's characteristic laughter, which carries profound undertones in Nietzsche's philosophy.

Vaget, Hans Rudolf. "Amazing Grace: Thomas Mann, Adorno, and the Faust Myth." In *Our "Faust"? Roots and Ramifications of a Modern German Myth,* edited by Reinhold Grimm and Jost Hermand, 168–89. Madison: University of Wisconsin Press, 1987.

> Examines Leverkühn's final composition, the *Lamentation of Doctor Faustus,* and argues that is an expression of Mann's fundamentally hopeful and musically conservative worldview, as distinct from Adorno's more pessimistic embrace of musical modernism.

Angress-Klüger, Ruth. "Jewish Characters in Thomas Mann's Fiction." In *Horizonte: Festschrift für Herbert Lehnert zum 65. Geburtstag,* edited by Hannelore Mundt, Egon Schwarz, and William J. Lillymann, 161–72. Tübingen: Max Niemeyer Verlag, 1990.

> Examines Mann's depiction of Jewish characters throughout his career and argues that he remained entangled in anti-Semitic stereotypes.

Scaff, Susanne von Rohr. "Unending Apocalypse: The Crisis of Musical Narrative in Mann's *Doktor Faustus.*" *Germanic Review* 65 (1990): 30–39.

> Examines the crisis of artistic production in which Leverkühn finds himself caught, arguing that his compositions up to the *Apocalipsis* illustrate the modernist "spatial form" described by literary theorist Frank Kermode.

Lehnert, Herbert, and Pfeiffer, Peter C., eds. *Thomas Mann's "Doctor Faustus": A Novel at the Margins of Modernism*. Columbia: University of South Carolina Press, 1991.

> Pathbreaking essay collection with contributions by almost all of the leading Mann scholars of the time. Contains essays on female and on Jewish characters in *Doctor Faustus*, on Mann's views of Adorno and of Joyce, on the treatment of narcissism and of melancholia in the novel, and on *Doctor Faustus*'s influence on contemporary literature. Originally delivered as lectures, each essay is followed by a short and cogent response.

Robertson, Ritchie. "Accounting for History: Thomas Mann, *Doktor Faustus*." In *The German Novel of the 20th Century: Beyond Realism*, edited by David Magley, 128–48. Edinburgh: Edinburgh University Press, 1993.

> Argues for *Doctor Faustus* as a novel that synthesizes realist, modernist, and mythic elements in an attempt to combat Mann's fear of creating art that would be defeated by its own intellectualism. Points out that the novel elevates to the level of social analysis many elements that previous fictions by Mann had applied to the merely personal.

Eisenstein, Paul. "Leverkühn as Witness: The Holocaust in Thomas Mann's *Doktor Faustus*." *The German Quarterly* 70, no. 4 (1997): 325–46.

> Applies psychoanalytic theories of Jacques Lacan and Slavoj Žižek to *Doctor Faustus*. Indicts Zeitblom's attempts to read German history through the lens of the Faust-pact as an "attempt to save an ordering system in the face of the catastrophe that shatters it." Argues that Leverkühn recognizes the fundamentally unsymbolizable dimension of murder and tries to bear witness to it through his music, thereby creating an opposition to Nazism.

Marx, Friedhelm. "Transfigurations of Christ in Thomas Mann." *Religion & Literature* 33, no. 2 (2001): 22–36.

> Examines the recurrence of Christ figures throughout Mann's oeuvre, including in *Doctor Faustus*. One of the earliest example of a resurgence of interest in the religious dimensions of Mann's arts over the past twenty-five years.

Cobley, Evelyn. "Avant-Garde Aesthetics and Fascist Politics: Thomas Mann's *Doctor Faustus* and Theodor Adorno's *Philosophy of New Music*." *New German Critique* 86 (2002): 43–70.

> A difficult essay, but perhaps the most important analysis of Mann's debt to Adorno's *Philosophy of New Music* available in English. Argues that the views of modernity and modern art articulated in *Doctor Faustus* are ultimately similar to those expressed by Adorno. (See the 2008 essay by Justice Krauss for a dissenting view.)

Cobley, Evelyn. "Ambivalence and Dialectics: Mann's *Doktor Faustus* and Kleist's "Über das Marionettentheater." *Seminar: a Journal of Germanic Studies* 39, no. 1 (2003): 15–32.

> Investigates the role that Kleist's "On the Marionette Theater" plays in *Doctor Faustus*, arguing that Mann used it to illustrate a Hegelian, dialectical model of history that he had borrowed from Adorno.

Crawford, Karin L. "Exorcising the Devil from Thomas Mann's *Doktor Faustus*." *The German Quarterly* 76, no. 2 (2003): 168–82.

> Revisionist study which argues that there is no devil's pact in *Doctor Faustus* and thus, by extension, also no damnation of Germany. The true Faustus figure is instead Serenus Zeitblom, and Mann's novel seeks to deliver a "message of compassionate love" emblematized by the relationship between narrator and protagonist.

Maar, Michael. "Teddy and Tommy: The Masks of *Doctor Faustus*." *New Left Review* 20, no. 20 (2003): 113–30.

> Examines the personal and emotional dimension of the collaboration between Mann and Adorno. Argues that in chapter XXV, the devil adopts the appearance not of Adorno but rather of Gustav Mahler, to whose works Mann scattered hitherto underappreciated hidden references throughout his novel.

Martin, Nicholas. "'Ewig verbundene Geister': Thomas Mann's Re-engagement with Nietzsche, 1943–1947." *Oxford German Studies* 34, no. 2 (2005): 197–203.

> Concise yet detail-rich examination of Mann's debts and allusions to Nietzsche both in *Doctor Faustus* and in his 1947 essay "Nietzsche's Philosophy in the Light of Contemporary Events."

Bahr, Ehrhard. "Evil Germany versus Good Germany: Thomas Mann's *Doctor Faustus*." In *Weimar on the Pacific: German Exile Culture and the Crisis of Modernism*, 242–64. Berkeley: University of California Press, 2007.

> Presents a highly readable summary of the composition history and the main themes of *Doctor Faustus*. Argues that the main significance of the novel lies in the fact that with it Mann overcame the originally Nietzschean (and therefore nineteenth-century) character of his art and fully turned to the problematic of modernism.

Jameson, Fredric, "Allegory and History: On Rereading *Doktor Faustus*." In *The Modernist Papers*, 113–36. London: Verso, 2007.

> Difficult yet immensely rewarding analysis of the four-fold allegorical structure in *Doctor Faustus* by America's leading Marxist literary critic. Argues for *Doctor Faustus* as a novel illustrating the transition from high to late modernity.

McFarland, James. "Der Fall Faustus: Continuity and Displacement in Theodor Wiesengrund Adorno and Thomas Mann's Californian Exile." *New German Critique* 34, no. 1 (2007): 111–39.

> Argues for 1945 as a "fulcrum" in the composition of *Doctor Faustus*, since in May of that year the Third Reich came to an end and in December Mann invited Adorno to collaborate on the description Leverkühn's works. The end of the Reich simultaneously marked the end of the historical period in which Mann felt at home, and his invitation to Adorno signaled a corresponding shift in authorial agency.

Kraus, Justice. "Expression and Adorno's Avant-Garde: The Composer in *Doktor Faustus*." *The German Quarterly* 81, no. 2 (2008): 170–84.

> Examines Mann's intellectual relationship to Theodor W. Adorno, arguing (in a break from most other writings on the topic) that Mann preserved his independence from the philosopher and articulated a view of modern artistic expression that is substantially different from Adorno's.

Ruehl, Martin, A. "A Master from Germany: Thomas Mann, Albrecht Dürer, and the Making of a National Icon." *Oxford German Studies* 38, no. 1 (2009): 61–106.

> Detailed discussion of Mann's debt to Albrecht Dürer. Arguably the most extensive study of this topic available in English.

Elsaghe, Yahya. "'La Rosenstiel' and Her Ilk: Jewish Names in Thomas Mann." *Publications of the English Goethe Society* 80, no. 1 (2009): 53–63.

> Places Leverkühn's admirer Kunigunde Rosenstiel in a long line of characters with markedly "Jewish" names that populate Mann's fiction and examines how the author deployed such names with anti-Semitic intentions.

Kontje, Todd. *Thomas Mann's World: Empire, Race, and the Jewish Question*. Ann Arbor: University of Michigan Press, 2011.

> Situates Mann within the context of nineteenth and early-twentieth-century imperialism, along with the attending racist and anti-Semitic prejudices. A nuanced discussion that points out the problematic aspects of Thomas Mann's thought while also honoring his fundamentally cosmopolitan outlook.

Ziolkowski, Theodore. "Leverkühn's Compositions and their Musical Realizations." *The Modern Language Review* 107, no. 3 (2012): 837–56.

> Provides descriptions of various real-life musical works that have been inspired by Leverkühn's fictional compositions, including the soundtracks created for the 1982 film adaptation by Franz Seitz and the 2007 radio play by Leonhard Koppelmann.

Rütten, Thomas. "Genius and Degenerate? Thomas Mann's *Doctor Faustus* and a Medical Discourse on Syphilis." In *Cotagionism and Contagious Diseases*, ed. Thomas Rütten and Martina King, 147–66. Berlin: De Gruyter, 2013.

> Investigates the symbolic overtones of Leverkühn's syphilitic infection, with particular reference to Paul Julius Möbius's 1902 study *On the Pathological in Nietzsche*, which Mann likely consulted in preparation for the novel.

Eagles, Peter. "The *Dunkelmänner* of *Doktor Faustus*: Humanists versus Theologians," *German Life and Letters* 75, no. 1 (2022): 98–115.

> Examines the origins of the theological materials in *Doctor Faustus*, especially in the Halle chapters (XI–XIV). Argues that the sixteenth-century struggle between Catholic humanists and the more extreme voices of the Protestant reformation is reenacted in the novel.

Kontje, Todd. "Saul Fitelberg's Failed Seduction: Worldliness in *Doktor Faustus*." *German Life and Letters* 75, no. 1 (2022): 78–97.

> Analyzes Mann's problematic depiction of the Jewish character Saul Fitelberg in chapter XXXVII and connects it to Mann's theory of cosmopolitanism as articulated in his radio addresses and other sources.

Figure 1. Albrecht Dürer, *Portrait of Philip Melanchthon* (Engraving, 1526). Image courtesy of the Metropolitan Museum of Art, Accession No. 19.73.117.

Figure 2. Albrecht Dürer, *Portrait of a Young Venetian Woman* (Painting, 1506). Image courtesy of Staatliche Museen zu Berlin, Gemäldegalerie, Identification No. 557G.

Figure 3. Albrecht Dürer, *The Master-Builder Jerome of Augsburg* (Drawing, 1506). Image courtesy of the Staatliche Museen zu Berlin, Kupferstichkabinett, Identification No. KdZ 2274.

Figure 4. Albrecht Dürer, *Knight, Death, and Devil* (Engraving, 1513). Image courtesy of the Raclin Murphy Museum of Art, University of Notre Dame, Accession No. 2916.030.

Figure 5. Albrecht Dürer, *The Apocalypse: The Torture of St. John the Evangelist* (Woodcut, 1511). Image courtesy of the Raclin Murphy Museum of Art, University of Notre Dame, Accession No. 2013.013.002.

Figure 6. Albrecht Dürer, *The Apocalypse: St. John Devouring the Book* (Woodcut, 1511). Image courtesy of the Raclin Murphy Museum of Art, University of Notre Dame, Accession No. 2013.013.010.

Figure 7. Albrecht Dürer, *The Apocalypse: The Hymn in Adoration of the Lamb* (Woodcut, 1511). Image courtesy of the Raclin Murphy Museum of Art, University of Notre Dame, Accession No. 2013.013.007.

Figure 8. Albrecht Dürer, *The Apocalypse: The Whore of Babylon* (Woodcut, 1511). Image courtesy of the Raclin Murphy Museum of Art, University of Notre Dame, Accession No. 2013.013.013.

Figure 9. Albrecht Dürer, *The Apocalypse: The Four Horsemen* (Woodcut, 1511). Image courtesy of the Raclin Murphy Museum of Art, University of Notre Dame, Accession No. 2013.013.005.

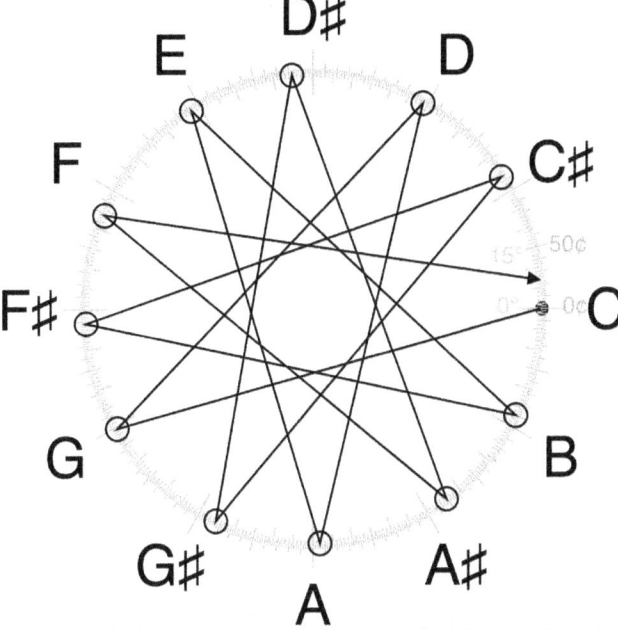

Figure 10. Pythagorean tuning system, showing Pythagorean comma and similarity to pentagram. Illustration courtesy of Wikimedia Commons Contributor Cmglee.

Figure 11. The Schweighart farm in Polling, Thomas Mann's model for the Schweigestill farm in Pfeiffering (Photograph, ca. 1920s, photographer unknown). Image courtesy of ETH-Bibliothek Zürich, Thomas-Mann-Archiv, Accession No. TMA_1809.

Figure 12. The parlor of the Schweighart farm, Thomas Mann's model for the "winged-victory-room" of the Schweigestill farm in Pfeiffering (Photograph, taken prior to 1915, photographer unknown). Image courtesy of Ms. Tina Mayr, Bernried.

Index

In subentries, *Doctor Faustus* is abbreviated as *DF.* Page references followed by an italicized *fig.* indicate illustrations.

Aachen (Germany), 52, 80n7, 135
"Abendständchen" (Brentano), 170
abstract expressionist art, 42
acoustics, 99, 132
Adorno, Theodor W., 17, 81, 210; on Beethoven, 105–6; as devil figure, 108, 108n20, 183; dialectical approach of, 141, 171; dissertation of, 55n9; early essays of, 206; influence on Mann, 8, 10n18, 26–27, 44, 84, 96, 139, 140, 141, 145, 171; jazz and, 204; as Jew, 69; as Mann's musical advisor, 55n9, 105, 200, 224, 226; Mann's relationship with, 105n13; as Mann's US neighbor, 8, 26, 55n9; montage technique and, 47; on musical vs. literary composition, 179; polyphony as defined by, 160; works by: "Late Style in Beethoven," 26, 105–6, 140, 160; *Noten zur Literatur,* 179. See also *Philosophy of New Music* (Adorno)
Adventures of Huckleberry Finn, The (Twain), 40
Albertus Magnus, 157
alchemy, 136, 137, 150, 157, 226
Alfred A. Knopf publishers, 28, 69
allegory, 78–79, 114–15. See also *Doctor Faustus* (Mann)—music theory and political allegory in; *Doctor Faustus* (Mann)—theological allegory in; *Doctor Faustus* (Mann)—typological allegory in
Also Sprach Zarathustra (Nietzsche), 131

ambiguity, 122
American Civil War, 193
American Guild for German Cultural Freedom, 78n1
American-German Review, The, 144
anabaptists, 87
Anbruch (music periodical), 206
Andersen, Hans Christian, 182, 229
Animal Farm (Orwell), 79
Antichrist figures, 118–19
anti-intellectualism, 149
anti-Semitism, 62, 174; *DF* references to, 5, 70–71; German language and, 195; of German student fraternities, 57; Mann and, 68–70, 128
Apocalipsis cum figuris (oratorio; Leverkühn): composition of, 65, 82, 84, 104, 199, 201; Dürer and, 82; as Leverkühn "middle period" piece, 84, 103, 107; modernity and, 104; musical description of, 200, 203–4; polyphonic technique in, 111–12; as premodern composition, 86, 109
Apocalipsis cum figuris (woodcut series; Dürer), 65, 82, 118, 199, 262–66 *figs. 5–9*
apostasy, 118
Arianna, L' (opera; Monteverdi), 225
"Art of the Novel, The" (Mann), 47
As You Like It (Shakespeare), 217
"At the Prophet's" (Mann), 66n23
Auerbach, Erich, 79
Auerbach's Inn (Leipzig, Germany), 159, 160
Auschwitz concentration camp, 68

Austria, 193
authoritarianism, 113
avant-garde culture, 47, 109, 209, 210
avant-garde music, 20, 96, 203, 206

Bach, Johann Sebastian, 10, 50, 53, 98, 99, 143, 158, 159, 164
Ballets Russes, 193, 210
barbarism, 101–2, 178
Bartók, Béla, 183
Basel (Switzerland), 169
Baudelaire, Charles, 189
Bavarian Soviet Republic, 63–64
BBC, 24
Beebee, William, 189
Beethoven (Bekker), 26
Beethoven, Ludwig van: as Christ figure, 118, 139; deafness of, 85, 85n20; death of, 85; *DF* lectures on, 87, 88, 139–41, 145, 172, 184, 227; *DF* typological allegory and, 84–86, 93, 105–8; "early period" of, 106, 139, 140; German music identity and, 10; "Heiligenstadter Testament" of, 85n20; homophony of, 67, 104–8; "late period" of, 85–86, 105–6, 139, 140, 178, 184, 222; Mann's research on, 26, 27; "middle period" of, 85, 106, 139, 140–41; patrons of, 142; redemption motif and, 195; spiritual liberation vs. political liberty, 94; as syphilitic, 85; "Tenth Symphony" of, 217; Wagner and, 145; works by: *Fidelio*, 85–86, 94, 121, 133, 147, 195; *Missa solemnis*, 88, 93, 118; Overture no. 3 ("Leonore"), 147, 195; String Quartet no. 13, 142; Symphony no. 3 ("Eroica"), 85; Symphony no. 8, 140. *See also* Piano Sonata no. 32 (Opus 111; Beethoven); Symphony no. 9 (Beethoven)
Beissel, Georg Conrad, 87–88, 93, 94, 95, 112–13, 139, 144

Bekker, Paul, 96, 101, 107, 139, 145; works by: *Beethoven*, 26; The *Story of Music*, 26, 99, 102, 146, 203
Benjamin, Walter, 81, 92
Berg, Alban, 226
Bergsten, Gunilla, 46
Berlioz, Hector: *Faust* adaptations of, 34, 35; as late Romantic composer, 162; Leverkühn and, 10; Mann's research on, 26; works by: *The Damnation of Faust*, 35, 137; *Symphonie Fantastique*, 35, 200, 213
Bermann-Fischer Verlag, 28, 69
Bertram, Ernst, 92, 155
Beßlich, Barbara, 38–39n9
Bible, 125
"Bilse and I" (Mann), 25, 46–47
black magic, 78, 156, 157
"Black Swan, The" (Mann), 114
Blake, William, 187
"Blood of the Walsungs" (Mann), 69
Blue Angel, The (H. Mann), 51
Blüher, Hans, 14–15, 14n24
bodily heat motif, 139, 145
bohemian vs. bourgeois dynamic, 59, 59n15
Böhm, Hans, 135
Bolshevism, 198, 206
Borchmeyer, Dieter, 81n12, 119, 119n6
bourgeois culture, 59, 173, 191, 196, 203
bourgeois humanism, 105, 200
Brahms, Johannes, 10, 166, 172, 217
breakthrough concept, 63, 121–22, 185, 192, 195, 228
Brecht, Bertolt, 78n1, 134, 224
Breisacher, Chaim (character), 100; as allegory, 74; biographical sketch, 231; conservatism as viewed by, 101–2; as Jewish character, 71, 73, 74, 102n11, 209; model for, 61n17, 190, 231; Riedesel vs., 190; *völkisch* ideology of, 61–62, 102n11, 103, 190

Brentano, Clemens, 164, 170, 217
Brentano Songs (Leverkühn), 57, 110, 167, 181, 217
Breuer, Stefan, 55n10
Brexit referendum, 5
Broch, Hermann, 70
"Brother Hitler" (Mann), 59n15
Brothers Karamazov, The (Dostoevsky), 180
Buchel farm, 42, 60, 89, 103, 118, 132, 170, 173
Buchenwald concentration camp, 5, 70, 223
Budapest (Hungary), 207
Buddenbrooks (Mann), 23; anti-Semitic dog-whistles in, 69; composition history, 176; decaying teeth motif in, 219; illness and allegory in, 114; montage technique in, 46
Bulgakov, Mikhail, 34
Bülow, Hans von, 10, 215, 216
Busoni, Ferruccio, 34
Buxtehude, Dietrich, 169

C major, 35
Calm Sea and Prosperous Voyage (Mendelssohn), 162
"Camps, The" (Mann), 68, 219, 223
Camus, Albert, 4, 38
Capercailzie, Mr. (character), 188
capitalism, 78n1
Catholic Church, 53–54, 157
chapbooks, 31. See also *Historia von D. Johann Fausten* (chapbook)
Charles V (Holy Roman Emperor), 30
Cherubini, Luigi, 162
Chladni, Ernst, 99, 130, 132
chords, 46
Christ figures, 139
Christian theorists, 79, 114, 115
chromaticism, 107, 108, 146
Chronicle of My Life (Mann), 161
church modes, 146, 165
classicism, 184
Clermont-Tonnère, Duchess de, 209
Cocteau, Jean, 211
coldness motif, 157, 161, 182, 185, 195
Colin, Saul C., 72, 233

collage technique, 48
collective memory, 24–25, 117
"Coming Victory of Democracy, The" (lecture; Mann), 95
communism, 104
concentration camps, 5, 68, 70, 223
Congress of Vienna (1814–1815), 85, 86
conservatism, 190
Conservative Revolution, 54, 149, 171
contritio, 122, 157
cosmopolitanism, 73, 133
counterpoint, 133, 141
Counter-Reformation, 54
courtship triangles, 193, 217
Cracow (Poland), 219
Crimea, Russian invasion of, 5
Crotus Rubanius of Dornheim, 127, 149
"cultic" vs. "cultural," 128, 129, 143, 144, 146
"cultural Bolshevism," 206
culture vs. barbarism, 178

Damnation of Faust, The (opera; Berlioz), 35, 137
Danse macabre (Saint-Saëns), 137
Dante Alighieri, 125, 127, 166, 200
Darwinism, sublimated, 65–66
David, Hans Theodore, 144
de Kooning, Willem, 42
de Man, Paul, 63n18
Death in Venice (Mann), 13n22, 23, 38n8, 114, 163
Debussy, Claude, 162
decaying teeth motif, 219
Delacroix, Eugène, 35
democracy, 14–15, 24, 94–95, 178, 202
"Democratic Vistas" (Whitman), 14
Denmark, 193
Derleth, Ludwig, 66, 66n23, 202
Deussen, Paul, 46, 57, 78, 88, 89
Deutschlin, Konrad (character), 56, 82, 155
devil: informal language used by, 180; Kierkegaard and, 55n11; Pythagorean comma and, 99

devil figures: Adorno, 108, 108n20, 183; in Chapbook, 181, 188; Fitelberg, 42, 53, 208; informal language used by, 180; Kretzschmar, 54; red-headed porter, 116; Schleppfuss, 41, 42, 54, 151, 160, 185; shape-shifting stranger, 179; in Weber *Der Freischütz*, 99n7; Zeitblom, 43n15

devil's pact theme: in Chapbook, 31–32, 158; in *DF*, 57, 116–17, 162, 179, 214; Paganini and, 165; syphilis and, 116–17, 179; in Weber *Der Freischütz*, 147, 195

Dialectic of Enlightenment (Adorno and Horkheimer), 143

digressions, 48, 49

"Disorder and Early Sorrow" (Mann), 154

dissonance, 99, 108, 111, 112, 146, 163

Divine Comedy (Dante), 200

Dnieper River, 168

Döblin, Alfred, 47

Doctor Faustus (Mann), 46, 154; anti-Semitism as addressed in, 70–71; Author's Note in, 16, 28, 110, 173, 230; central theme of, 4–5; chapter divisions in, 41–44; characters in, 231–42; Christological aspects of, 119, 142, 148, 156, 176, 177, 194, 227; composition history, 23–27, 30, 31–32, 89, 126; devil's pact theme in, 57, 116–17, 162, 179, 214; edition choice, 16–18; extra-German dimension of, 10, 10n19; geographical references in, 13n22; as German vs. American novel, 29; historical lateness of, 44n19; humor in, 4, 11–12, 56, 129, 166; Jewish characters as portrayed in, 68, 71–74, 102n11, 209; laughter motif in, 131; literary parallels, 4, 12; Mann's acquaintances as characters in, 164, 165; Mann's intentions for, 3–4, 3n2, 4nn4–5, 44n19, 48, 92; montage in, 26–27; narrative structure of, 34, 168; as "Nietzsche novel," 57, 89, 194; parody in, 7, 109, 159, 169, 212; publication history, 27–29, 43; questions to consider, 19–20; redemption motif in, 35; research behind, 25–27, 80–81, 87, 189, 222; Rodde episodes in, 58–59; structure of, 10; timeline of, 50, 243–48; vagueness of, 5

Doctor Faustus (Mann)—as modernist novel: Faust tradition and, 36; Joyce and, 37–38; medium specificity in, 41–44; montage technique in, 46–49, 136–37; narration style and, 12, 38–44, 48–49; polyphonic technique in, 44–46, 49, 77–79

Doctor Faustus (Mann)—current relevance of: democratic backsliding and, 4–6, 8–9; music as allegory, 6–11, 42–44, 43n15; politics of inevitability/eternity and, 8–9; as queer text, 12–15, 13n22

Doctor Faustus (Mann)—historical settings of: German Revolution (1918-1919), 63–65, 69–70; Halle an der Saale (Germany), 53–57; Kaisersaschern (fictional), 50–53, 80, 80n7; Leipzig (Germany), 57; montage technique and, 50–51; Munich (Germany), 58–59, 60–62; Palestrina (Italy), 59–60; Pfeiffering (fictional Bavarian town), 60; significance of, 50; World War I, 62–63. *See also specific historical setting*

Doctor Faustus (Mann)—music theory and political allegory in: homophony and, 104–8; polyphony and political culture, 100–103; Pythagorean music theory and, 97–100; significance of, 96–97; strict style and, 108–13

Doctor Faustus (Mann)—theological allegory in: illness and, 114, 115–17; lamentation and redemption, 119–22; Leverkühn as Christ figure, 117–19

Doctor Faustus (Mann)—typological allegory in: Beethoven and, 84–86, 105–8; Beissel and, 87–88; difficulty of, 91–92; Dürer and, 80–82, 134; Kaisersaschern and, 79–80, 134; Luther and, 82–84; Nietzsche and, 88–91; polyphonic technique and, 77–79
dodecaphony. *See* twelve-tone music
Dostoevsky, Fyodor, 180
Doyle, Arthur Conan, 38n8
Dürer, Albrecht, 11; death of, 85; *DF* typological allegory and, 80–82, 93; historical settings and, 50, 134, 136; Italian travels of, 181; Leverkühn works inspired by, 65, 199; Mann's research on, 26; Nietzsche and, 82, 155; portraits of, 115, 130, 133; as syphilitic, 115; works by: *Apocalipsis cum figuris*, 65, 82, 118, 199, 262–65 *figs. 5–9*; *Knight, Death, and the Devil*, 82, 155, 161, 165, 261 *fig. 4*; *Master-Builder Jerome of Augsburg*, 136, 260 *fig. 4*; *Melencolia I*, 11, 81–82, 150; *Portrait of a Young Venetian Woman*, 133, 259 *fig. 2*; *Portrait of Philip Melanchthon*, 258 *fig. 1*; "Self-Portrait at Twenty-Eight," 80
Ecce Homo (Nietzsche), 117, 149, 161, 225
Eichendorff, Joseph von, 139
Eisenach (Germany), 154
Eisenstein, Sergei, 47
Eisleben (Germany), 50
Eisner, Kurt, 63, 64
El Greco, 229
elegy, 195
Elizabethan literary conventions, 32–33
Ellison, Ralph, 4, 38
"End, The" (Mann), 219
"end of history" thesis, 9
Enlightenment, 222

Ephrata community (United States), 87, 103, 112–13, 139, 144
epic tradition, 50
Erb, Karl, 204
Esmeralda (character): biographical sketch, 232; devil's pact theme and, 57, 162; foreshadowings of, 152, 205, 207; in Hugo *Hunchback of Notre Dame*, 133; Hungarian background of, 207; Leverkühn contracts syphilis from, 57, 115, 162; Leverkühn's first encounter with, 78, 158; Wagner *Parsifal* and, 163
Esméralda (unfinished opera; Massenet), 211
eternity, politics of, 8–9, 11, 48, 113, 121
"Evening Song" (Brentano), 170
Everyman's Library edition, 16
eye motif, 45, 171, 174, 214, 216, 220, 222

fascism, 48, 202; ethos of, 235; German youth culture and, 154; Leverkühn and, 119, 235; Nietzsche and, 89–90, 93
Faust (Goethe): *DF* allusions to, 155, 159, 160, 171, 172, 206, 209, 225; influence on *DF*, 33–34; operatic adaptation of, 211; pentagram in, 98–99
Faust (opera; Gounod), 35, 211
Faust myth: apostasy themes and, 118; historical origins of, 30–31; in literature, 31–34, 127; melancholia and, 81, 81n12; in music, 34–35
Faustus (historical figure), 30–31
"Festival of Spring, The" (Klopstock), 187–88
Fidelio (opera; Beethoven), 85–86, 94, 121, 133, 147, 195
fifths, circle of, 97–99, 100, 112, 136, 138
figura, 79, 81
Finnegans Wake (Joyce), 7, 109

Firebird Suite (Stravinsky), 162
Fischer, Ernst, 52
Fitelberg, Saul (character), 32; as allegory, 74; biographical sketch, 233; chapter devoted to, 207–12; as devil figure, 42, 53, 208; as Jewish character, 72–73, 74, 209; models for, 72, 233
flagellants, 116
Fleurs du mal, Les (Baudelaire), 189
Flying Dutchman, The (opera; Wagner), 35, 163
Fontane, Theodor, 50
Ford, Ford Madox, 12
Förster-Nietzsche, Elizabeth, 89
France, 193
Francke, August Hermann, 53
Frank, Bruno, 198
Frankfurt School, 105n13
fraternities, 55–57, 153
"Frederick the Great and the Grand Coalition" (Mann), 193
Freideutsche Position, Die (fraternity newsletter), 56–57, 154
Freischütz, Der (opera; Weber), 35, 99n7, 147, 160, 181, 195
French music, 53, 155, 162
French Revolution, 105
From Caligari to Hitler (Kracauer), 51
fugue, 142, 172
Fukuyama, Francis, 9

Gay Science, The (Nietzsche), 235
Generation of 1914, 153, 173, 191, 192
generational identity, 56, 154
geometry, 81–82
"German Catastrophe," 4, 4n5
German culture: as cosmopolitan, 52; fascism and, 154; Luther and, 149; youth culture, 154
German film, 51
German identity, 180, 211
German Pietism, 53
German Revolution (1918-1919), 24, 63–65, 69–70, 82, 86, 206
German Romanticism, 164
German Studies, 105n13
German university life, 54–57
Germanness vs. Jewishness, 72–73
Germany: as "belated nation," 155; Second Reich, 193. *See also* Nazi Germany
"Germany and the Germans" (lecture; Mann), 89, 92; on Luther and German culture, 83, 94, 152; on music as order/chaos, 97; on Nazism and the German character, 77–78, 219, 224
Gesammelte Werke (GW) edition, 16–17, 17n2
Gesta Romanorum, 33, 63, 181, 193
Gesta Romanorum (puppet opera; Leverkühn), 120, 192, 194, 195
Gestapo, 185
Gewandhaus (Leipzig, Germany), 160
Godeau, Marie (character): biographical sketch, 233; *DF* dramatic focus and, 34; eyes of, 45, 214, 216; Leverkühn's relationship with, 43, 177, 214, 215, 216, 217; love triangle involving, 177, 193, 216; marriage of, 217–18; models for, 233; as mother figure, 214; Zeitblom as narrator and, 39
Goebbels, Joseph, 39, 229
Goethe, Johann Wolfgang von: Mann and, 50, 80; works by: *Poetry and Truth*, 148; *Tame Xenias*, 219; *Wilhelm Meister*, 213. See also *Faust* (Goethe)
Goldberg, Oskar, 61n17, 190
Goldhagen, Daniel, 117, 223
Good Soldier, The (Ford), 12
Göring, Hermann, 168
Gounod, Charles, 34, 35, 211
Great Depression, 5
Greenberg, Clement, 42
Grétry, André, 162
Grimmelshausen, Christoffel von, 46, 148, 150, 156
Große kommentierte Frankfurter Aufgabe (GKFA) edition, xi, 16–17, 17n2
Gründgens, Gustav, 157
Gumpert, Martin, 116

Half Mile Down (Beebee), 189
Halle an der Saale (Germany), 53–57, 148–56, 159
Hamburger, Käte, 194, 195
Händel, Georg Friedrich, 99
harmony, 82, 99–100, 141, 145, 146, 172
Haydn, Franz Josef, 100, 226
"Heiligenstadter Testament" (Beethoven), 85n20
Heine, Heinrich, 34, 35n7
Helen of Troy, 129, 167, 228
hell, 185, 188
Helmstetter, George, 30
Hentsch, Richard, 194
Herz, Ida, 194
Herzog, Wilhelm, 70
Hetaera Esmeralda, 39–40, 57, 130, 131, 158, 167
Hindemith, Paul, 107–8
Histoire du soldat, L' (Stravinsky), 195
Historia von D. Johann Fausten (chapbook): *DF* allusions to, 32, 129–30, 131, 132, 136, 142, 150, 157, 158, 171, 179, 180, 181, 185–86, 188, 219, 225, 226, 227, 228, 229; *DF* chapter numbering and, xi; Faust myth as portrayed in, 31–32, 116–17, 127, 129–30, 140, 148, 181, 188; formatting of, xi; geographical confines of, 58; literary influence of, 31, 32–34; Mann and, 31, 32, 33–34, 33n5, 227; melancholia in, 81; popularity of, 32
History of the Damnable Life and Deserved Death of Doctor John Faustus, The, 32
Hitler, Adolf, 24; bohemian vs. bourgeois dynamic and, 59, 59n15; death of, 229; *DF* references to, 164; election returns (1932), 52; Leverkühn and, 60, 113, 139, 185; Mussolini and, 198; Nietzsche and, 93; Poland invasion plans of, 168; rise of, 60; Strauss *Salome* performance and, 163
Hitler's Willing Executioners (Goldhagen), 223

Hoeckner, Berthold, 43n15
Hoffmann, Heinrich, 221
Holocaust, the, 5, 68, 70
Holy Roman Empire, 52–53, 80n7
Holy Sinner, The (Mann), 195
Homer, 13, 167
homoeroticism, 12–15, 13n22, 163, 178, 197
homophony, 46, 67, 104–8, 112, 121, 141, 143
Horkheimer, Max, 143
Huber, Kurt, 168
Hugo, Victor, 133, 211
"Humaniora und Humanismus" (Mann), 145
humanism vs. anti-humanism, 189
Hunchback of Notre Dame, The (Hugo), 133, 211
hyperinflation of 1923, 5, 58, 196, 206

"Ideas of 1914," 192
illiberalism, 3
illness as allegory, 114, 114n3
"Illness as Metaphor" (Sontag), 114, 114n2
impressionism, literary, 48
Independent Socialist Party, 63
inevitability, politics of, 8–9
Inferno (Dante), 125, 127, 166
Institoris, Helmut (character), 13, 191, 196, 234
Institoris, Henricus, 32, 130
intellectual anomie, 93
International Society for Contemporary Music, 204
Invisible Man, The (Ellison), 4
irony, 147, 154
Italian music, 53

jazz, 204
Jesus Christ: Beethoven and, 142; *DF* allusions to, 161, 225; Dürer and, 80; laughter motif and, 131; Leverkühn and, 117–19; pietà motif and, 156; typological allegory and, 81
"Jewish Question, The" (Mann), 69, 69n5

Jewishness vs. Germanness, 72–73, 211
John (apostle), 199, 225
John, Gospel of, 225
Joseph tetralogy (Mann), 24, 69, 79, 199, 201
Joyce, James, 7; as literary modernist, 184; Mann and, 37–38, 108–9, 184; as Paris avant-garde member, 209; Schoenberg and, 8; works by: *Finnegans Wake*, 7, 109; *A Portrait of the Artist as a Young Man*, 108–9; *Ulysses*, 7, 109
Judaism: Mann and, 68–70; Zeitblom and, 128. *See also* anti-Semitism
Jünger, Ernst, 67

Kafka, Franz, 37
Kahler, Erich, 47
Kähler, Martin, 55n10, 235
Kaisersaschern (fictional), 80–82, 128, 134, 135, 150, 199
Kaufmann, Fritz, 80
Keats, John, 187
Kierkegaard, Søren, 55n11, 155, 185
Kleist, Heinrich von, 63, 63n18, 192, 194
Klemperer, Otto, 108, 204
Klopstock, Friedrich Gottlieb, 187–88
Knight, Death, and the Devil (engraving; Dürer), 82, 155, 161, 165, 261 *fig.* 4
Kontje, Todd, 73
Kracauer, Siegfried, 51, 51n2
Kretzschmar, Hermann, 234
Kretzschmar, Wendell (character): Beethoven lectures of, 27, 85, 88, 97, 105–6, 139–41, 172, 184, 227; biographical sketch, 234; as devil figure, 54; Ephrata brethren lectures of, 87, 95, 103; Leverkühn as student of, 57, 84, 156, 158; model for, 234
Kridwiss, Sixtus (character), 3n2, 201, 235
Kridwiss Circle (fictitious proto-fascist group), 24, 59; Conservative Revolution and, 66–67; Mann and, 202; members of, 65–66, 101; models for, 90, 201; as "pre-fascist" group, 65n22
Kumpf, Ehrenfried (character): archaic idiom of, 150; biographical sketch, 235; German culture and, 149; models for, 54, 82, 149; montage technique and, 46; as professorial caricature, 55

Lagarde, Paul de, 92
lamentation and redemption, 119–22
Lamentation of Doctor Faustus, The (symphonic cantata; Leverkühn): Adorno and, 224; anti-Semitism and, 72, 195; Beethoven and, 84–85, 86, 113, 121, 225; composition of, 218–19, 223; elegy and, 195; genre of, 158, 162; Kridwiss Circle and premiere of, 67; as Leverkühn "late period" piece, 84–85, 103, 110, 119; Leverkühn's piano performance of, 116, 118, 226–27; musical description of, 224, 226; as redemption, 119–22
Langbehn, Julius, 92
Lasso, Orlando di, 10
"Late Style in Beethoven" (Adorno), 26, 105–6, 140, 160
laughter motif, 131, 175
Lebensraum, 169
Leipzig (Germany), 57–58, 115, 158–60, 173
leitmotifs, 45, 111
Les Six, 211
Lesser, Jonas, 4n4
Lessing, Gotthold Ephraim, 72, 233
Letters of Obscure Men, The (Crotus Rubanius), 127
Leverkühn, Adrian (character): biographical sketch, 235; birth of, 4, 50; childhood mentor of, 84; as Christ figure, 117–19, 119n6; death of, 228–29; devil's pact of, 158, 162; Dürer and, 80–82, 81n12; as Generation of 1914 member, 192; goal of, 34;

health problems of, 197, 218; Hitler and, 60, 113, 139, 185; as homosexual, 161, 205; irrational/demonic aspects of, 78; life of, and twelve-tone musical theory, 42–44, 43n15; lifespan of, 4; love triangle involving, 217; Luther and, 82–84; melancholic temperament of, 128; "middle period" of, 65; models for, 225, 228, 230; as modern figure, 189; Munich salon society and, 100; music education of, 133, 138–39; name of, 235; pact with the devil, 100, 104, 116–17, 221–22; paralytic stroke suffered by, 227, 228; patrons of, 142; polyphonic technique and, 45–46, 77; puppet opera by, 33; self-identification of, as Christian, 126; "strict style" of, 48, 67, 88, 97, 100, 119, 134, 139, 170, 220; suicide attempt of, 228, 229; as syphilitic, 64–65, 93, 104, 115–17, 158, 162, 179, 197, 207, 224; theology studies of, 122, 147–48; tragic relationships of, 43; twelve-tone music and, 6; as university student, 53, 55–56, 148–56; Zeitblom's relationship with, 12–14, 145, 147, 161, 170

Leverkühn, Adrian (character)—as artist/intellectual: Beethoven and, 84–86, 104–8; Beissel and, 87–88; Dürer and, 79–82; Luther and, 82–84; Nietzsche and, 88–91; polyphonic technique and, 77–79, 100–104; typological allegory and, 79, 91–95

Leverkühn, Adrian (character)—as fascist: homophony and, 104–8; music as order/chaos, 97–100; music theory and political allegory and, 96–97; polyphony and political culture, 100–103; strict style and, 108–13, 139

Leverkühn, Adrian (character)—compositions: Brentano Songs, 57, 110, 167, 181, 217; early period (1905-1906), 84, 107, 247; first performances of, 205; late period (1919-1930), 84–85, 111, 248; *Love's Labor Lost*, 84; *Marvels of the Universe*, 187–88; middle period (1906-1918), 65, 84, 103, 107–8, 247–48; *Phosphorescence of the Sea*, 84, 107, 162, 210. See also *Apocalipsis cum figuris* (oratorio; Leverkühn); *Lamentation of Doctor Faustus, The* (symphonic cantata; Leverkühn); Violin Concerto (Leverkühn)

Leverkühn, Elsbeth (character), 118, 132, 133, 156, 214, 236

Leverkühn, Jonathan (character), 88, 130, 137, 236

Leverkühn, Nikolaus (character), 136–37, 236

Levin, Harry, 37–38

Lewisohn, Ludwig, 5n7

liberal culture, regression into irrationality, 4–6; politics of inevitability/eternity and, 8–9, 48

Library of Congress (Washington, DC): Beissel manuscripts at, 87, 144; Mann's lectures at, 9–10, 89 (*see also* "Germany and the Germans" (lecture; Mann))

Life and Opinions of Tristram Shandy, Gentleman, The (Sterne), 40, 145

Linderhof Castle (Bavaria), 215

Liszt, Franz, 34

"Little Mermaid, The" (Andersen), 182, 229

logograms, 164, 167, 170

Lolita (Nabokov), 12

London (England), 197

Longfellow, Henry Wadsworth, 125

Lortzing, Albert, 34

Los Angeles Philharmonic, 204, 206

love triangles, 193, 217

Love's Labour's Lost (opera; Leverkühn), 84

Love's Labour's Lost (Shakespeare), 164, 166, 171, 176, 214, 216

Löwenstein, Hubertus zu, 78n1

Lowe-Porter, Helen Tracy, 16, 28, 43, 174

Loyal Subject, The (H. Mann), 51
Lübeck (Germany), 51, 80n7
Luder, Frau (character), 133
Ludwig II (King of Bavaria), 215, 216
Ludwig III (King of Bavaria), 63
Lukács, Georg, 35
Luther, Martin: Bible translation of, 125; character modeled on, 54, 82, 235; on *contritio*, 157; devil encounter of, 84, 151; *DF* typological allegory and, 82–84; Faust myth and, 30–31; historical settings and, 50, 128, 132, 154; Mann's research on, 26; montage technique and, 46, 150; quotations from, in Faust Chapbook, 179; spiritual liberation vs. political liberty, 94, 152; "table talks" of, 31, 54
Lutheranism, 82, 83, 127
"Lyric Suite" (Berg), 226

Magic Mountain, The (Mann): illness and allegory in, 96–97, 114; music in, 130, 138; *nunc stans* concept in, 135; success of, 3, 23; Wagner's influence on, 44–45; WWI and, 24–25
magic square, 11, 43, 82, 134, 150, 172
Malleus Maleficarum, 26, 130, 137, 151, 152, 227, 242
Manlius, Johannes, 31, 118
Mann, Carla (sister), 27, 58, 59, 120, 205, 238
Mann, Frido (grandson), 120, 220, 221, 239
Mann, Heinrich (brother), 51, 176, 198, 224
Mann, Julia Elizabeth (sister), 58, 238
Mann, Julia (mother), 58, 174, 175, 196, 238
Mann, Katia Pringsheim (wife), 69, 233
Mann, Klaus (son), 34, 35n7, 157
Mann, Michael (son), 26, 96, 193, 239

Mann, Thomas, 195; Adorno and, 105n13; birth of, 23; democracy theory of, 14–15, 24, 94–95; diaries of, 25, 185; health problems of, 27, 201; as "high modernist" writer, 37–38; hometown of, 51; as homosexual, 25; interviews given by, 5n7; Joyce and, 37–38, 108–9, 184; Judaism and, 68–70, 128; lectures of, 24, 89, 95, 175, 178, 202 (*see also* "Germany and the Germans" (lecture; Mann); literary reputation of, 3, 23–25; marriage of, 69; as music lover, 96, 96n1; Nietzsche and, 80, 88n27; notebooks of, 23, 30; as political exile, 3, 24, 27–28, 78n1, 180, 201; propaganda broadcasts of, 24; religious beliefs of, 83; Sontag and, 114nn2–3; speeches of, 68; travels of, 209; ultra-nationalist critics of, 214; as US citizen, 28; works by: "The Art of the Novel," 47; "At the Prophet's," 66n23; "Bilse and I," 25, 46–47; "Blood of the Walsungs," 69; "Brother Hitler," 59n15; "The Camps," 68, 219, 223; *Chronicle of My Life*, 161; *Death in Venice*, 13n22, 23, 38n8, 114, 163; "Disorder and Early Sorrow," 154; "The End," 219; "Frederick the Great and the Grand Coalition," 193; *The Holy Sinner*, 195; "Humaniora und Humanismus," 145; "The Jewish Question," 69, 69n5; *Joseph* tetralogy, 24, 69, 79, 199, 201; *Reflections of a Non-Political Man*, 23, 192; *Sorrows and Greatness of Richard Wagner*, 193; *The Story of a Novel*, 10n18, 27, 44, 45, 108–9; "The Tables of the Law," 24, 69; "Thoughts in Time of War," 143; *Tonio Kröger*, 23, 183; *Tristan*, 69. See also *Buddenbrooks* (Mann); *Doctor Faustus* entries; *Magic Mountain, The* (Mann)

Mann, Thomas—correspondence of: Adorno, Theodor W., 141; Broch, Hermann, 70; Kahler, Erich, 47; Lesser, Jonas, 4n4; Meyer, Agnes E., 3; Preetorius, Emil, 3n2, 47; Reeb, Otto, 65n22; Rohde, Erwin, 213; Rosenau, Fred H., 48n28; Tillich, Paul, 149, 153
Mann, Thomas Johann Heinrich (father), 238
Marble Statue, The (Eichendorff), 139
Marcuse, Ludwig, 33n5, 224
Marlinière, Riccault de la, 72
Marlowe, Christopher, 32–33
Martin Secker publishers, 28
Marvels of the Universe (orchestral fantasy; Leverkühn), 187–88
Marxism, 78n1, 134
Massenet, Jules, 211
Massine, Léonide, 211
Master-Builder Jerome of Augsburg, The (drawing; Dürer), 136, 260 fig. 3
Matthew, Gospel of, 118, 171, 176
medium specificity, 41–44
Meistersinger, Die (opera; Wagner), 10, 169
melancholia, 81–82, 81n12, 131, 150
Melanchthon, Philip, 31, 130, 258 fig. 1
Melani, Jacopo, 224
Melencolia I (woodcut; Dürer), 11, 81–82, 150
Méliès, Georges, 34
melody, 82, 99–100, 145, 146, 172
Mendelssohn, Felix, 53, 158, 160, 162
meningitis, 114, 120, 221, 222
Mephisto (K. Mann), 157
Mer, La (Debussy), 162
Merseburg (Germany), 52
Metamorphoses (Ovid), 187, 220
Meyer, Agnes E., 3
Meyerbeer, Giacomo, 174
Midsummer Night's Dream, A (Mendelssohn), 161
Midsummer Night's Dream, A (Shakespeare), 171

Milhaud, Darius, 107–8
Minna von Barnhelm (Lessing), 233
Missa solemnis (Beethoven), 88, 93, 118
Möbius, Paul Julius, 89
Moderne Orchester, Das (Volbach), 137
modernism: as barbarism, 101–2; international, 211; literary, 178; musical, 203, 210; poetry, 189
modernity, 104–5, 112, 189
Moeller Van den Bruck, Arthur, 54
Moltke, Helmuth von (the Elder), 194
Moltke, Helmuth von (the Younger), 194
monophony, 101
montage: defined, 27; *DF* historical settings and, 50–51, 136–37, 159; *DF* polyphonic structure and, 46, 47–48; ethical problems of, 120; Mann's use of, 26–27, 28, 46–47, 156; Schoenberg and, 28, 110, 173, 230
Monteux, Pierre, 193
Monteverdi, Claudio, 10, 225
Moretti, Franco, 34
Moses, Julius, 69n5
mother figures, 207, 214
Much Ado about Nothing (Shakespeare), 193, 217, 218
Mühsam, Erich, 64
Munich (Germany): Allied bombing raids in, 45; chapters occurring in, 13, 58–59, 60–62, 173–76; council movement in, 198; democratic backsliding in, 60–62; gay cruising area in, 13n22, 197; German Revolution in (1918-1919), 63–64; Mann's residence in, 206; post-WWI cultural life in, 217–18; salon society in, 61–62, 100, 189–90, 213, 238; Wagner cult in, 175
Munich Royal Opera, 206
Munich Secession, 174, 176
Munich Soviet Republic, 64, 65
Münzer, Thomas, 52
Murnau, F. W., 34

music: "absolute" vs. programmatic, 166; alchemy and, 226; as allegory, 6–11, 42–44, 43n15 (*see also Doctor Faustus:* (Mann)—music theory and political allegory in); horizontal vs. vertical aspects of, 82, 99–100, 110, 141, 145, 172
music and mathematics motif, 132
"music of the spheres," 139
musica riservata, 169
"musical Bolshevism," 206
Musical Encyclopedia (Riemann), 204
"musical prose," 219
Mussolini, Benito, 168, 198

Nabokov, Vladimir, 12
Nadler, Josef, 66
Napoleon, 85
Narrated Time, 45
narrative style: heterodiegetic, 38n8; homodiegetic, 38–41
National People's Party, 62, 100–101, 190
National Socialist Party, 60, 190, 224
nationalism, 56–57, 72–73; Bach and, 158; conservatism and, 190; *völkisch,* 61, 102, 102n11, 103, 135, 155
naturalism, 48
Naumburg (Germany), 80n7, 229
Nazi Germany: fall of, 27; German public blame for, 134; liberation vs. self-liberation of, 224; Mann as commentator on, 3; Mann writings banned in, 27–28; quotidian life in, 134; WWII military defeats, 167, 186; WWII surrender of, 187, 223
Nazism, 3; art as used in, 143, 144, 157; Conservative Revolution and, 54; defeat of, 12, 27; election returns (1932), 52; genesis of, 5; German character and, 77–78, 224; German "devil's pact" and, 117; history and, 4–5; intellectual/cultural factors behind rise of, 67, 92, 92n37; *Lebensraum* concept of, 169; Mann as commentator on, 68–69, 219; medieval German history and, 51–52, 134, 135; propaganda of, 126; resistance to, 168; rise of, 6–7, 24, 48–49, 127, 224; Romanticism and, 63n18; Schoenberg and, 6–7; student movements infiltrated by, 57; twelve-tone music and, 7n11, 113, 226; *Volk* concept and, 135; Zeitblom and, 39, 48–49, 121, 126, 134, 168, 223
neoclassicism, 48, 183
Newman, Ernest, 26, 85, 96
Nietzsche, Friedrich, 161, 213, 235; Basel teaching position of, 169; "blond beasts"/"ascetic priests" dualism of, 58–59, 191; *DF* typological allegory and, 88–91, 93, 149; Dürer and, 82, 155; fascism and, 89–90, 93; health problems of, 131; historical settings and, 51; Hitler and, 93; Leverkühn and, 57, 78, 225, 230; Mann and, 80, 88n27; Mann's research on, 26, 183; montage technique and, 46, 47; mood swings of, 181; postures affected by, 227; return to Naumburg, 229; spiritual liberation vs. political liberty, 94; as syphilitic, 93, 117, 181, 218, 227; as university student, 57; women and, 89; works by: *Also Sprach Zarathustra,* 131; *Ecce Homo,* 117, 149, 161, 225; *The Gay Science,* 235; *On the Genealogy of Morals,* 58–59, 191
Nietzsche: Attempt at a Mythology (Bertram), 155
"Nietzsche's Philosophy in the Light of Contemporary Events" (lecture; Mann), 89
Nikolaus II, Prince Esterhazy, 142
1984 (Orwell), 4
"Nobleman with a Hand on His Chest" (painting; El Greco), 229
Nonnenmacher, Kolonat (character), 97, 237
Noten zur Literatur (Adorno), 179
nunc stans (standing now), 80, 135

Nuremberg (Germany), 50, 80, 134, 136, 168, 199

Oberammergau (Bavaria), 215
Odyssey, The (Homer), 13, 167
Oedipus Rex (Stravinsky), 200
On the Genealogy of Morals (Nietzsche), 58–59, 191
"On the German Republic" (lecture; Mann), 178, 202
"On the Marionette Theater" (Kleist), 63, 63n18, 192, 194
Orfeo, L' (opera; Monteverdi), 225
Origin of the German Mourning Play (Benjamin), 81
Orwell, George, 4, 38, 79
Otto II (Holy Roman Emperor), 150
Otto III (Holy Roman Emperor), 52–53, 80n7, 135, 150
Overture no. 3 ("Leonore"; Beethoven), 147, 195
Ovid, 187, 220

Pacific Palisades (CA, USA): Mann's residence in, 3, 8, 24, 206
Paganini, Niccolò, 165
Pale Fire (Nabokov), 12
Palestrina (Italy), 59–60, 84, 116, 176, 179
Palestrina, Giovanni Pierluigi da, 10, 176
Panofsky, Erwin, 81
paresis, 116, 117
Paris (France), 209, 210, 211, 217
parody, 7, 109, 159, 169, 178, 212
Parsifal (opera; Wagner), 131, 143, 144, 163
Patton, George S., 223
peasant uprisings (1520s), 65, 94
pentagram, 98–99, 100, 103, 138, 267 *fig. 10*
Pessoa, Fernando, 34
Peter, Gospel of, 171
Pfeiffering (fictional Bavarian town): Buchel counterparts in, 132; *Lamentation of Doctor Faustus* performed in, 67; Leverkühn arrives in, 60; Leverkühn's final days in, 85, 187–88, 197, 220; real-world model for, 60, 196; Schweigestill farm in, 173, 175, 268–69 *figs. 11–12*; significance of, 60
Philosophy of New Music (Adorno): influence on *DF*, 26, 44, 146, 170, 173, 183–84; polyphony as defined in, 160; on Schoenberg, 8; on subjectivism in music, 107, 110–11, 112, 112n27, 119–20; on twelve-tone music, 119, 173
Phosphorescence of the Sea (symphonic fantasy; Leverkühn), 84, 107, 162, 210
Piano Sonata no. 32 (Opus 111; Beethoven): Adorno and, 27, 108, 139, 140; *DF* lectures on, 27, 97, 105, 108; as late-period piece, 140; Mann and, 172; third movement lacking in, 105
pietà motif, 118, 156, 228
Pirckheimer, Willibald, 168
plagiarism, 28, 47, 173
Plague, The (Camus), 4
Plessner, Helmut, 155
Poetry and Truth (Goethe), 148
pogroms, 52
Poland, German invasion of, 168
Polling (Germany), 175, 196, 268–69 *figs. 11–12*
Pollock, Jackson, 42
polyphony: defined, 101, 141, 143; *DF* structure and, 44–46, 49, 77–79; dissonance and, 146; "imitative," 132, 133; Leverkühn and, 67, 133, 146, 189; political culture and, 100–103; "strict style" in, 110n22, 111–12
Portrait of a Young Venetian Woman (painting; Dürer), 133, 259 *fig. 2*
Portrait of Philip Melanchthon (engraving; Dürer), 258 *fig. 1*
Portrait of the Artist as a Young Man, A (Joyce), 108–9
Pound, Ezra, 209
Praetorius, Michael, 140
Preetorius, Emil, 3n2, 47, 201

Pressburg (Hungary), 115, 162
Princeton University, 24
Pringsheim, Katia, 69
Pringsheim, Klaus, 69, 96
Proclamations (Derleth), 202
prostitution, 114, 131, 158, 160
Protestant Reformation, 53–54, 127
Proust, Marcel, 37
Prussia, Kingdom of, 50
puppet theaters, 32–33, 63
Pushkin, Alexander, 34, 35n7
Pythagoras, 143
Pythagorean comma, 98–99, 100, 112, 267 *fig. 10*
Pythagorean music theory, 97–100, 139, 267 *fig. 10*

queerness, 12–15, 13n22

Recollections of Nietzsche (Deussen), 57, 88
redemption motif, 35, 63, 119–22, 119n6, 195
Reeb, Otto, 65n22
Reflections of a Non-Political Man (Mann), 23, 192
Reflections on Violence (Sorel), 202
Reisinger, Hans, 15, 164, 165, 167, 239
revolutions of 1848, 52
Rheingold, Das (opera; Wagner), 144, 169
rhombohedron, 81–82
Riedesel, Baron von (character), 61–62, 100–102, 190, 237
Riefenstahl, Leni, 52
Riemenschneider, Tilmann, 26, 235
Rimsky-Korsakov, Nikolai, 161
Ring of the Nibelung (opera series; Wagner), 144, 169
Rodde, Clarissa (character): biographical sketch, 238; bohemian vs. bourgeois dynamic and, 59, 173; Generation of 1914 and, 173, 191; Mann's montage technique and, 27; model for, 27; Munich salon society and, 61; suicide of, 204

Rodde, Frau Senatorin (character), 58, 61, 174, 238
Rodde, Inez (character), 58, 61, 173, 191, 196, 204, 238
Rohde, Erwin, 213
Roman Empire, 101, 102
Romanticism, 63n18, 111, 140, 160, 162, 164, 178, 184
Rosenau, Fred H., 48n28
rounds (musical genre), 102, 132, 134
Russian Revolution, 198

S. Fischer Verlag, xi, 16
Saale River, 128
Saint-Saëns, Camille, 120, 120n8, 137, 213
Salome (opera; R. Strauss), 163
Salonmusik, 213
Salzburg Festival, 206
Samson and Delilah (opera; Saint-Saëns), 120, 120n8, 213
San Francisco Symphony, 96, 193
Sartre, Jean-Paul, 38
Satie, Erik, 210
Saturday Review of Literature, 96n1
Scheidemann, Philipp, 63
Schildknapp, Rüdiger (character): as anti-Semitic, 70–71; biographical sketch, 239; *DF* dramatic focus and, 34; eyes of, 216; as homosexual, 167; Leverkühn's relationship with, 59, 164, 215; Leverkühn/Zeitblom relationship and, 13; model for, 15, 165, 239; name of, 165, 167, 239
Schindler, Anton, 85, 89, 140, 142
Schlaginhaufen salon (fictitious Munich salon), 24, 189–90, 239
Schleiermacher, Friedrich, 53
Schleppfuss, Eberhard (character): as devil figure, 41, 42, 54, 151, 160, 185; Faust myth and, 39; montage technique and, 32, 151; name of, 151; as private lecturer, 151–52; as professorial caricature, 55; Zeitblom narration and, 41
Schmitt, Carl, 54, 67

Schneidewein, Nepomuk (character), 120, 121, 220, 221–22, 226, 239
Schoenberg, Arnold: German cultural hubris and, 6–7; Mann's montage technique and, 28, 110, 173, 230; "musical prose" term and, 219; as twelve-tone music inventor, 170, 173; works by: *Transfigured Night,* 162; Trio for Violin, Viola, and Cello, 219; writings by: *Theory of Harmony,* 26, 96. *See also* twelve-tone music
Schoeps, Hans-Joachim, 154
Schopenhauer, Arthur, 80, 135, 191
Schritt vom Wege, Der (film; 1939), 157
Schubert, Franz, 34, 130
Schuh, Willi, 214
Schumann, Robert, 10, 34
Schütz, Heinrich, 140
Schwarz, Egon, 68, 71–72
Schweigestill, Frau (character), 207, 208
Schweigestill farm, 173, 175, 220, 268–69 *figs. 11–12*
Schweighart farm (Polling, Germany), 175, 268–69 *figs. 11–12*
Schwerdtfeger, Rudi (character), 39; death of, 218, 226; DF dramatic focus and, 34; eyes of, 45, 174, 216; as homosexual, 13, 205; Leverkühn violin concerto composed for, 35, 99, 109, 197, 205; Leverkühn's relationship with, 43, 57, 109, 205, 217, 218; love triangle involving, 193, 216, 217; marriage of, 217–18; name of, 14, 174; Rodde (Inez) and, 191, 196; Zeitblom-Leverkühn relationship and, 12–13
Second Reich, 193
"Self-Portrait at Twenty-Eight" (Dürer), 80
sentimenalism, literary, 188
Shakespeare, William: *Gesta Romanorum* as influence on, 193; Leverkühn and, 145; Wagner and, 145; works by: *As You Like It,* 217;

Love's Labour's Lost, 164, 166, 171, 176, 214, 216; *Much Ado about Nothing,* 193, 217, 218; sonnets, 177, 214; *The Tempest,* 121, 220, 222; *Twelfth Night,* 193; *Two Gentlemen of Verona,* 193, 217
Shostakovich, Dmitri, 164
Simplicius Simplicissimus (Grimmelshausen), 46, 148, 150, 156
Snyder, Timothy, 8–9, 11, 113, 121
Social Democratic Party, 24, 51, 63
sonata form, 139, 172
Sontag, Susan, 114, 114n2–3
Sorel, Georges, 202
Sorrows and Greatness of Richard Wagner (Mann), 214
Spender, Stephen, 12
Spengler, Oswald, 35, 54, 67, 90
Spies, Johann, 31–32, 33
Spirit of 1914, 62–63, 194
Stachorski, Stephan, 17
Stein, Gertrude, 34
Sterne, Laurence, 40, 145
Stockholm edition, 16–17, 28
Story of a Novel, The (Mann), 10n18, 27, 44, 45, 108–9
Story of Music, The (Bekker), 26, 99, 102, 146, 203
Strauss, Richard, 163
Stravinsky, Igor: avant-garde culture and, 210; Leverkühn and, 10, 107–8; Mann's research on, 26, 96; memoirs of, 26, 96, 161, 209, 233; musical innovations of, 107–8; as neoclassic composer, 48, 183; works by: *Firebird Suite,* 162; *L'Histoire du soldat,* 195; *Oedipus Rex,* 200
stream of consciousness, 48
"strict style": in music history, 110n22, 142
String Quartet no. 13 (Beethoven), 142
Struwwelpeter, Der (Hoffmann), 221
subjectivity, 106, 107–8, 110–12, 113, 141, 184, 226
"Suffering and Greatness of Richard Wagner" (lecture; Mann), 175

Suhrkamp edition, 16, 28, 230
Switzerland, 24, 201
symbolism, 48
Symphonie Fantastique (Berlioz), 35, 200, 213
Symphony no. 1 (Brahms), 217
Symphony no. 3 ("Eroica"; Beethoven), 85
Symphony no. 8 (Beethoven), 140
Symphony no. 9 ("Choral"; Beethoven): *DF* lectures on, 139; intellectual anomie and, 93; Leverkühn *Lamentation* and "taking back" of, 84–85, 113, 121, 225; progressive/universalist aspirations of, 113, 121, 147; redemption and, 86, 195; spiritual liberation vs. political liberty, 86, 88, 94; symphonic form overcome by, 139
Symphony no. 45 ("Farewell"; Haydn), 226
syphilis: devil's pact and, 116–17; Dürer and, 80–81; historical reputation of, as punishment, 114n3; Mann's montage technique and, 46, 47; Mann's research on, 26; primary, 115; secondary, 115–16; symptoms of, 103, 117, 131, 181, 197, 224; tertiary, 64–65, 116, 197, 221, 224, 227

"Tables of the Law, The" (Mann), 24, 69
Tame Xenias (Goethe), 219
Tannhäuser (opera; Wagner), 156
Tartini, Giuseppe, 198
Tempest, The (Shakespeare), 121, 220, 222
Theory of Harmony (Schoenberg), 26, 96
Thomas Mann: Werk und Zeit (Borchmeyer), 81n12
Thomson, Virgil, 210
"Thoughts in Time of War" (Mann), 143
Thuringia (Germany), 84
Tillich, Paul, 26, 55–56, 55n9, 55n10, 149, 153, 155, 235

Time of Narration, 45
Tissot, James, 35
Tobin, Robert, 13n22, 197
Tokyo Chamber Symphony, 96
Toller, Ernst, 64
Tolna, Frau von (character), 152, 158, 205, 207, 232, 241
Tolstoy, Leo, 50
Tonio Kröger (Mann), 23, 183
Tragical History of Doctor Faustus, The (Marlowe), 32–33
Transfigured Night (Schoenberg), 162
Treaty of Versailles, 197
Trio for Violin, Viola, and Cello (Schoenberg), 219
Tristan (Mann), 69
Tristan and Isolde (opera; Wagner), 137
Trithemius, Johannes, 30
Triumph of the Will (film; 1935), 52
Trump, Donald, 5
Turgenev, Ivan, 34, 35n7
Twain, Mark, 40
Twelfth Night (Shakespeare), 193
twelve-tone music: as allegory, 6–11; defined, 146; four-fold division of, as structuring device, 42–44, 43n15; Leverkühn and, 84, 110–11, 134, 146, 170, 173; Mann's research on, 26; montage technique and, 28, 110; in Nazi Germany, 7n11, 113, 226
Two Gentlemen of Verona (Shakespeare), 193, 217
typological allegory, 79

ultra-nationalism, 56–57, 214
Ulysses (Joyce), 7, 109
Unconscious Beethoven, The (Newman), 26, 85
Unitarianism, 83
United States: Beissel in, 93; Civil War in, 193; exiled German intellectual community in, 55n9, 206; German Studies in, 105n13; Mann's arrival in, 180
University of Cracow, 219
University of Gießen, 53

University of Halle, 53, 148–56
University of Jena, 53
University of Notre Dame (South Bend, IN), 4
University of Wittenberg, 53, 148

Vaget, Hans Rudolf, 4n5, 51n2, 52, 120n8
Vienna edition, 16–17
Vintage edition, xi, 16, 17
Violin Concerto (Leverkühn): Beethoven and, 165; commissioning of, 197; first performance of, 205; as late-period piece, 84; Munich salon society and, 213; musical description of, 35, 40, 99, 212–13; parody and, 109
Violin Concerto no. 1 (Shostakovich), 164
Virgil, 166
Volbach, Fritz, 26, 96, 136, 137
Volk, 135
völkisch rhetoric, 61, 102, 102n11, 103, 135, 155
Voss, Richard, 187

Waetzoldt, Wilhelm, 80, 81, 242
Wagner, Cosima, 216
Wagner, Richard: *DF* references to, 10, 10n18; Faust myth and, 35; leitmotifs used by, 44–45, 111; lodestars of, 145; love affairs of, 216; Mann and, 80, 175; Munich cult of, 175; patrons of, 215; programmatic music of, 166; works by: *The Flying Dutchman*, 35, 163; *Die Meistersinger*, 10, 169; *Parsifal*, 131, 143, 144, 163; *Das Rheingold*, 144, 169; *Tannhäuser*, 156; *Tristan and Isolde*, 137
Walter, Bruno, 96, 206
Wartburg Castle (Germany), 84, 154
Weber, Carl Maria von, 35, 99n7, 147, 160, 181, 195
Weber, Max, 155
Wedekind, Frank, 34, 35n7
Weilheim (Germany), 175

Weimar Republic: collective memory struggles in, 24–25; Conservative Revolution in, 171; constitution of, 24; court system in, 202; cultural high point of, 206; democratic backsliding in, 65; far-right intellectuals in, 55n10; as first German democracy, 86; generational identity in, 56, 154; Jewish literary critics in, 70, 74; Mann's support of, 202; political culture in, 5, 55n10, 56, 100–101, 190
Weissenfels (Germany), 130
Well-Tempered Clavier, The (Bach), 143
White Rose resistance group, 168
Whitman, Walt, 14, 15, 193
Wilde, Oscar, 34
Wilhelm II (German emperor), 63, 192
Wilhelm Meister (Goethe), 213, 220
Wilhelmine Empire, 86, 145, 193
Wimmer, Ruprecht, 17
Winfried (fictional student fraternity), 13, 15, 55–56, 149, 153
Wingolf (student fraternity), 149, 153
Wirklichkeit der Hebräer, Die (Goldberg), 190
witchcraft trials, 78
Wittelsbach dynasty, 63
Wittenberg (Germany), 31, 32, 53, 132, 148
Wolf, Hugo, 10, 26, 181, 228, 230
Wolfenbüttel (Germany), 50
Woods, John E., xi, 16, 17, 102n11, 125, 138, 141
Woolf, Virginia, 37
World War I: chapters devoted to, 62–63; end of, 197; German responsibility for, 197; German university life and, 56; intellectual/cultural factors behind outbreak of, 3; *The Magic Mountain* and, 24–25; Munich salon society and, 62; outbreak of, 192, 197; Zeitblom's military service during, 192, 194

World War II: chapters devoted to, 167–70; *DF* composition history and, 24–25, 186; German resistance movements following, 223; German surrender, 187, 223; German V-1 rocket used in, 197

xenophobia, 149

Zeitblom, Bartholomäus, 80
Zeitblom, Serenus (character): Apostolic function of, 85; biographical sketch, 242; birth of, 4, 50; Breisacher and, 190; comic relief function of, 33; as devil figure, 43n15; final words of, 92; as Generation of 1914 member, 192; as "good German," 12; as homosexual, 161; Leverkühn's relationship with, 12–14, 145, 147, 161, 170; lifespan of, 4; marriage of, 129, 170; models for, 140; Munich salon society and, 100; name of, 242; as narrator, 25, 38–44, 38–39n9, 48–49, 126–30, 134; Nazism and, 39, 48–49, 121, 126, 134, 168, 223; as novel's hero, 12; polyphonic technique and, 45–46, 77; prayer for the fatherland, 229; retirement of, 127; temperament of, 128; "thoughtlessness"/ "suffering" dualism of, 58–59; travels of, 58; as university student, 53, 55–56, 153–54; WWI military service of, 192, 194

Zionism, 68–69, 69n4, 71
Zurich (Switzerland), 214

www.ingramcontent.com/pod-product-compliance
Lightning Source LLC
Chambersburg PA
CBHW051117160426
43195CB00014B/2244